Texas
Ties

▪▪▪▪▪▪

Recipes And
Remembrances
From
The Junior League Of
North Harris County, Inc.

Texas Ties

This cookbook is a collection of favorite recipes,
which are not necessarily original recipes.

Texas Ties
Recipes And Remembrances
From The Junior League Of North Harris County, Inc.

Library of Congress Catalog Number: 97-071435
ISBN: 0-9657063-0-3

Edited, Designed and Manufactured by
Favorite Recipes® Press
an imprint of

FRP™

P.O. Box 305142, Nashville, Tennessee 37230
800-358-0560

Designer and Art Director: Steve Newman
Book Project Manager: Debbie Van Mol

Manufactured in the United States of America
First Printing: 1997   10,000 copies
Second Printing: 1997   7,500 copies

*The Junior League of North Harris County, Inc.
is an organization of women
committed to promoting voluntarism,
developing the potential of women,
and improving communities
through the effective action and leadership
of trained volunteers.
Its purpose is exclusively educational
and charitable.*

Contents

Preface

Texas Ties was developed with the idea that food is more than simple nourishment for the body; it nourishes the spirit as it is prepared and shared with those whose company we enjoy. Food is often a central element in our gatherings, whether it is a weekday meal with family members or a holiday dinner with our circle of friends. Each provides an opportunity to connect with the special people in our lives. We share ourselves when we plan, prepare and enjoy a meal with family and friends.

Our sense of smell has the ability to trigger memories associated with the foods we eat. The familiar smells that accompany the preparation of favorite recipes, those that have survived several generations, bring to mind where we were and who we were with when they were served. The traditions represented by these inherited recipes keep us connected to our past, bring a richness to our present and, through our children, are preserved for the future.

Texas Ties is a cookbook that celebrates the importance of the connections we have with our families and friends. The blending together of recipes that have been passed down from one generation to the next with new recipes that reflect the influence of the diverse cultures in our community will provide each of you the opportunity to create memories of your own. Personal essays and short recollections throughout the cookbook serve to remind us that food is a reflection not only of our culture, but of our unique family traditions.

More than 1200 recipes were submitted to the cookbook by members and friends of The Junior League of North Harris County. Each recipe went through an extensive process of testing and evaluation before being selected for this book. The recipes chosen for *Texas Ties* are indeed the best of the best. We want to acknowledge the contribution of everyone who shared recipes and personal memories, as they have helped to make this a very special book. We invite you to join us in celebrating our *Texas Ties*.

Texas Ties Committee

Karen Brosky Cate, Chair
Linda J. Martens, Editor
Vickie Johnson Hamley, Storywriter
Gwenda Crane Baker, Testing Coordinator
Linda J. Martens, Administrative Coordinator
Sustaining Advisors:
    Kaye Hill-Birkholz
    Kathy Silverberg
Jill Johnson Roberson, Production Coordinator
Marketing and Sales Coordinators:
    Deborah Isbell Holt
    Jennifer Little Harvey
    Cynthia Mueller Jarosh
    Jane Habel Price
Section Coordinators:
    Susan Crocker, Entrées
    Sheila Jortner, Brunch and Breads
    Janelle Potin Lundy, Appetizers
    Leanne Alexander Savage, Desserts
    Jan Rutland Sheehy, Comfort Foods
    Mary Beth Williams, Complements
    Cindy Kidder Wood, Soups and Salads
Kim Shaw Klein, Administrative Secretary
Art Design Committee:
    Susan Crocker
    Cynthia Mueller Jarosh
    Kim Shaw Klein
    Jill Johnson Roberson
Rhonda Pellerin Chenet, Editor, June 1995 to October 1996

Acknowledgements

Amedeo's Restaurant
Dr. and Mrs. Jack Bell
Jack Burgher
Captain's Choice Seafood Market
Linda Cassidy
Chez Nous
Clementine's Restaurant
Custom Pies by Janice
Mrs. Jerry Holditch
Dr. and Mrs. Alex Klein
Joe Klein—Klein Supermarket in Tomball
Mr. and Mrs. Tom Klos and Tahoe
The Knight Family
La Madeleine
Mr. and Mrs. James Lipetska
Maxim's
Michelangelo's
Mr. and Mrs. Richard Mueller
Mr. and Mrs. Gavin Parrish of Chrislyn Farm
Randall's Supermarkets
Raveneaux Country Club
Saigon Palace
Teddi's Tea Room
Wunsche Bros. Cafe

9

Cookbook Contributors

Julie L. Adamis
Michele Huser Adriance*
Karyn Altshuler
Martha Dugas Andersen
Sheila Fry Anderson*
Jane Andrus
Robyn Austin*
Sanette H. Austin*
Jana Earnshaw Babitt
Gwenda Crane Baker*
Julie Fuerstenau Batsche
Shirley R. Bazata
Denise Mallory Bell*
Gail Keathley Bielitz*
Marla Mitchell Bierman
Sally Booth Bierman
Kaye Hill-Birkholz*
Christie Paris Birney
Shelley Rose Blanche
Juli Bledsoe*
Sarah Oliver Bonassin
Lisa Casey Bowman*
Carolyn Torregrossa
    Brandon*
Cinda Lumsden Brown*
Debra Fitch Brown*
Diane Hughes Brown*
Ann Teefy Brumm
Wendy Wright Bruner*
Mary Buettner
Cynthia S. Burger*
Shirley Fischer Burns
Sandra Cahee
Paige Harkins Caldwell*
Katie Callahan
Laura Baxter Cannetti*

Karen Bottoms Cappolino*
Barbara Calhoun Cargill
Kara E. Carlton*
Cheryl J. Castagno*
Karen Brosky Cate*
Dala Shapley Cathey
Janet Evans Cavanaugh*
Robin Rupley Charlesworth
Rhonda Pellerin Chenet*
Alicia Kervin Collins
Caroline Tyre Cookingham*
Susan Kay Cooper
Martha Maxfield
    Cottingham
Joann Mierendorf Crawford*
Melinda Ward Crawford
Ann Green Crews
Susan Witmer Crocker*
Pamela Nies Cross
Debbie Hinze Crum
Sara Sumner Davidson*
Lisa R. dell'Anno
Laura Taylor den Boer*
Teresa Hughes Dernick
Becky Knowlton Dickson*
Susan Tegethoff Diehl*
Erica Donnalley
Vicki Buehrig Downing
Melissa Fredrickson Doyle
Carol Garcia Drake
Leanne Weed Drake
Laura Dronette*
Valerie Eagle
Gina Nelson Ebers*
Suzy Sullivan Englert
Liz Padgett Espenan*

Patti Everett*
Tamala Wikes Finger
Eileen Foerster
Sharon Fore
Michele Frankson*
Wendy Keck Fryfogle
Kathy Helms Gahm
Annette Wagnon Geffert
Claudia Smith Gifford*
Kallie Shivers Gilbreath
Fritzi Glover*
Debra Martin Godbold
Audrey Martinak Gomez*
Susan Hartley Gotliboski*
Melissa Bond Grabois
Patricia Graves Gray
Connie Gregston*
Vickie Johnson Hamley*
Cindy Rose Hardin*
Vicky Williams Harrison
Linda Harvard
Jennifer Little Harvey*
Joan Loeffel Hayes
Sue Wagner Hearne*
Beverly Youdal Heaton*
Lisa Henthorn
Brenda Herod
Lucy Smith Hofmann
Lorel Brown Hohl
DeDe Holbrook
Deborah Isbell Holt*
Karen Holzem*
Deborah Powell
    Houghtaling*
Shawn Howell
Shelly Carnahan Hubble*

Valerie Huddleston
Holly Hitchcock Hulbert
Pamela Hunkin
Tony Aguillard Jansky
Shelly Janszen
Cynthia Mueller Jarosh*
Kathy E. Jaska*
Jan Foster Jewell*
Yvette Cornelius Jircik
Liz Dolle Johnson
Virginia Tuttle Johnson
Mary Andrea Jones
Kristin Marconi Jones*
Sheila Fine Jortner*
Janet Lee Laiser*
Karen Fruge Keener*
Kimberly Kelley
Paula Chapman Kercheval
Shannon Crawford Kidd*
Nancy Seknicka Kimberlin*
Anita Sloan Kittridge*
Kim Shaw Klein*
Christy Hartmangruber
    Knapp
Deborah Barnes Krummel
Ruby Wong Kuhmichel*
Carol H. Lauck
Gena Giles Lillis
Melinda Jones Little
Nancy Doerer Lombardo*
Kimberly Jett Luck
Zoe Ann Newman Ludlum
Christine Fries Lummus*
Janelle Potin Lundy*
Marti Lundy*
Allison Tinsley Maier*

Jennifer Locke Mally
Linda J. Martens*
Brenda Amstutz Martin
Joy Williamson Martin
Michelle H. Mason
Bilinda Cox Matusek
Paige Patteson Mays*
Gayle McConnell*
Mary Callanan McCoy
Lesa Fink McDonald
Judy Adams McGown
Gayelene Kilgore McIngvale
Jillian Cowan Meaux*
Tina Melcher
Kathleen Delaney Merchant*
Jennifer Hoemig Merkel*
Mary Tichenor Metzinger*
Courtney McAninch Miller*
Julie Scott Miracle
Sally Payne Mitchell
Brenda Higgins Mizell
Barbara Wessels Montgomery
Stefanie Montgomery*
Melissa Vaughn Moran*
Nancy Nowlin Morgan
Sandy Hurta Morris*
Susan Morrison*
Diana Motl
Carol Cicconi Mumma
Karla Johnson Neal
Janlyn Brooks Nentwig*
Debbie Hill Nelson*
Nancy Niehous*
Ginger Graham Nieman*
Kate Ogletree
Karen F. Olsen

Kathy E. Olsen
Kathryn Kidd Organ*
Anita Condel Otto*
Kelly Overton
Kathryn Hood Owen*
Patricia Neal Parham*
Suzi Parzych
Lucia Herrera Perez
Debi Wilson Peters*
Greta Peterson
Carol Pfeiffer*
Suzette Phillips
Amy Cooper Pickron*
Louise Wheeler Pinkston*
Susan Adams Pluhowski
Marianne Pompili
Jane Habel Price*
Priscilla Dickson Primavera*
Cheryl Roper Pritzen
Molly Marshall Pryor*
Susan L. Pugliese
Becky Raney
Sharon Stohr Reece*
Lisa Claridy Reed*
Ruth Reitmeier
Marian Maier Richards*
Jill Johnson Roberson*
Rhonda Robicheaux
Pam Romesser*
Cindy Henry Russell
Lisa Henson Rutter
Amy Mauldin Ryan
Nance Hooper Ryer
Sarah Cash Sanders*
Tracy Olson Santoro*
Lynden Lagraize Sartain

Leanne Alexander Savage*
Billie Sue Brogden Schaefer*
Susan Nelson Schatz
Lori Coldwell Schefke*
Mickey Carney Schwartz
Karen DelVentura Scott
Patti Perkins Seefeldt
Jan Rutland Sheehy*
Sherrie Eller Sherertz
Allison Smith Shoffner
Lauren Bourg Simmons*
Sandra Putman Sipes
Kerrie Lyn Smith*
Pamela Brown Smith*
Paula Snyder*
Diane Hess Spear
Jodie Ward Spitzer
Adria Grainge Stacha*
Erika C. Steuterman
Marcia Stibbs*
Laura Sauder Stout
Mary McLennon Stuart*
Mary Thomas Stuart*
Marlene Summers
Diane Keil Summerville*
Jill Wright Sweeney
Angela Sydow
Robin Sydow
Laurel Armet Taylor*
Kathryn Kilgore Thibeaux*
Vanessa Dunbar Thompson*
Luann Walker Tietze
Debbie Tramel*
Amy Becker Vross
Kimberly Butz Wallace
Kathryn Kelly Watkins

Karol Kirkpatrick Watson*
Penny Barnhart Watson*
Stacey Webb
Shauna Webster*
Darcel Atwill Weller
Patty Whited Welte
Vickie Brodbeck Wendt*
Molly Thornberry
   Whisenant*
Charlene Toland White
Pamela Kelly White
Lynne Andrews Whitelaw*
Jennifer Jones Wiemer*
Leesa Holbrook Williams
Lisa Caudle Williams*
Mary Beth Williams*
Sandy Williamson
Sally Kaduk Willms*
Chris Wilson
Mary French Wilson*
Mara Winkler
Kathleen Wollin*
Cindy Kidder Wood*
Holly Bauerschlag Wood*
Kathy Kelly Woodward
Meredith Wurtzler*
Celia Signor Wyatt
Dana Erickson Wyman
Nita York*
Leslie Lochridge Young*

*Denotes Recipe Testers

11

Professional Credits

Byra Vion, *Photographer*

Byra Vion, a resident of Houston for over ten years, specializes in black and white candid portraits. Ms. Vion is a member of numerous professional organizations, including the Professional Photographers of America and the Professional Photographers Guild of Houston. Two of her prints were accepted into the General Collection of the Professional Photographers of America, and one print was accepted into the prestigious Traveling Loan Collection of the Professional Photographers of America. Most recently, Ms. Vion had two photographs selected for the *Professional Photographers of America Exhibit '96 Book*. Working closely with the Art Design Committee for *Texas Ties*, Ms. Vion beautifully interpreted the layouts for the cover and section pages. Each of the photographs was hand-tinted for emphasis.

Kim Cogburn, *Artist*

Kim Cogburn, a resident of The Woodlands for seven years, created the borders for the photographs. Ms. Cogburn is a member of The Woodlands Art League and has won awards for her work in juried shows. Her art is in private collections in Texas, Florida and Kansas. The mixed medium of black and white photography with Ms. Cogburn's watercolors creates a unique effect.

Appetizers

Texas Ties

by Jennifer Little Harvey

We have often heard the old adage, "There's nothing permanent in the world except change." Change is a constant and it affects all areas of our lives, including the family. The days when grandparents, aunts and uncles lived close to each other, keeping alive traditions and providing support, have long since passed. Most of us now spend our adult lives away from our families. Friends and neighbors, though unable to claim blood kinship, become like family because of shared time and experiences. For me, the concept of "Texas Ties" touches on many areas as I consider the ties that join me to the people in my life.

Since I do not live close to my own family, I am thankful for the relationships I have with my friends and neighbors. The support of neighbors who have helped rear my children and shared carpools, and the friends who have provided food during difficult times, has been an important part of my life. We have shared not only the keys to our homes, but our joys and sorrows through the years as well. These special people are my Texas ties.

I appreciate our family traditions, which are a mixture of those I grew up with and those my children and I have developed through the years. We have learned not to resist the change, but to build on it to make something stronger. We have found joy in joining old ways with new ones to create something that is uniquely ours. These traditions are our Texas ties.

Considering the relationships that have impacted me, I am reminded of the many people who so willingly shared their knowledge and experiences with me through the years. Like surrogate parents and grandparents, I considered their advice and treasured their support. These relationships are also my Texas ties.

In a larger sense, I have ties with the community in which I live. Through church, work and school, I have formed relationships that are an important part of my life. Although we come from diverse backgrounds and cultures, we have many similarities: our beliefs, the job we perform, the hopes and concerns for our children. These are the ties that unite, rather than divide, us.

I am particularly reminded of the wonderful women in the League who unselfishly touch so many lives with their caring spirits. The positive changes brought about by their volunteer efforts ripple throughout the community. Their investment of time makes a difference in the lives of people whose ties need strengthening. I count these women as my Texas ties, also.

As the years have passed, I have come to realize that, whatever our differences may be, there is a common thread between us all—we are indeed tied by the incredible journey of life.

Jennifer Little Harvey supplied extensive research on cookbook trends, which was instrumental in creating a focus for this book. She is a sustaining member of the League.

Chiles Rellenos with Mango Salsa

4 poblanos
2/3 cup shredded
   Monterey Jack cheese
2/3 cup shredded
   mozzarella cheese
1/2 cup crumbled feta
   cheese
Mango Salsa (at right)

Char the chiles over a gas flame or under a broiler until blackened on all sides. Place the chiles in a sealable plastic bag immediately; seal tightly. Let stand for 10 minutes. Peel the chiles. Cut slits in each chile; discard the seeds. Combine the Monterey Jack cheese, mozzarella cheese and feta cheese in a bowl and mix well. Spoon the cheese mixture evenly into each chile. Arrange the chiles on a baking sheet. Broil until the cheese melts and the chiles are heated through. Arrange on a serving platter; spoon the Mango Salsa over the chiles. Serve immediately.
Yield: 4 servings.

Note: May prepare the chiles 1 day in advance, chill overnight and broil just before serving.

Prepare Mango Salsa by combining 3/4 cup chopped mango, 1/4 cup chopped red onion, 1/4 cup chopped red bell pepper, 2 tablespoons chopped fresh cilantro and 1 tablespoon fresh lime juice in a bowl and mixing gently. Chill, covered, until serving time. May be prepared up to 6 hours in advance.

Chicken Flautas

2 1/2 cups chopped
   cooked chicken
1 cup shredded Cheddar
   cheese
1 cup shredded
   Monterey Jack cheese
2/3 cup picante sauce
1/3 cup sliced green
   onions
3/4 teaspoon cumin
Vegetable oil for frying
35 corn tortillas

Combine the chicken, Cheddar cheese, Monterey Jack cheese, picante sauce, green onions and cumin in a bowl and mix well. Pour oil into a skillet to a depth of 1/2 inch. Heat until hot but not smoking. Fry the tortillas in the hot oil for 3 seconds per side or until softened; drain. Spoon 1 1/2 tablespoons of the chicken mixture down the center of each tortilla. Roll to enclose the filling; secure with a wooden pick. Arrange seam side down in a baking pan. Bake at 400 degrees for 18 to 20 minutes or until heated through. Serve warm with additional picante sauce, sour cream and/or guacamole. Great served with Guacamole Layer Dip found on page 29.
Yield: 24 servings.

Note: May substitute crab meat for the chicken.

Toasted Crab Puffs

1 1/2 cups chopped crab
   meat
8 ounces cream cheese,
   softened
1/2 cup mayonnaise
1/3 cup freshly grated
   Parmesan cheese
2 tablespoons chopped
   fresh chives
1 tablespoon grated
   onion
1/2 teaspoon cayenne
1/4 teaspoon garlic
   powder
8 English muffins, split

Combine the crab meat, cream cheese, mayonnaise, Parmesan cheese, chives, onion, cayenne and garlic powder in a bowl and mix well. Spread the mixture over the cut sides of the muffins. Arrange cut side up on a baking sheet. Bake at 350 degrees for 15 minutes. *Yield: 16 servings.*

Note: May prepare in advance, freeze and bake just before serving. Substitute shrimp for the crab meat for variety.

Crawfish Elegante

1 pound crawfish tail
   meat
3/4 cup butter
1/2 cup chopped fresh
   parsley
1/3 cup chopped green
   onions
3 tablespoons flour
2 cups half-and-half
3 tablespoons sherry
Salt to taste
Cayenne to taste
24 petite pastry shells,
   baked

Place the crawfish on a paper towel. Wipe gently to remove excess fat. Sauté the crawfish in 1/4 cup of the butter in a skillet for 10 minutes; drain. Sauté the parsley and green onions in the remaining 1/2 cup butter in a skillet. Stir in the flour. Add the half-and-half gradually, stirring constantly until thickened. Stir in the crawfish and sherry. Season with salt and cayenne. Spoon into the pastry shells. Serve immediately. *Yield: 24 servings.*

Note: May freeze for future use.

Without a doubt, the best Parmesan cheese is Parmigiano-Reggiano. It is imported from Italy and is expensive. Its sweet, yet nutty flavor virtually melts in your mouth. This cheese is worth the money and surpasses any other Parmesan cheese on the market. Grate only the amount you plan on using and tightly wrap the remainder and store in the refrigerator for up to several months.

Stuffed Grilled Doves

16 dove breast halves,
   boned, skinned
32 jalapeño slivers
32 thin mozzarella
   cheese strips
Seasoned salt to taste
16 slices bacon

Rinse the doves and pat dry. Pound between sheets of waxed paper with a meat mallet until flattened. Place 2 jalapeño slivers and 2 cheese strips in the center of each dove breast; roll to enclose. Sprinkle with seasoned salt. Wrap each dove breast with a slice of bacon; secure with a wooden pick. Grill over hot coals for 10 minutes or until the bacon and dove breasts are cooked through.
Yield: 16 servings.

Gruyère Puffs

1 cup water
5 tablespoons butter
1¹/₂ teaspoons salt
¹/₂ teaspoon freshly
   ground nutmeg
¹/₈ teaspoon freshly
   ground pepper
1 cup flour
1 cup grated Gruyère
   cheese
5 eggs, at room
   temperature
1¹/₂ teaspoons water

Bring 1 cup water, butter, salt, nutmeg and pepper to a boil in a saucepan; stir until the butter melts. Reduce the heat to simmer. Stir in the flour. Simmer for 1 minute, stirring constantly. Remove from heat. Add the cheese and mix well. Add 4 of the eggs 1 at a time, beating well after each addition. Beat until the mixture is firm and smooth. Drop by spoonfuls onto a lightly greased baking sheet. Beat the remaining egg and 1¹/₂ teaspoons water in a bowl until blended. Brush the puffs with the egg mixture. Place the baking sheet on an oven rack in the upper third of the oven. Bake at 425 degrees for 15 to 20 minutes or until golden brown. Serve hot or at room temperature. *Yield: 36 servings.*

When I was growing up, we spent the school year in Maine and the summers in Texas. I can remember how excited we would be to head south where we spent the days crabbing, swimming, and eating homemade ice cream at my grandmother's house. My clearest memories are of my dad, the "Grill Master," as he set about the work of cooking on the grill. Framed by gigantic baskets of ferns, he would arrange the charcoal, light and tend the fire, and constantly check the meat cooking on the grill. His efforts always paid off with a "Grill Master Specialty" that was delicious and, oh, so memorable.

    ~ *Susan Cooper* ~

19

Oysters Raveneaux

2 slices white bread
6 ounces bacon
1/2 medium onion, finely
    chopped
2 cloves of garlic, minced
1 cup whipping cream
1/2 cup white wine
2 ounces cream cheese
1 teaspoon chicken base
Salt to taste
White pepper to taste
6 ounces fresh spinach
1 egg
12 oysters on the half
    shell

Tear the bread into small pieces. Fry the bacon in a skillet until crisp; drain. Crumble the bacon. Return the bacon to the skillet. Add the onion and garlic. Cook for 2 minutes, stirring frequently. Stir in the whipping cream, white wine and cream cheese. Cook over medium heat for 5 minutes, stirring frequently. Add the chicken base and mix well. Season with salt and white pepper. Remove from heat. Add the spinach and bread and mix well. Let stand for 30 minutes. Stir in the egg. Spoon the spinach mixture over the oysters on a baking sheet. Bake at 350 degrees for 10 to 12 minutes.
Yield: 12 servings.

This hot appetizer, prepared by Chef Roy Quezada at Raveneaux Country Club, is a favorite.

Herbed Pea Pods

8 ounces cream cheese,
    softened
1/2 cup butter, softened
4 teaspoons tarragon
    wine vinegar
1 teaspoon coarsely
    ground pepper
2 cloves of garlic, minced
4 teaspoons minced fresh
    parsley
1/2 cup whipping cream
1 pound pea pods

Process the cream cheese, butter, tarragon wine vinegar, pepper and garlic in a blender or food processor until blended. Combine the mixture with the parsley in a mixer bowl and mix well. Add the whipping cream, beating until creamy. Chill, covered, for 2 hours. Steam the pea pods in a steamer for 3 to 5 minutes. Drain and pat dry. Make a slit in the top of each pea pod. Fill each pea pod with 1 teaspoon of the cheese mixture using a pastry tube. Arrange on a serving platter. Chill, covered, for up to 8 hours before serving.
Yield: 12 servings.

Red Salmon Caviar Pinwheels

1/4 cup unsalted butter
1/2 cup flour
1/8 teaspoon salt
2 cups milk, heated
4 egg yolks, beaten
1 1/4 teaspoons sugar
4 egg whites, stiffly
    beaten
5 ounces cream cheese,
    softened
1/4 cup sour cream
7 ounces red salmon
    caviar

Heat the butter in a saucepan until melted. Stir in the flour and salt. Cook for 1 minute, stirring constantly. Add the warm milk gradually and mix well. Cook for 3 minutes or until thickened, stirring constantly. Remove from heat.

Stir a small amount of the hot mixture into the egg yolks; stir the egg yolks into the hot mixture. Add the sugar and mix well. Fold in the egg whites. Spread in a buttered 10x15-inch baking pan.

Bake at 325 degrees for 35 minutes or until golden brown. Invert onto a tea towel. Let stand until cool.

Beat the cream cheese and sour cream in a bowl until blended. Fold in the caviar. Spread over the baked layer; roll as for a jelly roll to enclose the filling. Chill, covered, in the refrigerator.

Cut into thin slices. Serve cold with lightly salted sour cream or reheat just until warm. *Yield: 16 servings.*

Note: May store, covered, in the refrigerator for up to 2 days and slice just before serving.

Fresh caviar is very perishable. Buy only as much as needed and keep cool in an insulated bag on the way home from the market. Fish eggs should have a fresh, briny smell and be firm, shiny, and separate.

Cilantro Ginger Shrimp

2 pounds medium
  shrimp, peeled,
  deveined
1 bunch cilantro,
  chopped
1/3 cup fresh lime juice
1/4 cup olive oil
1/4 cup finely chopped
  fresh gingerroot
5 cloves of garlic, finely
  chopped

Combine the shrimp, cilantro, lime juice, olive oil, gingerroot and garlic in a bowl and mix well. Marinate, covered, in the refrigerator for 3 hours, stirring occasionally; drain. Soak 12 bamboo skewers in water for 5 to 10 minutes; drain. Thread the shrimp on the skewers. Grill over medium-hot coals until the shrimp are pink, turning occasionally.
Yield: 12 servings.

To remove onion or garlic odor from your fingers, place your fingers on the handle of a stainless steel spoon and run cold water over them. The smell will disappear in seconds.

Orange Thai Shrimp

1 pound large shrimp,
  cooked, peeled,
  deveined
Sections of 3 oranges,
  seeded, cut into bite-
  size pieces
10 mint leaves, coarsely
  chopped
4 cloves of garlic, minced
1/2 teaspoon salt
1/2 teaspoon dried red
  chili flakes
Juice of 1 lime
1/2 teaspoon fish sauce
Peel of 1 orange, cut into
  thin strips

Combine the shrimp and oranges in a bowl and mix well. Stir in the mint, garlic, salt and red chili flakes. Add the lime juice, fish sauce and orange peel and mix well. Marinate, covered, in the refrigerator for 1 hour or longer, stirring occasionally. Spoon onto a glass platter or into a crystal bowl. *Yield: 8 servings.*

Shrimp Nachos

12 ounces shrimp,
  cooked, peeled,
  deveined
1¹/₂ cups shredded
  Cheddar cheese
¹/₂ cup chopped drained
  green chiles
¹/₃ cup sliced green
  onions
¹/₄ cup sliced drained
  black olives
¹/₂ cup mayonnaise
6 dozen round tortilla
  chips

Chop the shrimp coarsely. Combine the shrimp, cheese, chiles, green onions and olives in a bowl and mix well. Stir in the mayonnaise. Arrange the chips on a baking sheet. Spoon 1¹/₂ teaspoons of the shrimp mixture on each chip. Bake at 350 degrees for 5 minutes or until the cheese melts. *Yield: 24 servings.*

South-of-the-Border Won Tons

24 won ton wrappers
2 tablespoons vegetable
  oil
1 pound mild pork
  sausage
1¹/₄ cups shredded sharp
  Cheddar cheese
1¹/₄ cups shredded
  Monterey Jack cheese
1 cup ranch salad
  dressing
¹/₂ cup chopped red bell
  pepper
¹/₄ cup sliced black olives

Grease 24 miniature muffin cups lightly with oil. Press 1 won ton wrapper into each cup; brush with 2 tablespoons oil. Bake at 375 degrees for 10 minutes or until golden brown. Remove from muffin cups. Arrange the won ton cups on a baking sheet. Brown the sausage in a skillet, stirring until crumbly; drain. Combine the sausage, Cheddar cheese, Monterey Jack cheese, salad dressing, red pepper and olives in a bowl and mix well. Spoon 1 tablespoon of the sausage mixture into each won ton cup. Bake at 325 degrees for 5 minutes or until bubbly.
Yield: 24 servings.

Mozzarella and Spinach Crostini

1 loaf thin French bread,
  cut lengthwise into
  halves
Garlic salt to taste
1 1/2 cups fresh spinach
4 ounces cream cheese,
  softened
8 ounces mozzarella
  cheese, thinly sliced

Arrange the bread cut side up on a baking sheet. Toast in a 350-degree oven. Sprinkle with garlic salt. Combine the spinach with a small amount of water in a saucepan. Cook until tender and drain. Squeeze the moisture from the spinach. Combine the spinach and cream cheese in a bowl and mix well. Spread the spinach mixture over the cut side of the bread; top with the mozzarella cheese. Broil until the cheese melts; slice. Serve immediately. *Yield: 24 servings.*

Fresh herbs provide a pizzazz unmatched by dried herbs. When purchasing fresh herbs, select those with a clean, fresh fragrance and a bright color.

Basil-Baked Tomatoes

18 small Roma tomatoes
3/4 cup chopped fresh
  basil
7 cloves of garlic, minced
1/3 cup olive oil
Salt to taste

Cut the tomatoes lengthwise into halves. Arrange cut side up in a shallow baking pan. Sprinkle with the basil and garlic; drizzle with the olive oil. Bake at 200 degrees for 2 to 2 1/2 hours; the tomatoes are done when shriveled but still moist. Cool to room temperature. Season with salt just before serving. Serve with baguette slices. Store leftovers, covered, in the refrigerator. *Yield: 9 servings.*

    Note: This versatile dish may be used as a pizza topping, a pasta topping, or as an addition to grilled cheese sandwiches or tossed green salads.

Avocado and Tomato Dip

3 large avocados
$^2/_3$ cup chopped fresh
   tomato
1 green onion with top,
   sliced
2$^1/_2$ tablespoons picante
   sauce
2 tablespoons fresh lime
   juice
2 teaspoons vegetable oil
$^1/_8$ teaspoon garlic salt
Salt to taste

Peel the avocados; mash in a bowl. Stir in the tomato, green onion, picante sauce, lime juice, oil, garlic salt and salt and mix well. Chill, covered, for 1 hour. Spoon into a serving bowl. Serve with tortilla chips.
Yield: 8 servings.

This is not your ordinary avocado dip!

Stuffed Cherry Tomatoes

12 ounces bacon
1 cup mayonnaise
1 green onion top, finely
   chopped
Pepper to taste
2 pints cherry tomatoes
Fresh chives, cut into
   1-inch strips
1 pint alfalfa sprouts

Fry the bacon in a skillet until crisp; drain. Crumble the bacon. Combine the bacon, mayonnaise, green onion and pepper in a bowl and mix well. Chill, covered, for 1 hour. Cut the top from each tomato and discard. Remove the seeds and pulp carefully, leaving a shell. Invert the tomato shells on a paper towel to drain. Arrange the tomatoes cut side up in a dish. Fill with the bacon mixture. Place the chive strips decoratively in the tomatoes. Spread the alfalfa sprouts on a serving platter; arrange the stuffed tomatoes over the sprouts.
Yield: 12 servings.

Black Bean Dip

2 cups drained rinsed
  black beans
²/₃ cup mild or hot salsa
2¹/₄ tablespoons lime
  juice
2 tablespoons chopped
  fresh cilantro
¹/₄ teaspoon cumin
¹/₈ teaspoon salt
Freshly ground pepper to
  taste

Combine the black beans, salsa, lime juice,
cilantro and cumin in a blender or food
processor container. Process until smooth.
Season with the salt and pepper. Spoon
into a serving bowl. Serve with tortilla
chips. *Yield: 1¹/₂ cups.*

Bleu Cheese Crumble

8 ounces bleu cheese
¹/₃ cup olive oil
2 cloves of garlic, minced
¹/₂ cup chopped red
  onion
¹/₂ cup minced fresh
  parsley
2 tablespoons red wine
  vinegar
1 tablespoon lemon juice
Freshly ground pepper
  to taste
Red and white endive

Crumble the bleu cheese evenly over the
bottom of a 6x8-inch dish. Drizzle with
a mixture of the olive oil and garlic.
Combine the red onion, parsley, wine
vinegar and lemon juice in a bowl and mix
well. Pour over the prepared layers. Chill,
covered, for 1 hour. Sprinkle with pepper.
Spoon onto an endive-lined serving
platter. Serve with pepper crackers.
Yield: 8 servings.

   Note: Serve this versatile dish as an
accompaniment to grilled meats, as a
topping for salads or with fresh fruits.
May also be served in a quiche dish or
decorative pie plate.

Bit of Brie

1 (14-ounce) round Brie
   cheese
1 tablespoon butter
1 cup finely chopped
   pecans, toasted
1/3 cup Kahlúa
1/4 cup packed brown
   sugar

Remove the top rind of the Brie. Place on a microwave-safe serving platter. Heat the butter in a saucepan until melted. Add the pecans and mix well. Cook for 5 minutes, stirring frequently. Stir in the Kahlúa and brown sugar. Spoon the pecan mixture over the Brie, spreading to the edge. Microwave on High for 1 minute; turn the platter. Microwave on High for 45 seconds longer or until bubbly. Serve with melba toast rounds. *Yield: 12 servings.*

Brie cheese should have a soft, creamy texture throughout when fully ripe. Rounds should be no more than 1 inch thick, otherwise they become overripe on the edges before ripening in the center. Let the Brie come to room temperature before serving.

Cashew Avocado Rounds

1 1/2 cups chopped
   cashews
1 cup mashed avocado
8 ounces cream cheese,
   softened
1/2 cup shredded sharp
   Cheddar cheese
2 teaspoons fresh lime
   juice
1/2 teaspoon
   Worcestershire sauce
1 clove of garlic, crushed
1/8 teaspoon Tabasco
   sauce
Paprika to taste

Combine the cashews, avocado, cream cheese, Cheddar cheese, lime juice, Worcestershire sauce, garlic and hot sauce in a bowl and mix well. Chill, covered, for 1 hour. Shape into 2 rounds; sprinkle with paprika. Chill, covered, for several hours before serving. Serve with assorted party crackers. *Yield: 24 servings.*

Dijon Crab Meat Dip

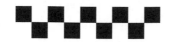

12 ounces cream cheese,
    softened
1/4 cup mayonnaise
2 tablespoons dry white
    wine
1 tablespoon Dijon
    mustard
3/4 teaspoon
    confectioners' sugar
1/4 teaspoon onion juice
1 clove of garlic, crushed
8 ounces crab meat
1/4 cup slivered almonds,
    toasted
2 tablespoons minced
    fresh parsley

Combine the cream cheese, mayonnaise, white wine, Dijon mustard, confectioners' sugar, onion juice and garlic in a saucepan. Cook until blended, stirring constantly. Flake the crab meat. Fold into the cheese mixture. Cook just until heated through, stirring frequently. Spoon into a chafing dish. Sprinkle with the almonds and parsley. Serve with assorted party crackers. *Yield: 12 servings.*

Savory Cheese Logs

1 pound extra-sharp
    Cheddar cheese
6 ounces each port wine
    cheese and jalapeño
    cheese
4 ounces bleu cheese
1 clove of garlic
1/2 cup minced onion
3 ounces cream cheese,
    softened
2 tablespoons
    Worcestershire sauce
1/4 cup minced green
    onions (optional)
2 tablespoons minced
    pimento (optional)
Finely chopped pecans
Chopped fresh parsley

Combine the Cheddar cheese, port wine cheese, jalapeño cheese and bleu cheese in a food processor. Process until blended. Mince the garlic. Mix with the Cheddar cheese mixture and onion in a bowl. Combine the cream cheese and Worcestershire sauce in a bowl and mix well. Add the green onions and pimento and mix well. Add the Cheddar cheese mixture and mix well. Shape into 3 logs. Sprinkle a sheet of waxed paper with pecans and parsley. Roll the logs in the pecan mixture until covered on all sides. Wrap the logs individually in plastic wrap. Chill until firm. Serve with assorted party crackers. *Yield: 16 servings.*

Note: May store in the refrigerator for several weeks or freeze for future use.

Guacamole Layer Dip

5 avocados, mashed
2 tablespoons
 mayonnaise
1 tablespoon fresh lemon
 juice
1 tablespoon dried
 minced onion
1 teaspoon each Tabasco
 sauce and
 Worcestershire sauce
3/4 teaspoon garlic
 powder
1/4 teaspoon salt
1/4 teaspoon pepper
1/2 teaspoon chopped
 fresh cilantro
3/4 cup chopped seeded
 tomato
1 cup sour cream
1/2 cup shredded Cheddar
 cheese
1/2 cup shredded
 Monterey Jack cheese
2 green onions, chopped

Combine the avocados, mayonnaise, lemon juice, minced onion, Tabasco sauce, Worcestershire sauce, garlic powder, salt, pepper and cilantro in a bowl and mix well. Spread in a shallow 2 1/2-quart dish. Layer the tomato, sour cream, Cheddar cheese, Monterey Jack cheese and green onions in the order listed over the prepared layer. Chill, covered, for 8 to 10 hours. Serve with tortilla chips or the Chicken Flautas on page 17.
Yield: 16 servings.

Keep guacamole from browning when prepared in advance by placing plastic wrap directly on the surface of the dip. It's oxygen that browns the avocado, so the less air that gets to the surface, the better. Store guacamole in the refrigerator until serving time.

Kahlúa Fruit Dip

8 ounces cream cheese,
 softened
3/4 cup sugar
1/3 cup Kahlúa
1 cup sour cream
1/3 cup chopped nuts

Beat the cream cheese in a mixer bowl until smooth. Add the sugar gradually, beating constantly for 5 minutes or until light and fluffy. Add the Kahlúa. Beat for 1 minute or until blended. Fold in the sour cream and nuts. Chill, covered, for 2 hours. Serve as a dip with fresh fruit.
Yield: 10 to 12 servings.

Salmon Mousse

2 envelopes unflavored
  gelatin
1/4 cup cold water
1/2 cup boiling water
3/4 cup mayonnaise
2 tablespoons fresh
  lemon juice
2 tablespoons finely
  grated purple onion
2 tablespoons chopped
  fresh dillweed
1 teaspoon hot red
  pepper sauce
1 teaspoon salt
1/2 teaspoon paprika
3 cups flaked boned
  poached fresh salmon
2 cups whipping cream

Garnish:
Capers
Sliced radishes
Sliced cucumbers
Purple onion strips
Sweet gherkins

Combine the gelatin and cold water in a bowl and mix well. Add the boiling water, stirring until the gelatin dissolves. Let stand until cool.

Whisk in the mayonnaise, lemon juice, grated purple onion, dillweed, red pepper sauce, salt and paprika. Chill just until partially set.

Fold in the salmon. Beat the whipping cream in a mixer bowl just until stiff peaks form. Fold into the salmon mixture. Spoon into a 1-quart fish-shape mold sprayed with nonstick cooking spray. Chill, covered, for 4 hours or until set.

Dip the mold in warm water until the sides loosen; invert onto a serving platter. Decorate with an olive slice or caper for the eye, paper-thin slices of radishes or cucumbers for the scales and thinly sliced strips of purple onion for the fins and tail.

Serve with baguette or black bread slices, slivered red onions and sweet gherkins. *Yield: 25 servings.*

Although this hors d'oeuvre may take a little extra effort, it can be prepared in advance and stored in the refrigerator until serving time. What a beautiful presentation!

Brandied Pâté

1 cup minced onion
2 tablespoons unsalted
　　butter
1 cup brandy
3 cloves of garlic, minced
2 teaspoons salt
1 teaspoon thyme
3/4 teaspoon freshly
　　ground pepper
1/2 teaspoon allspice
12 ounces ground pork
8 ounces ground veal
3/4 cup chopped
　　pistachios
2 eggs, beaten
1 bay leaf
8 thin slices bacon

Sauté the onion in the butter in a skillet over medium heat for 10 minutes or until golden brown. Transfer the onion mixture to a bowl. Add the brandy to the skillet. Simmer for 6 minutes or until reduced to 1/4 cup. Pour the brandy over the onion mixture. Stir in the garlic, salt, thyme, pepper and allspice. Add the ground pork, ground veal, pistachios and eggs and mix well.

Place the bay leaf in the center of a 5x9-inch loaf pan. Line the pan with the bacon slices, arranging crosswise and allowing the ends to drape over the sides of the pan. Spoon the pork mixture into the pan; smooth the top. Fold the bacon ends over the top.

Place the loaf pan in a 9x13-inch baking pan. Add hot water to the baking pan to a depth of 1 1/2 inches. Bake at 350 degrees for 1 1/2 hours or until a meat thermometer inserted in the center of the pâté registers 180 degrees; the bacon may appear raw, but it is cooked through.

Remove the loaf pan from the water. Drain any liquid from the pâté; cover with foil. Place a small pan atop the pâté; fill with heavy objects to weight down.

Chill for 8 to 10 hours. Invert onto a serving platter. Serve with baguette slices or assorted party crackers. *Yield: 15 servings.*

Feta Cheese Torte

8 ounces cream cheese,
  softened
8 ounces feta cheese,
  softened
1 1/2 cups butter, softened
1 cup pesto, drained
1 cup minced drained
  sun-dried tomatoes

Beat the cream cheese, feta cheese and
butter in a mixer bowl until fluffy. Place 1/3
of the cheese mixture in a 9-inch springform pan. Layer the pesto and remaining
cheese mixture 1/2 at a time in the prepared
pan, ending with the cheese mixture. Top
with the sun-dried tomatoes. Chill, covered,
for 2 hours. Serve at room temperature with
baguette slices. *Yield: 16 servings.*

*To curl fresh vegetables
such as celery and
carrots, cut the
vegetables lengthwise
into strips and soak
in ice water until
serving time.*

Sun-Dried Tomato Dip

2 cups drained garbanzo
  beans
1 cup drained oil-pack
  sun-dried tomatoes
1/2 cup mayonnaise
1/3 cup freshly grated
  Parmesan cheese
2 tablespoons fresh
  lemon juice
2 cloves of garlic,
  chopped
1/4 teaspoon basil
1/4 teaspoon ground red
  pepper

Garnish:
Chopped sun-dried
  tomatoes

Process the garbanzo beans, sun-dried
tomatoes, mayonnaise, Parmesan cheese,
lemon juice, garlic, basil and red pepper in
a blender or food processor fitted with a
knife blade until smooth. Spoon into a
serving bowl. Chill, covered, for 2 hours.
Garnish with chopped sun-dried tomatoes.
Serve with assorted fresh vegetables.
Yield: 8 servings.

Soups and
Salads

A Mahogany Memorial

by Kristina Gaiser Conner

As the seasons change, I find myself in our dining room continuing a Gaiser family tradition: placing seasonal decorations on a runner on our dining room table. This was my parents' table and it holds so many memories—sort of a mahogany "Ghost of Celebrations Past."

When I was a little girl, the table was the herald of things to come. Usually, it sat quietly in our dining room with one or two leaves inserted. But every once in a while the table would almost come to life and it would tell me that good times were nearly here. When the table suddenly became larger than life, much as Alice experienced in Wonderland, with a perfectly starched white runner topped with an abundance of rabbits and rainbow-colored baskets, it meant Easter was nearly here with egg decorating and hunting and chocolate bunnies. Family and friends would join us for a hunt through

"Alice's Magical Gardens," followed by a brunch featuring a three-dimensional coconut lamb cake. Each November the table blossomed with fruit and nuts overflowing a cornucopia— a sure sign that Thanksgiving with turkey and dressing and all the good things to eat was just ahead. The final course was Mother's Mincemeat Pie… a bit strong for the under-twelve palate. Occasionally, the table was draped in a white cloth with balloons and bunting overhead: one of us was having a birthday party with friends and cake, ice cream and presents. The celebrant would sit at the head of the table in my father's chair. When it was my turn, I felt like a queen sitting in that august throne.

The table would also tell me that company was coming. Sometimes formal company, men in suits and ladies in dresses, would be heralded by complete table settings for twelve. This told me that I would be able to look, but I would have to be on my best behavior—there would be no staying up or sneaking

down the stairs this night. Other times the table, festooned with ribbons and bows, would tell me that it was time for one of my mother's special parties: everyone in attendance would don outrageous hats, which Mother rescued from rummage sales from around the state. Strapping on her accordion, Mother would play while she and her friend Grace sang slightly ribald songs they had composed, some on the spur of the moment. Those nights were truly special. A friend and I would sneak under the table, knowing that no one could possibly see us there. And we would giggle quietly while the adults laughed. It seemed that those parties went on forever, and what wisdom my friend and I acquired!

Best of all each year was when the table suddenly sprouted a long red runner, covered with hundreds of little wooden German figurines, music boxes and candles. It made no difference what the calendar or the weatherman said: this was the sign that Christmas was coming. The table told of cookies to bake and candy to make, of presents to wrap and gifts to bake. For us, Christmas Day itself was very special as we opened gifts with all the family members present, but the caroling party we held the week before Christmas is what I remember most of all.

We would invite all our relatives and friends for punch and wassail, eggnog and sundry drinks. A huge pot of rich, burgundy beef stew would bubble on the stove while fresh bread baked in the oven; two large salad bowls overflowing with greens were dressed with garlic, oil and vinegar—olfactory overload in the Gaiser kitchen!

When everyone was very mellow, my Father would get out his zither. Mrs. Raynor would sit at the piano and the caroling would begin. Dad and two of his brothers would sing some of the old German carols, in German, and we would all join in on the choruses. The high point of the evening came when the Gaiser brothers would sing "We Three Kings," each taking the part of one king. When all the carols were sung and our guests were about to depart, each child received a gingerbread man, baked with his or her name on it—a special Gaiser treat which was never known to last much beyond the doorstep.

Now, the caroling is done, the funny hats have been put away, and Mom and Dad and most of their friends have long since gone to rest. Still the table remains to tell of the good times we had. And I still set the table first. Before the tree can be trimmed or the lights lit, the runner must be placed down the center of the table and the figurines, candles and bows carefully arranged. Only then can the recipes be recreated and the party begun. I do not know why, but that is the way it has to be. It is the Gaiser way.

Kristina Gaiser Conner was a founding member of The Junior League of North Harris County. She considers herself a dreamer and has seen firsthand what can be accomplished when you start with a dream and are willing to work to make it happen.

White Chili

1 pound dried White
    Northern beans or
    any large white beans
7 cups chicken broth
1 cup chopped onion
2 cloves of garlic, minced
1 cup chopped onion
1 tablespoon vegetable
    oil
1 (8-ounce) can mild
    green chiles, drained,
    chopped
2 teaspoons cumin
1 1/2 teaspoons oregano
1 teaspoon salt
1/2 teaspoon cayenne
1/4 teaspoon ground
    cloves
4 1/2 cups chopped
    cooked chicken breast

Garnish:
Shredded Monterey Jack
    cheese
Chopped fresh tomatoes
Sour cream
Chunky salsa
Chopped avocado

Sort and rinse the beans. Combine the beans with enough cold water to cover in a bowl. Let stand for 8 to 10 hours. Drain and rinse. Combine the beans with the broth, 1 cup onion and garlic in a stockpot. Bring to a boil and stir; reduce heat.

Simmer for 3 hours or until the beans are tender, stirring occasionally.

Sauté 1 cup onion in the oil in a skillet until tender. Stir in the green chiles, cumin, oregano, salt, cayenne and cloves. Add to the beans and mix well. Stir in the chicken.

Simmer for 1 hour, stirring occasionally. Ladle into chili bowls. Garnish with shredded Monterey Jack cheese, chopped fresh tomatoes, sour cream, chunky salsa and/or chopped avocado. *Yield: 6 servings.*

Add a pinch of baking soda when cooking dried beans to prevent the beans from becoming mushy.

Black Bean Soup with Tomato Salsa

1 pound dried black
  beans
1 ham hock
1 onion, chopped
2 tablespoons olive oil
3 cloves of garlic, minced
1 tomato, peeled,
  chopped
2 fresh jalapeños, seeded,
  chopped
$1/2$ teaspoon oregano
$1/4$ teaspoon salt
$1/4$ teaspoon freshly
  ground pepper
Tomato Salsa

Garnish:
Sour cream

Sort and rinse the beans. Combine the beans and ham hock with enough cold water to cover in a stockpot. Bring to a boil; reduce heat. Simmer for 3 hours or until the beans are tender, stirring occasionally. Remove the ham hock.

Sauté the onion in the olive oil in a skillet until tender. Add the garlic and mix well. Cook for 1 minute, stirring constantly. Stir in the tomato, jalapeños, oregano, salt and pepper. Cook for 5 minutes, stirring frequently. Add to the beans and mix well. Simmer for 25 minutes, stirring occasionally.

Process the bean mixture in a blender or food processor until puréed. Pour the purée into a saucepan. Cook just until heated through, stirring frequently. Ladle into soup bowls. Top with Tomato Salsa and sour cream. May add additional chicken stock for a thinner consistency. *Yield: 8 to 10 servings.*

Tomato Salsa

3 tomatoes, peeled,
  chopped
$1/3$ onion, chopped
$1/2$ cup chopped fresh
  cilantro
Juice of 1 lime
1 fresh jalapeño, seeded,
  chopped
1 clove of garlic, minced

Combine the tomatoes, onion, cilantro, lime juice, jalapeño and garlic in a bowl and mix gently.

Creamy Cauliflower Soup

5 cups chopped
   cauliflower
$1/2$ cup chopped onion
$1/4$ cup butter
2 cups chicken broth
$1/2$ teaspoon marjoram
$1/2$ teaspoon fines herbes
$1/4$ teaspoon salt
$1/4$ teaspoon pepper
1 bay leaf
1 cup shredded Cheddar
   cheese
$1^1/2$ cups half-and-half

Sauté the cauliflower and onion in the butter in a saucepan until the vegetables are tender. Add the broth, marjoram, fines herbes, salt, pepper and bay leaf and mix well. Cook until of the desired consistency, stirring frequently. Discard the bay leaf. Process the cauliflower mixture in a blender until puréed. Return the soup to the saucepan. Add the cheese and mix well. Cook over low heat until the cheese melts, stirring frequently. Stir in the half-and-half. Cook just until heated through; do not boil. Ladle into soup bowls.
Yield: 8 to 10 servings.

Cheese and Artichoke Soup

1 cup chopped onion
1 cup sliced carrot
1 cup chopped celery
$1/4$ cup butter
$1/4$ cup flour
$1^1/2$ tablespoons
   cornstarch
$1/8$ teaspoon baking soda
4 cups chicken broth
4 cups milk
2 cups extra-sharp
   shredded Cheddar
   cheese
1 teaspoon pepper
$3^1/2$ cups chopped
   drained artichoke
   hearts
Salt to taste

Sauté the onion, carrot and celery in the butter in a saucepan until tender. Stir in a mixture of the flour, cornstarch and baking soda. Add the broth gradually, stirring constantly. Stir in the milk. Bring to a boil. Boil until thickened, stirring constantly; reduce heat. Add the cheese and pepper and mix well. Cook until the cheese melts, stirring constantly. Stir in the artichokes and salt. Cook just until heated through, stirring constantly. Ladle into soup bowls.
Yield: 12 servings.

Note: May sprinkle each serving with additional shredded cheese, chopped fresh parsley and/or paprika.

Never boil soup or sauces that contain cheese. The protein in the cheese coagulates and tends to separate from the fat and water. If the soup or sauce is boiled, it will be watery and grainy. Reduced temperatures and cooking times are the true secrets to success when cooking with cheese.

Italian Knife-and-Fork Soup

8 ounces sweet Italian
   pork sausage, sliced
8 ounces hot Italian pork
   sausage, sliced
1/4 cup water
2 tablespoons olive oil
4 potatoes, thinly sliced
1 red pepper, cut into
   strips
1 green bell pepper, cut
   into strips
1 red onion, chopped
4 cloves of garlic, minced
1 teaspoon oregano
1/2 teaspoon rosemary
4 cups chicken stock
3/4 cup tomato paste
1/4 cup water
Salt and pepper to taste

Garnish:
Minced green onions
Grated Parmesan cheese
Croutons

Combine the sausage and 1/4 cup water in a saucepan. Simmer, covered, for 4 minutes; drain.

Brown the sausage in the saucepan. Remove the sausage with a slotted spoon to a bowl. Discard the pan drippings; wipe the saucepan with a paper towel.

Heat the olive oil in the saucepan until hot. Sauté the potatoes, red pepper, green pepper, onion, garlic, oregano and rosemary in the hot oil for 5 minutes. Stir in the stock, tomato paste, 1/4 cup water and sausage.

Cook, covered, for 10 minutes, stirring occasionally. Season with salt and pepper. Ladle into soup bowls. Garnish with green onions, Parmesan cheese and croutons. *Yield: 8 servings.*

Creole Corn and Crab Bisque

4 ears of yellow corn
^{1}/$_2$ cup unsalted butter
^{1}/$_2$ cup flour
3 cups shrimp stock
2 cups chicken stock
1 teaspoon liquid crab
 boil
1 cup whipping cream
1 pound fresh lump crab
 meat, flaked
1 tablespoon Creole
 seasoning
1 teaspoon lemon pepper
^{1}/$_4$ teaspoon salt
^{1}/$_4$ teaspoon pepper
^{3}/$_4$ cup chopped green
 onions

Shuck the corn and remove the silk. Cut the tops of the corn kernels with a sharp knife into a bowl, scraping the cob to remove the milk. Heat the butter in a saucepan. Stir in the flour. Cook just until the flour begins to stick, stirring constantly. Add the stocks and crab boil and mix well. Bring to a boil, stirring constantly; reduce heat. Simmer for 10 minutes, stirring frequently. Add the corn kernels and milk. Cook for 10 minutes. Stir in the whipping cream gradually. Fold in the crab meat, Creole seasoning, lemon pepper, salt, pepper and ^{1}/$_2$ of the green onions. Let stand for 20 minutes. Ladle into soup bowls. Sprinkle with the remaining green onions. *Yield: 6 servings.*

In the summer, my family would go to a nearby cornfield and pick bushels of corn to put up for the following year. As children, we would run through the rows of corn, stacking the ears so we could take them home to shuck. For our efforts, we set aside several ears of the fresh-picked corn to boil for dinner that evening. Corn on the cob never tasted so good!

~ Rhonda Chenet ~

Chili Con Queso Soup

12 ounces cream cheese
5 tablespoons unsalted
 butter
1 cup chopped onion
7 cups chopped drained
 plum tomatoes
1^1/$_2$ cups chopped mild
 drained green chiles
3^1/$_2$ cups chicken broth
3 cups half-and-half
2 tablespoons fresh
 lemon juice
^{1}/$_8$ teaspoon cayenne
^{1}/$_8$ teaspoon salt

Garnish:
Julienned corn tortillas
Chopped onions
Shredded cheese

Cut the cream cheese into cubes. Let stand at room temperature until softened. Heat the butter in a saucepan over medium heat until melted. Add the onion and mix well. Cook until tender, stirring frequently. Stir in the tomatoes and chiles. Cook until the liquid has evaporated, stirring occasionally. Add the cream cheese. Cook until the cream cheese melts, stirring constantly. Stir in the broth, half-and-half, lemon juice, cayenne and salt. Cook just until heated through. Ladle into soup bowls. Garnish with tortilla strips, onions and cheese. *Yield: 6 to 8 servings.*

Perfect French Onion Soup

1/4 cup unsalted butter
2 tablespoons olive oil
6 cups chopped yellow
  onions
4 cloves of garlic, minced
1 teaspoon sugar
1/3 cup Cognac
1 tablespoon Dijon
  mustard
1/2 teaspoon thyme
3 tablespoons flour
3 quarts beef stock
1 1/2 cups dry white wine
1/4 teaspoon freshly
  ground pepper
1/4 teaspoon salt
French Bread Croutons
8 ounces Gruyère
  cheese, grated
8 ounces smoked
  mozzarella cheese,
  shredded
4 ounces Parmesan
  cheese, grated

8 thick slices French
  bread
1/4 cup unsalted butter,
  softened
1/4 cup olive oil
2 cloves of garlic, minced

Heat the butter with the olive oil in a
stockpot until melted. Sauté the onions in
the hot butter mixture over high heat for
10 minutes; reduce heat to medium. Add
the garlic and sugar. Cook for 30 minutes
or until the onions are light brown, stirring
occasionally. Stir in the Cognac.

Cook until warm; flame with a match.
Stir in the Dijon mustard and thyme when
the flames have subsided. Stir in the flour.
Cook until smooth, stirring constantly.
Add the stock and white wine gradually
and mix well. Stir in the pepper and salt.
Simmer over medium heat for 1 hour,
stirring occasionally.

Arrange 8 ovenproof soup bowls on a
baking sheet. Fill the bowls 3/4 full. Place 1
crouton on top of each serving.

Combine the Gruyère cheese, mozzarella cheese and Parmesan cheese in a
bowl and mix well: Sprinkle over each
crouton. Broil 6 inches from the heat
source until bubbly. Serve immediately.
Yield: 8 servings.

French Bread Croutons

Arrange the French bread in a single layer
on a baking sheet. Spread with the butter;
drizzle with the olive oil. Sprinkle with the
garlic. Bake at 350 degrees for 15 minutes
or until light brown.

*For our fifth wedding
anniversary, my
husband and I decided
to have a special dinner
at home. I spent days
planning the menu,
which was to begin
with French Onion
Soup. As I prepared the
soup, the aroma was
wonderful, and it
slowly filled the house. I
did notice however that
the soup did not look
like I thought it should,
but the aroma was
divine! I ladled the soup
into the soup bowls,
and the first course was
served. My husband,
ever the diplomat,
commented on the
consistency of the
onions . . . he had never
had a French Onion
Soup quite like this.
And, no wonder; the
onions were whole,
uncooked, and hard as
rocks! What a dinner!*

↤ *Linda Martens* ↦

Soups and Salads

Fresh Mushroom Bisque

1/2 cup butter
1 1/2 cups sliced green
    onions
1 leek, chopped
3 tablespoons flour
5 cups chicken stock
8 ounces fresh
    mushrooms, chopped
1 cup whipping cream
1/4 cup dry sherry
1/4 teaspoon salt
1/4 teaspoon white pepper

Garnish:
Sliced mushrooms

Heat the butter in a saucepan until melted. Add the green onions and leek. Simmer for 15 minutes, stirring frequently; do not brown. Whisk in the flour. Cook for 1 minute, stirring constantly. Add the stock gradually and mix well. Bring to a boil; reduce heat. Stir in the mushrooms. Cook for 10 minutes, stirring occasionally. Process the mushroom mixture in a blender or food processor until smooth. Return the soup to the saucepan. Add the whipping cream and sherry gradually, stirring until blended. Cook just until heated through. Season with the salt and white pepper. Ladle into soup bowls. Garnish each serving with sliced mushrooms. *Yield: 6 to 8 servings.*

Keep mushrooms fresh by storing them unwashed in paper or damp cloth bags. This allows them to breathe and stay fresh longer.

Holiday Soup

2 tablespoons butter
1 cup chopped onion
1 pound mild Italian link
    sausage, diagonally
    sliced
5 1/2 cups beef broth
3 1/2 cups whole
    tomatoes, chopped
1 1/2 cups burgundy
1 teaspoon basil
2 cloves of garlic,
    chopped
Chopped fresh parsley to
    taste
Salt and pepper to taste
2 cups sliced zucchini
2 cups rigatoni, cooked,
    drained

Heat the butter in a saucepan until melted. Add the onion. Sauté until tender. Brown the sausage in a skillet. Drain, reserving 1/2 cup of the pan drippings. Stir the sausage, reserved pan drippings, broth, tomatoes, burgundy, basil, garlic, parsley, salt and pepper into the onion mixture and mix well. Cook for 15 minutes, stirring occasionally. Add the zucchini and mix well. Cook for 10 minutes or until the zucchini is tender, stirring occasionally. Stir in the pasta just before serving. Ladle into soup bowls. *Yield: 6 to 8 servings.*

Note: This easy, hearty soup is great to serve on Christmas Eve. The red and green color is so festive!

Creamy Potato Soup

3 tablespoons butter
1/3 cup flour
4 slices bacon
3/4 cup chopped carrot
3/4 cup minced onion
1/2 cup chopped celery
1/3 cup minced green
   onions
1 teaspoon seasoned salt
1 teaspoon minced garlic
1/2 teaspoon white pepper
1/2 teaspoon cracked
   black pepper
2 tablespoons olive oil
4 1/2 cups (1/2-inch cubes)
   peeled baking potatoes
2 2/3 cups whipping cream
2 cups water
2 teaspoons chicken
   bouillon granules
12 ounces Swiss cheese,
   shredded

Heat the butter in a saucepan over low heat until melted. Stir in the flour. Cook until smooth or of roux consistency, stirring constantly. Fry the bacon in a heavy saucepan over medium heat until crisp; drain. Crumble the bacon. Combine the carrot, onion, celery, green onions, seasoned salt, garlic, white pepper and black pepper in a bowl and mix well. Sauté the vegetable mixture in the olive oil in a saucepan over medium-low heat until the vegetables are tender. Add the potatoes. Cook until the potatoes are tender, stirring occasionally. Add the whipping cream, water and bouillon granules gradually and mix well. Cook for 5 minutes or until the bouillon granules dissolve, stirring constantly. Stir in the cheese. Add the roux and mix well. Simmer for 15 minutes, stirring occasionally. Ladle into soup bowls. Sprinkle with the bacon.
Yield: 6 servings.

The flavor of this soup is enhanced if prepared one day in advance, chilled overnight, and reheated just before serving.

Peasant Potato Soup

6 tablespoons butter
4 cups chopped potatoes
1 cup water
2/3 cup chopped onion
2 cloves of garlic,
   crushed
1 tablespoon salt
1/4 teaspoon pepper
4 cups milk
3 tablespoons chopped
   fresh parsley
Salt and pepper to taste

Heat the butter in a saucepan until melted. Stir in the potatoes, water and onion. Add the garlic, 1 tablespoon salt and 1/4 teaspoon pepper. Cook, covered, over low heat until the potatoes are tender, stirring occasionally. Mash the potato mixture until of the desired consistency. Add the milk and mix well. Cook over low heat until heated through, stirring occasionally. Stir in the parsley. Season with salt and pepper if desired.
Yield: 6 servings.

Chunky Cream of Pumpkin Soup

1 small pumpkin
2¹/₂ cups chicken broth
2 cups solid-pack
  pumpkin
2 tablespoons butter
2 tablespoons flour
2 tablespoons butter
1 onion, chopped
1 teaspoon nutmeg
¹/₂ teaspoon fresh lemon
  juice
¹/₄ teaspoon allspice
¹/₈ teaspoon white pepper
¹/₈ teaspoon black pepper
1 bay leaf
1 cup half-and-half

Cut the top from the pumpkin and discard; remove the seeds and stringy portions. Place the pumpkin in a large baking pan; add hot water to a depth of 1 inch. Tent the pumpkin with foil. Bake at 400 degrees for 1¹/₂ hours or until the pumpkin is tender and the inside walls scrape easily.

Bring the broth to a boil in a saucepan. Stir in the canned pumpkin. Simmer, covered, for 30 minutes, stirring occasionally. Heat 2 tablespoons butter in a saucepan until melted. Add the flour and mix well. Cook until thickened, stirring constantly. Add to the pumpkin mixture and mix well.

Heat 2 tablespoons butter in a saucepan until melted. Sauté the onion in the butter until tender. Stir into the pumpkin mixture. Add the nutmeg, lemon juice, allspice, white pepper, black pepper and bay leaf and mix well.

Simmer, covered, for 30 minutes, stirring occasionally. Add the half-and-half. Cook just until heated through, stirring occasionally. Discard the bay leaf.

Arrange the hot pumpkin on a serving platter; do not allow the pumpkin to cool. Pour the soup into the pumpkin. Scrape the cooked pumpkin with a metal spoon into the soup and mix well. Serve immediately. *Yield: 6 to 8 servings.*

Note: If pumpkins are not available, steam six to eight acorn squash and use them as soup bowls.

Select pumpkins specifically grown for their eating qualities, such as the sugar pumpkin, that are firm, heavy, and without noticeable blemishes or cracks. Look for a strong orange color and an attached stem. Such a pumpkin will have more meat, less waste, and a sweeter flavor.

Fresh Seafood Gumbo

1/3 cup olive oil
1/3 cup flour
2 cups chopped onions
2 cups chopped celery
2 cups (1/4-inch slices) okra
1 cup chopped green bell pepper
1/4 cup chopped fresh parsley
2 cups water
1 3/4 cups chicken broth
1/2 cup tomato sauce
2 tablespoons Worcestershire sauce
1 tablespoon thyme
1 tablespoon Kitchen Bouquet
2 teaspoons garlic salt
2 teaspoons freshly ground pepper
3 bay leaves
Hot sauce to taste
2 pounds cooked medium shrimp, peeled, deveined
1 pound crab meat, flaked
Hot cooked rice

Heat the olive oil in a heavy skillet until hot but not smoking. Whisk in 1/2 of the flour. Add the remaining flour and mix well.

Cook until smooth and dark in color, stirring constantly. Add the onions, celery, okra, green pepper and parsley. Cook over low heat for 5 minutes, stirring constantly. Stir in the water, broth and tomato sauce.

Simmer for 1 hour, stirring occasionally. Add the Worcestershire sauce, thyme, Kitchen Bouquet, garlic salt, pepper, bay leaves and hot sauce and mix well.

Simmer for 20 minutes, stirring occasionally. Add the shrimp and crab meat. Cook just until heated through, stirring occasionally. Discard the bay leaves. Ladle over hot cooked rice in soup bowls. *Yield: 8 to 10 servings.*

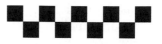

To correct overseasoning, add a raw, peeled, and quartered potato and simmer for 15 minutes. Remove from the heat and discard the potato before serving.

Sherried Wild Rice Soup

6 tablespoons butter
1/3 cup chopped onion
1/2 cup flour
4 cups chicken broth
1 cup whipping cream
1/3 cup dry sherry
1 1/2 cups cooked wild
  rice
1/2 teaspoon salt
1/2 teaspoon freshly
  ground pepper

Heat the butter in a saucepan over medium heat until melted. Stir in the onion. Cook until tender, stirring constantly. Add the flour and mix well. Cook for 1 minute, stirring frequently. Add the broth gradually, whisking constantly until mixed. Add the whipping cream and sherry gradually and mix well. Stir in the wild rice, salt and pepper. Simmer for 5 minutes or until slightly thickened, stirring frequently. Ladle into soup bowls. *Yield: 6 to 8 servings.*

Fresh Spinach Soup

4 ounces fresh
  mushrooms, chopped
2 scallions, chopped
5 tablespoons unsalted
  butter
5 tablespoons flour
2 cups chicken broth
2 cups milk
1 cup shredded Swiss
  cheese
4 ounces cream cheese,
  cubed, softened
1/2 teaspoon salt
1/4 teaspoon nutmeg
Freshly ground pepper
  to taste
12 ounces fresh spinach,
  cooked, drained,
  chopped

Sauté the mushrooms and scallions in the butter in a saucepan until tender. Whisk in the flour. Add the broth gradually and mix well. Add the milk gradually and mix well; reduce heat. Cook until thickened, stirring constantly. Stir in the Swiss cheese, cream cheese, salt, nutmeg and pepper. Cook until the cheese melts, stirring constantly. Add the spinach and mix well. Cook just until heated through, stirring gently. Ladle into soup bowls. *Yield: 4 to 6 servings.*

Texas Tortilla Soup

1 (3-pound) chicken
10 cups water
2 onions, cut into halves
6 ribs celery, cut into
    halves
8 sprigs of cilantro
4 chicken bouillon cubes
12 corn tortillas, torn
2 jalapeños, seeded,
    chopped
2 cloves of garlic

Garnish:
Fried corn tortilla strips
Shredded Cheddar and
    Monterey Jack cheese
Chopped fresh cilantro

Rinse the chicken. Combine the chicken, water, onions, celery, cilantro and bouillon cubes in a stockpot. Bring to a boil; reduce heat. Simmer for 1 hour or until the chicken is tender. Drain, reserving the stock and discarding the vegetables. Shred the chicken, discarding the skin and bones. Process 2 cups of the reserved stock, tortillas, jalapeños and garlic in a blender until puréed. Pour into the stockpot with the remaining stock. Stir in the chicken. Simmer over low heat for 30 minutes or until slightly thickened, stirring occasionally. Ladle into soup bowls. Garnish each serving with corn tortilla strips, Cheddar cheese, Monterey Jack cheese and cilantro. *Yield: 6 to 8 servings.*

White Gazpacho

2 cups chopped peeled
    cucumbers
1 cup chicken broth
2 cloves of garlic,
    chopped
1 cup fat-free sour cream
1 cup low-fat sour cream
1/2 cup each fat-free and
    low-fat plain yogurt
3 tablespoons white
    vinegar
1 teaspoon salt
1/4 teaspoon white pepper
2 cups chicken broth

Garnish:
Chopped green onions
Chopped fresh tomatoes

Process the cucumbers, 1 cup broth and garlic in a blender or food processor until puréed. Add the sour cream, yogurt, white vinegar, salt and white pepper. Process until puréed. Add 2 cups broth. Process on medium speed just until blended. Chill, covered, in the refrigerator. Ladle into soup bowls. Garnish with green onions and tomatoes. *Yield: 6 to 8 servings.*

As an Irish bride newly arrived in America, my mother set out to impress her Texan husband with her cooking skills. As my father left for work in the morning, she started preparations for an authentic Texas dish. He returned at noon to find my mother still in her nightgown standing over the stockpot. When he asked her if there was a problem, she replied that she was holding the chicken down under the water because it kept floating to the top!

⌐ Lisa Harrison ⌐

Soups and Salads

Curried Pea Soup

1 1/2 cups fresh green
   peas
1 cup chicken broth
1 cup sliced peeled white
   potato
3/4 cup sliced celery and
   celery leaves
1/2 cup sliced onion
1/2 cup sliced carrot
1 teaspoon salt
1 teaspoon curry powder
1 clove of garlic
1 cup chicken broth
1 cup whipping cream

Combine the peas, 1 cup broth, potato, celery, onion, carrot, salt, curry powder and garlic in a saucepan. Bring to a boil; reduce heat. Simmer, covered, for 15 minutes, stirring occasionally. Remove from heat. Let stand until cool. Process the pea mixture in a blender until puréed. Add 1 cup broth and whipping cream gradually, processing constantly at low speed until blended. Pour into a bowl. Chill, covered, in the refrigerator. Ladle into soup bowls. *Yield: 6 servings.*
   Note: This is a great alternative to gazpacho in the summer. May be served hot or cold.

Squash Soup with Nutmeg

1 cup chopped onion
1/4 cup unsalted butter
4 cups sliced yellow
   squash
2 cups chicken stock
1 leek, chopped
1/4 teaspoon sugar
2 cups whipping cream
1/4 teaspoon freshly
   grated nutmeg
1/8 teaspoon saffron
Salt and white pepper to
   taste

Garnish:
Chopped fresh chives or
   dillweed

Sauté the onion in the butter in a saucepan until tender. Add the squash, stock, leek and sugar and mix well. Cook until the vegetables are tender, stirring occasionally. Cool to room temperature. Process the squash mixture in a blender or food processor until puréed. Add the whipping cream, nutmeg, saffron, salt and white pepper gradually, processing constantly at low speed just until blended. Pour into a bowl. Chill, covered, for 4 hours. Ladle into soup bowls. Garnish with chives or dillweed. *Yield: 6 to 8 servings.*

Chilled Strawberry Soup

5 cups sliced fresh strawberries
2½ cups freshly squeezed orange juice
½ cup plus 1 teaspoon Grand Marnier
½ cup Crème Fraîche
2 teaspoons (about) superfine sugar
6 fresh strawberries with caps
6 sprigs of mint

Process 5 cups strawberries in a blender or food processor until puréed. Combine the strawberry purée and orange juice in a bowl, whisking until blended. Whisk in the Grand Marnier. Whisk in the Crème Fraîche.

Chill, covered, for 4 hours or until thoroughly chilled. Stir in the sugar just before serving, adjusting according to taste. Spoon into chilled dessert cups or chilled wine glasses.

Cut four parallel slices from the tip of each strawberry to just below the cap with a sharp knife; fan the slices gently. Arrange 1 mint sprig and 1 strawberry fan on top of each serving. Serve immediately.
Yield: 6 servings.

Note: Do not make any substitutions for the fresh orange juice.

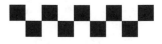

This soup is great for a bridal shower or summer luncheon.

Crème Fraîche

½ cup sour cream
½ cup whipping cream

Combine the sour cream and whipping cream in a bowl and mix well. Spoon into a jar with a tightfitting lid; seal. Let stand at room temperature for 12 hours or until thickened. Chill for 24 hours. Crème Fraîche is available in some supermarket dairy cases.

Chilled Tomatillo Soup

8 ounces fresh
tomatillos, husks
removed, rinsed
1/2 cup chopped onion
2 tablespoons chopped
seeded poblanos
11/2 tablespoons fresh
lime juice
2 teaspoons chopped
fresh cilantro
1/2 teaspoon cumin
1/8 teaspoon salt
1/8 teaspoon sugar
1 clove of garlic
1 cup half-and-half
1 cup finely chopped
peeled jicama

Garnish:
Sliced tomatillos
Sprigs of cilantro
Sliced almonds

Combine the tomatillos with enough water to cover in a saucepan. Bring to a boil. Boil for 5 minutes or until tender; drain.

Process the tomatillos, onion, poblanos, lime juice, cilantro, cumin, salt, sugar and garlic until smooth. Combine the tomatillo mixture with the half-and-half and jicama in a bowl and mix well. Chill, covered, in the refrigerator.

Ladle into soup bowls. Garnish each serving with sliced tomatillos, cilantro sprigs and/or sliced almonds.

Yield: 8 servings.

Note: For a smoother soup, add the jicama to the blended mixture and pulse until of the desired consistency. Stir in the half-and-half.

Tomatillos are a small, olive-green fruit often called Mexican green tomatoes. Tomatillos are not related to tomatoes however. The texture is similar to the tomato, but with lots of seeds. The tomatillo is acidic and resembles a lemon or apple.

Fresh Fruit Salad with Rum Raisin Sauce

1 cantaloupe, coarsely
   chopped
1 honeydew melon,
   coarsely chopped
1 pint strawberries,
   sliced
2 cups grapes
Rum Raisin Sauce

2 cups sour cream
1/2 cup packed light
   brown sugar
1 tablespoon plus
   1 teaspoon light rum
1 tablespoon Irish
   whiskey
1/3 cup raisins

Combine the cantaloupe, honeydew melon, strawberries and grapes in a crystal serving bowl and mix gently. Serve with Rum Raisin Sauce. *Yield: 4 servings.*

Note: May substitute any of your favorite fruits for the cantaloupe, honeydew melon, strawberries and grapes.

Rum Raisin Sauce

Combine the sour cream, brown sugar, rum and Irish whiskey in a bowl, whisking until blended. Fold in the raisins. Chill, covered, for 2 hours or longer.

Here's a favorite from the Wunsche Bros. Cafe, a local, historic establishment dating back to 1902.

Cool Watermelon Salad

8 cups (3/4-inch cubes)
   seeded watermelon,
   chilled
1 cup crumbled feta
   cheese
1/3 cup chopped mint
   leaves
1/4 cup extra-virgin olive
   oil
Juice of 2 limes
Freshly ground pepper to
   taste

Combine the watermelon, feta cheese, mint, olive oil, lime juice and pepper in a bowl, tossing to mix. Serve immediately. *Yield: 12 servings.*

This unique salad is very colorful and is a great accompaniment to grilled beef, poultry and seafood.

Home-Style Chicken Salad

4 large boneless skinless
    chicken breast halves
1 small onion, cut into
    quarters
1 rib celery with top
5 chicken bouillon cubes
2 cups seedless red grape
    halves
1 cup drained crushed
    pineapple
1 cup chopped celery
    (optional)
2/3 cup slivered almonds
3 hard-cooked eggs,
    chopped
2 cups mayonnaise
Salt and pepper to taste

Rinse the chicken. Combine the chicken, onion, 1 rib celery and bouillon cubes with enough water to cover in a stockpot. Cook until the chicken is tender. Drain, discarding the vegetables. Chop the chicken into bite-size pieces or shred, discarding the skin and bones. Combine the chicken, grapes, pineapple, 1 cup celery, almonds and eggs in a bowl and mix gently. Stir in the mayonnaise, salt and pepper. Chill, covered, until serving time. *Yield: 6 servings.*

This chicken salad may be used as a sandwich spread, or served as an entrée in lettuce cups garnished with sliced pineapple and strawberries. Spoon into miniature puff pastries for ladies luncheons and showers.

Tropical Chicken Salad

3 cups chopped cooked
    chicken
1 cup sliced celery
2 tablespoons chopped
    green onions
2 tablespoons fresh
    lemon juice
1 teaspoon salt
1/2 cup mayonnaise
1/2 teaspoon grated lemon
    peel
1 1/4 cups drained
    mandarin oranges
1 cup drained pineapple
    chunks
1/2 cup slivered almonds,
    toasted
Assorted salad greens

Combine the chicken, celery and green onions in a bowl and mix well. Stir in the lemon juice and salt. Chill, covered, for 8 to 10 hours. Add the mayonnaise and lemon peel and mix well. Stir in the mandarin oranges, pineapple and almonds gently just before serving. Line 6 salad bowls with the salad greens. Spoon the chicken salad into the bowls. *Yield: 6 servings.*

Chicken Pasta Salad

1 pound mixed fusilli, cooked al dente
4 boneless skinless chicken breasts, grilled, chopped
2 carrots, cut into $1/8$-inch slices
2 zucchini, cut into $1/4$-inch slices
2 yellow squash, cut into $1/4$-inch slices
1 head broccoli, cut into bite-size pieces
4 ounces snow peas
1 tomato, chopped
$1^1/2$ cups Creamy Dressing
1 head green leaf lettuce
1 head iceberg lettuce, torn

Garnish:
Sliced tomato wedges
Olives

Combine the pasta, chicken, carrots, zucchini, yellow squash, broccoli, snow peas and tomato in a bowl and mix gently. Add the chilled Creamy Dressing, tossing to coat.

Reserve 8 outside leaves of the leaf lettuce. Tear the remaining leaf lettuce into bite-size pieces. Combine the leaf lettuce and iceberg lettuce in a bowl, tossing to mix.

Line 8 salad bowls with the reserved lettuce leaves. Fill each bowl $1/2$ full with the lettuce mixture. Arrange the chicken salad over the lettuce. Garnish with sliced tomato wedges and olives. *Yield: 8 servings.*

Creamy Dressing

$1^1/2$ cups mayonnaise
$1/4$ cup red wine vinegar
$1/4$ cup vegetable oil
$1/4$ cup confectioners' sugar
$3/4$ teaspoon minced garlic
$1/4$ teaspoon salt
$1/8$ teaspoon freshly ground pepper

Process the mayonnaise, wine vinegar, oil, confectioners' sugar, garlic, salt and pepper in a blender or food processor until smooth. Chill, covered, in the refrigerator.

Marinated Shrimp and Artichoke Salad

3¹/2 cups drained water-
    pack artichoke hearts
1¹/2 pounds medium
    shrimp, cooked,
    peeled, deveined
¹/2 cup vegetable oil
¹/2 cup olive oil
¹/2 cup wine vinegar
1 egg, beaten
2 tablespoons Dijon
    mustard
2 tablespoons minced
    chives
2 tablespoons minced
    green onions
¹/2 teaspoon salt
¹/2 teaspoon sugar
¹/8 teaspoon pepper

Cut the artichokes hearts into quarters. Combine with the shrimp in a bowl and mix gently. Combine the vegetable oil, olive oil, wine vinegar, egg, Dijon mustard, chives, green onions, salt, sugar and pepper in a bowl and mix well. Pour over the shrimp mixture, tossing to coat. Marinate in the refrigerator for 6 hours or longer; drain. Spoon into a serving bowl. May store, covered, in the refrigerator for up to 2 days. *Yield: 8 to 10 servings.*

    Note: To avoid raw eggs that may carry salmonella use an equivalent amount of commercial egg substitute.

Bulgur Vegetable Salad

1¹/2 cups broccoli florets
¹/2 cup plus 2 tablespoons
    chicken stock
3 tablespoons plus
    ¹/2 teaspoon red wine
    vinegar
1¹/2 teaspoons Dijon
    mustard
³/4 teaspoon coarse salt
1 clove of garlic, minced
¹/4 teaspoon freshly
    ground pepper
1 cup medium bulgur
¹/3 cup chopped radishes
¹/3 cup chopped celery
¹/4 cup sliced green
    onions
1¹/2 tablespoons olive oil

Cut the broccoli into bite-size pieces. Steam in a steamer until tender-crisp. Drain and pat dry. Bring the stock, wine vinegar, Dijon mustard, salt, garlic and pepper to a boil in a saucepan. Stir in the bulgur; reduce heat. Cook, covered, for 30 minutes. Mix the broccoli, radishes, celery and green onions in a bowl. Add the bulgur mixture, tossing to mix. Drizzle with the olive oil. Chill, covered, for 2 hours. *Yield: 6 to 8 servings.*

Shrimp sizes vary greatly. A recipe will usually dictate which is the most desirable size. For a finger food served with a dipping sauce, jumbo or extra-large shrimp are best. Medium to large shrimp are most commonly used with vegetable or pasta dishes served as entrées. Small shrimp are the sweetest and most time-consuming to peel. If you have the patience, they are excellent served in salads or soups.

Crunchy Rice Salad

1 cup white rice
1 1/3 cups drained
    mandarin oranges
1 cup chopped green
    onions
1 cup diagonally sliced
    celery
1 cup water chestnuts
1/2 cup sliced fresh
    mushrooms
1/4 cup rice vinegar
1/4 cup vegetable oil
1/4 cup soy sauce

Cook the rice using package directions, omitting the salt. Let stand until cool. Combine the rice, mandarin oranges, green onions, celery, water chestnuts and mushrooms in a bowl, tossing to mix. Combine the rice vinegar, oil and soy sauce in a bowl, whisking to mix. Pour over the rice mixture and mix gently. Chill, covered, until serving time.
Yield: 10 to 12 servings.

To make rice fluffier and drier, place a slice of dry bread on top of it after cooking.

Fresh Vegetable and Rice Salad

1 1/2 cups long grain rice
2 bay leaves
2 teaspoons salt
1/4 teaspoon saffron
1 cup chopped onion
1 cup chopped celery
1 cup chopped green bell
    pepper
2/3 cup chopped tomato
2/3 cup chopped fresh
    parsley
1/2 cup raisins
1/3 cup vegetable oil
5 teaspoons red wine
    vinegar
1 cup roasted peanuts

Combine the rice, bay leaves, salt and saffron in a saucepan. Cook using package directions. Drain and discard the bay leaves. Combine the rice, onion, celery, green pepper, tomato, parsley, raisins, oil and wine vinegar in a bowl and mix gently. Chill, covered, in the refrigerator. Mix in the peanuts just before serving.
Yield: 6 to 8 servings.

Chinese Noodle Salad

1/2 cup slivered almonds
3 ounces ramen noodles
2 tablespoons sesame
   seeds
2 tablespoons olive oil
1/2 head Chinese
   cabbage, thinly sliced
2 cups torn fresh spinach
1/2 cup chopped green
   onions
Soy Dressing

Sauté the almonds, ramen noodles and sesame seeds in the olive oil in a skillet until brown; drain. Chill in the refrigerator. Layer the cabbage, spinach and green onions in a salad bowl. Chill, covered, until serving time. Sprinkle with the noodle mixture and drizzle with the chilled Soy Dressing just before serving.
Yield: 6 to 8 servings.

Soy Dressing

1/3 cup white vinegar
1/3 cup sugar
1/3 cup vegetable oil
2 tablespoons soy sauce
1 tablespoon sesame oil

Whisk the vinegar, sugar, vegetable oil, soy sauce and sesame oil in a bowl until mixed. Chill, covered, in the refrigerator.

Minted Green Bean Salad

1 1/2 pounds fresh green
   beans, trimmed, cut
   into halves
3/4 cup extra-virgin olive
   oil
1/2 cup fresh mint leaves
1/4 cup white wine
   vinegar
1/2 teaspoon salt
1 clove of garlic, chopped
1/4 teaspoon freshly
   ground pepper
1 cup walnuts, toasted
1 cup chopped red onion
1 cup crumbled feta
   cheese

Parboil the beans in boiling water in a saucepan for 5 minutes; drain. Plunge into ice water in a bowl for 5 minutes; drain. Chill in the refrigerator. Whisk the olive oil, mint, wine vinegar, salt, garlic and pepper in a bowl until blended. Mix the chilled green beans, walnuts, red onion and feta cheese gently. Drizzle with the dressing. Chill, covered, for 2 hours. Toss lightly just before serving.
Yield: 6 to 8 servings.

Nutty Coleslaw

¹/₂ cup slivered almonds
¹/₂ cup sunflower kernels
1 tablespoon butter
6 tablespoons rice
　vinegar
¹/₄ cup sugar
1 teaspoon salt
1 teaspoon freshly
　ground pepper
³/₄ cup salad oil
8 cups packaged
　shredded coleslaw mix
¹/₂ cup sliced scallions
2 (3-ounce) packages
　ramen noodles,
　broken

Sauté the almonds and sunflower kernels in the butter in a skillet for 2 to 3 minutes; drain. Combine the rice vinegar, sugar, salt, pepper and oil in a bowl and mix well. Toss the almond mixture, coleslaw mix, scallions and ramen noodles in a salad bowl. Add the dressing, tossing to coat. Serve immediately. *Yield: 10 to 12 servings.*

　Note: May prepare in advance and store, covered, in the refrigerator until serving time.

Spicy Cajun Slaw

3 slices bacon
1 head purple cabbage,
　sliced
1 cup sliced purple onion
1³/₄ cups diced tomatoes
　with green chiles
¹/₂ cup sugar
¹/₂ cup cider vinegar

Fry the bacon in a skillet until crisp. Drain, reserving the pan drippings. Crumble the bacon. Sauté the cabbage and purple onion in the reserved pan drippings in a skillet just until tender. Stir in the tomatoes, sugar and vinegar. Cook over low heat for 10 to 15 minutes or just until heated through, stirring frequently. Do not overcook; cabbage should be tender-crisp. Serve warm. *Yield: 6 to 8 servings.*

Green Salad Italiano

1/2 cup salad-variety
    gourmet vinegar
1 1/2 teaspoons pepper
1 teaspoon salt
1 teaspoon dry mustard
4 cloves of garlic, minced
1 1/3 cups vegetable oil
1 head romaine, torn
1 head iceberg lettuce,
    torn
8 green onion tops,
    chopped
1 cup freshly grated
    Parmesan cheese
1 cup slivered almonds,
    toasted

Combine the vinegar, pepper, salt, dry mustard and garlic in a bowl and mix well. Add the oil in a thin stream, whisking constantly until mixed. Chill, covered, in the refrigerator. Combine the romaine, iceberg lettuce, green onion tops, cheese and almonds in a salad bowl and mix gently. Pour the chilled dressing over the salad greens just before serving, tossing to coat. Serve immediately.
Yield: 8 to 10 servings.

One medium head of iceberg lettuce equals approximately ten cups torn. One pound of spinach, stems removed, will equal approximately twelve cups.

Harvest Tossed Salad

3/4 cup vegetable oil
1/4 cup vinegar
1 head red leaf lettuce,
    torn
1 head green leaf lettuce,
    torn
1 head Boston lettuce,
    torn
1/2 cup grated Parmesan
    cheese
1/2 cup grated carrot
1/4 cup sesame seeds,
    toasted
1/4 cup sunflower
    kernels, toasted
1/4 cup pumpkin seeds,
    toasted
1/4 cup almonds, toasted

Whisk the oil and vinegar in a bowl. Chill, covered, for 1 hour. Combine the lettuce, cheese, carrot, sesame seeds, sunflower kernels, pumpkin seeds and almonds in a bowl, tossing to mix. Drizzle with the chilled oil and vinegar dressing and toss gently. Serve immediately.
Yield: 10 to 12 servings.

Mixed Greens with Lump Crab Meat

8 cups torn mixed salad
  greens
1/4 cup chopped avocado
1/4 cup chopped hearts of
  palm
1/2 cup French Dressing
4 tablespoons lump crab
  meat

Garnish:
Tomato wedges
Green onions

3/4 cup olive oil
1/2 cup red wine vinegar
1/4 cup red wine
4 anchovy fillets
2 tablespoons chopped
  red onion
2 teaspoons cracked
  black peppercorns
1 teaspoon
  Worcestershire sauce
1 teaspoon salt
1/4 teaspoon tarragon
1/4 teaspoon oregano
1/4 teaspoon thyme
3 cloves of garlic
4 sprigs of parsley

Toss the salad greens in a salad bowl.
Add the avocado, hearts of palm and the
chilled French Dressing and toss gently.

Arrange the salad mixture on 4
individual salad plates; top each salad with
1 tablespoon crab meat.

Garnish with chilled tomato wedges
and green onions. Serve immediately.
Yield: 4 servings.

French Dressing

Combine the olive oil, wine vinegar, red
wine, anchovies, red onion, black peppercorns, Worcestershire sauce, salt, tarragon,
oregano, thyme, garlic and parsley in a
blender or food processor container.
Process until blended. Chill, covered, in
the refrigerator.

*Recrisp limp greens
by rinsing and placing
in a sealable plastic
bag while still damp.
Chill for ten hours or
longer before using.*

Romaine and Pine Nut Salad

1/4 cup pine nuts
1 tablespoon butter
1/4 cup fresh lemon juice
2 tablespoons freshly
    grated Parmesan
    cheese
1 clove of garlic, cut into
    halves
1/4 teaspoon oregano
3/4 cup olive oil
1/4 cup peanut oil
Salt and freshly ground
    pepper to taste
1 1/2 pounds romaine,
    torn
4 ounces endive, torn

Sauté the pine nuts in the butter in a skillet lightly; drain. Combine the lemon juice, cheese, garlic and oregano in a bowl, whisking until mixed. Add a mixture of the olive oil and peanut oil in a fine stream, whisking constantly until mixed. Season with salt and pepper; discard the garlic. Combine the romaine, endive and dressing in a salad bowl, tossing to mix. Sprinkle with the pine nuts. Serve immediately. *Yield: 6 to 8 servings.*

Pine nuts are small seeds from one of several pine tree varieties. They have a sweet, faint pine flavor. Pine nuts will turn rancid quickly, so store them in an airtight container in the refrigerator for up to two months or in the freezer for up to six months.

Romaine Citrus Salad with Almonds

1/4 cup vegetable oil
2 tablespoons vinegar
2 teaspoons sugar
1 1/2 teaspoons chopped
    fresh parsley
1/2 teaspoon salt
1/8 teaspoon Tabasco
    sauce
1/3 cup slivered almonds
3 tablespoons sugar
1 head romaine, torn
1 cup chopped celery
2 green onions, chopped
1 avocado, chopped
1 1/4 cups drained
    mandarin oranges

Combine the oil, vinegar, 2 teaspoons sugar, parsley, salt and Tabasco sauce in a bowl, whisking until mixed. Chill, covered, in the refrigerator. Combine the almonds and 3 tablespoons sugar in a skillet and mix well. Cook over medium heat until the almonds are coated and light brown, stirring constantly. Let stand until cool. Combine the romaine, celery and green onions in a bowl and toss well. Add the almonds, avocado, mandarin oranges and chilled dressing just before serving, tossing to mix. *Yield: 4 servings.*

Oriental Salad

1 head red leaf lettuce,
   chopped
2 cups chopped broccoli
1 cup chopped green
   onions
1 cup chopped walnuts
1 (3-ounce) package
   ramen noodles,
   broken
2 tablespoons butter
Oriental Vinaigrette

Combine the lettuce, broccoli and green
onions in a bowl, tossing to mix. Sauté the
walnuts and ramen noodles in the butter
in a skillet for 5 minutes; drain. Add to the
lettuce mixture and mix well. Drizzle with
the chilled Oriental Vinaigrette and toss
gently. Serve immediately.
Yield: 4 to 6 servings.

Oriental Vinaigrette

1 cup vegetable oil
1/2 cup sugar
1/2 cup red wine vinegar
3 tablespoons soy sauce
Freshly ground pepper to
   taste

Combine the oil, sugar, wine vinegar, soy
sauce and pepper in a bowl, whisking until
blended. Chill, covered, in the refrigerator.

New Potato Salad

12 unpeeled new
   potatoes
3/4 cup mayonnaise
1/4 cup whipping cream
2 teaspoons chopped
   fresh dillweed
1/2 teaspoon salt
1/2 teaspoon white pepper
2 cloves of garlic, minced

Steam the new potatoes in a steamer just
until tender; do not overcook. Let stand
until cool. Cut into quarters. Combine
the mayonnaise and whipping cream in a
bowl and mix well. Stir in the dillweed,
salt, white pepper and garlic. Add the
potatoes, tossing gently to mix. Adjust the
seasonings. Chill, covered, until serving
time. *Yield: 4 servings.*

Picnic Potato Salad

3 pounds unpeeled white
   potatoes
1¹/₂ teaspoons salt
¹/₂ cup vegetable oil
¹/₂ cup chopped green
   onions
¹/₄ cup cider vinegar
1¹/₂ teaspoons salt
1 teaspoon dry mustard
¹/₈ teaspoon black pepper
¹/₈ teaspoon cayenne
1 cup coarsely chopped
   celery
¹/₂ cup sliced radishes
¹/₂ cup green olive halves
3 hard-cooked eggs,
   coarsely chopped
Boiled Dressing
Lettuce leaves

Garnish:
Sliced cucumbers
Hard-cooked egg wedges
Radish roses
Sliced onion

Pour just enough boiling water to cover the potatoes in a 5-quart heavy saucepan. Stir in 1¹/₂ teaspoons salt. Bring to a boil; reduce heat. Simmer, covered, for 30 to 35 minutes or just until the potatoes are fork-tender; do not overcook. Drain. Cool for 20 minutes. Peel the potatoes; cut into ¹/₄-inch slices.

Combine the oil, green onions, vinegar, 1¹/₂ teaspoons salt, dry mustard, black pepper and cayenne in a bowl and mix well. Pour over the warm potatoes in a bowl, tossing gently to coat. Chill, covered, for 2 hours or longer, tossing several times. Add the celery, radishes, green olives and eggs to the potato mixture 1 hour before serving and mix gently. Add the Boiled Dressing, tossing gently to mix. Chill, covered, until serving time.

Spoon the potato salad into a lettuce-lined salad bowl. Garnish with cucumbers, hard-cooked egg wedges, radish roses and sliced onion. *Yield: 12 servings.*

Note: Substitute red potatoes for the white potatoes for variety. May substitute a good quality mayonnaise for the Boiled Dressing.

Boiled Dressing

2 teaspoons sugar
1 teaspoon flour
1 teaspoon salt
1¹/₄ cups milk
3 egg yolks, lightly
   beaten
¹/₄ cup cider vinegar
1 teaspoon prepared
   mustard
2 teaspoons butter

Mix the sugar, flour and salt in a saucepan. Add the milk gradually, whisking constantly. Bring to a boil over medium heat, stirring constantly. Boil for 1 minute. Remove from heat. Stir a small amount of the hot mixture into the egg yolks; stir the egg yolks into the hot mixture. Add the vinegar and mustard and mix well. Bring to a boil, stirring constantly. Remove from heat. Stir in the butter. Let stand until cool. Chill, covered, until serving time.

The Fourth of July holiday is filled with memories for me. When I was growing up, we always attended a family reunion over the holiday. My family is so large that the gatherings were held at a local park or on a family member's huge lawn. I remember tables and tables of food. No one ever left hungry, because there was always enough food for everyone to eat all day and well into the evening.

⁀ *Leanne Savage* ⁀

Red Potato and Artichoke Salad

1 1/2 pounds unpeeled red
    potatoes
1/3 cup olive oil
3 tablespoons deli-style
    mustard
2 tablespoons lemon juice
1 teaspoon salt
3/4 teaspoon oregano
1/8 teaspoon pepper
6 ounces marinated
    artichoke hearts
1/2 cup pitted black olives
2 hard-cooked eggs, cut
    into quarters
1 small red pepper,
    chopped
3 green onions, sliced

Cut the potatoes into 3/4-inch cubes. Steam in a steamer for 8 to 10 minutes or just until tender; do not overcook. Spoon into a bowl. Let stand until cool. Combine the olive oil, mustard, lemon juice, salt, oregano and pepper in a jar with a tightfitting lid and shake to blend. Pour over the cooled potatoes, tossing to coat. Drain the artichoke hearts and cut into quarters. Add the artichokes, black olives, eggs, red pepper and green onions to the potato mixture and mix gently. Chill, covered, until serving time.
Yield: 6 servings.

Snow Pea Salad with Sesame Dressing

1 head iceberg lettuce
1 pound snow peas,
    blanched
1/2 cup chopped fresh
    parsley
Sesame Dressing
Red leaf lettuce

Shred the lettuce into a salad bowl. Add the snow peas and parsley and toss to mix. Add the chilled Sesame Dressing, tossing to coat. Spoon the salad onto salad plates lined with red leaf lettuce.
Yield: 6 to 8 servings.

Sesame Dressing

2/3 cup vegetable oil
2 tablespoons fresh
    lemon juice
2 tablespoons vinegar
2 tablespoons sugar
1 1/2 teaspoons salt
1 clove of garlic, crushed
1/4 cup sesame seeds,
    toasted

Combine the oil, lemon juice, vinegar, sugar, salt and garlic in a blender or food processor container. Process until smooth. Pour into a jar with a tightfitting lid. Add the sesame seeds and seal tightly. Shake to mix. Chill until serving time.

Soups and Salads

Sumptuous Raspberry and Spinach Salad

8 cups spinach,
   stemmed, torn into
   bite-size pieces
1 cup fresh raspberries
3/4 cup chopped
   macadamia nuts
3 kiwifruit, sliced
Raspberry Dressing

2 tablespoons raspberry
   vinegar
2 tablespoons seedless
   raspberry jam
1/3 cup vegetable oil

Combine the spinach, $1/2$ of the raspberries, $1/2$ of the macadamia nuts and $1/2$ of the kiwifruit in a salad bowl and toss gently.

Sprinkle with the remaining raspberries, remaining macadamia nuts and remaining kiwifruit. Serve immediately with the Raspberry Dressing.
Yield: 8 servings.

Raspberry Dressing

Combine the raspberry vinegar and jam in a blender container. Add the oil gradually, processing constantly until blended. Chill, covered, until serving time.

Note: Fresh strawberries, strawberry jam and strawberry vinegar provide a nice substitution.

To protect a wooden salad bowl, wash it quickly in lukewarm water and dry completely. Rub the entire bowl inside and out with waxed paper to give luster to the wood.

Celebration Spinach Salad

3 bunches spinach,
   stemmed, torn into
   bite-size pieces
1 pound bacon, crisp-
   fried, crumbled
3 cups croutons
8 ounces fresh
   mushrooms, sliced
8 hard-cooked eggs, sliced
Poppy Seed Dressing

1 cup vegetable oil
3/4 cup sugar
1/3 cup white vinegar
3 tablespoons grated
   onion
1 1/2 tablespoons poppy
   seeds
1 teaspoon salt
1 teaspoon dry mustard

Combine the spinach, bacon, croutons, mushrooms and eggs in a salad bowl, tossing gently to mix.

Add the desired amount of the chilled Poppy Seed Dressing just before serving and mix gently.

Store leftover dressing in the refrigerator or serve on the side.
Yield: 10 to 12 servings.

Poppy Seed Dressing

Combine the oil, sugar, vinegar, onion, poppy seeds, salt and dry mustard in a jar with a tightfitting lid and seal tightly. Shake to mix. Chill until serving time.

Zucchini and Apple Salad

1/3 cup vegetable oil
2 tablespoons white wine
    vinegar
1 tablespoon fresh lemon
    juice
1 teaspoon sugar
1 teaspoon basil
3/4 teaspoon salt
1/4 teaspoon pepper
2 medium Golden
    Delicious apples,
    peeled, chopped
1 medium Red Delicious
    apple, peeled, chopped
1 pound zucchini, thinly
    sliced
1/2 cup red onion, thinly
    sliced
1 cup julienned green
    bell pepper

Combine the oil, wine vinegar, lemon juice, sugar, basil, salt and pepper in a bowl and mix well. Add the Golden Delicious apples and Red Delicious apples, tossing to coat. Stir in the zucchini, red onion and green pepper. Chill, covered, until serving time. Toss again just before serving.
Yield: 10 to 12 servings.

   Note: The flavor is enhanced if the salad is prepared early in the day.

Homemade Croutons

16 slices fresh or dry
    white bread
2/3 cup butter
3 tablespoons freshly
    grated Parmesan
    cheese

Remove the crusts from the bread and cut the bread into 1-inch cubes. Heat the butter in a skillet until foamy: do not burn. Add the bread cubes, stirring to moisten. Remove the bread cubes with a slotted spoon to a baking sheet. Arrange in a single layer; do not allow bread cubes to touch. Bake at 250 degrees for 35 minutes or until golden brown and crisp. Cool slightly. Pour the cheese into a sealable plastic bag. Add the croutons, tossing to coat. Store in an airtight container.
Yield: 4 cups.

   Note: Croutons are an excellent garnish for soups and salads.

Every summer, my family heads for Alabama to spend several weeks with my parents. My mother welcomes my three rambunctious children and allows her home to be a gathering place for my friends and their kids. To accommodate the unpredictable schedule and variety of appetites, we have made "peach basket picnics" a tradition for the kids. Using small chipwood baskets collected from the roadside produce stands, we create individual picnic baskets filled with fried chicken, peanut butter sandwiches, chips, fruit, cookies, and juice boxes. The kids have their picnics on quilts under the trees outside, allowing my friends and me time to visit.

⇠ *Jan Sheehy* ⇢

Seasoned Bread Crumbs

2 cups fine dry bread
   crumbs
1 teaspoon salt
$1/2$ teaspoon pepper
$1/2$ teaspoon paprika
$1/8$ teaspoon ginger
$1/8$ teaspoon nutmeg

Combine the bread crumbs, salt, pepper, paprika, ginger and nutmeg in a bowl and mix well. Store in an airtight container. *Yield: 2 cups.*

Chill salad ingredients, salad plates, and salad bowls for a great-tasting salad.

Curried Pumpkin Seeds

$1^2/3$ cups warm water
$1/3$ cup curry powder
Juice of 1 lime
1 teaspoon salt
1 clove of garlic, finely
   minced
$2^1/3$ cups hulled
   pumpkin seeds
Butter to taste
Salt to taste

Combine $2/3$ cup of the warm water and curry powder in a saucepan and mix well. Add the lime juice, 1 teaspoon salt and garlic, stirring until blended. Stir in the remaining 1 cup warm water. Cook until heated through, stirring constantly. Add the pumpkin seeds and mix well. Simmer for 5 minutes, stirring frequently; do not boil. Drain and spread the pumpkin seeds in a single layer on a baking sheet. Dot with butter; sprinkle with salt to taste. Bake at 250 degrees until crisp. Let stand until cool. Store in an airtight container. *Yield: $2^1/3$ cups.*

Roasted Pumpkin Seeds

Pumpkin seeds
Butter to taste
Salt to taste

Rinse the pumpkin seeds and pat dry. Spread in a single layer on a baking sheet. Roast at 375 degrees for 25 minutes or until dry. Dot with butter. Roast at 400 degrees for 10 minutes or until brown, stirring frequently. Sprinkle with salt. Let stand until cool. Store in an airtight container. *Yield: variable.*

Entrées

A Timeless Toast

by Sarah Oliver Bonassin

We had just sat down to a table spread with slowly smoked pork ribs and all the trimmings when a dinner guest raised his glass with a toast:

"Salud, amor, pesetas y tiempo para gustarlos."

To life, love, wealth and the time to enjoy them…the same words my father often spoke before special dinners and gatherings of loved ones. I had not heard the familiar toast in many years, and the sound of it brought pleasant memories of childhood: the smell of fresh basil from the garden drying in the oven; Mother studying mountains of cookbooks in September for Thanksgiving recipes; Daddy steadying a purple-stained cheesecloth dripping juice for dewberry jelly into a white enamel pot; bubbles breaking the surface of sweet batter for crepes prepared in an iron skillet; making do with Kentucky bourbon when there was no banana liqueur for spur-of-the-moment Bananas Foster.

Eating good food—and the planning and preparation of it—was a favorite family pastime when I was growing up in a small town in central Texas. With three children active in school, scouting, church and other extracurricular activities, schedules were often hectic. My father, a sculptor by hobby and a chemical engineer by trade, somehow found time between running the family ranch and insurance agency to be active in various community organizations; he became mayor the year I graduated from high school. Mother stayed busy as a full-time homemaker, volunteer, gardener, decorator, family chauffeur, seamstress, teacher, counselor and confidante. Nevertheless, meals were adventures to be enjoyed and shared daily. It seemed there was always a new recipe to try, a more interesting disguise for leftovers or simply a garnish to take the ordinary out of the most mundane of meals.

Holidays put these culinary efforts to the test, and as the family expanded to include new in-laws, grandchildren, nieces and nephews, the "feeding frenzy" increased in force and intensity. Thanksgiving, for example, meant a solid week of elaborate meals and hors d'oeuvre in between, all carefully planned by Mother, who welcomed the chance to squeeze in a few more chairs at the table to accommodate visiting relatives. Our "Olympics of Eating," as we jokingly referred to the annual gathering, climaxed with Thursday's dinner, a marathon meal eaten at linen-covered card tables because there was no room for plates on the heavily laden dining room table.

Growing up in this atmosphere, trying new foods was a habit we all took for granted. As children, we were accustomed to nibbling on smoked oysters, homemade caponata, Mother's pate and such when she and Daddy entertained. Preparing the food in anticipation of "company" was almost as much fun as tasting the seemingly endless creations from the kitchen.

Visiting our relatives in a New Orleans suburb opened more doors for experimentation. Avid cooks themselves, Uncle Emmett and Aunt Louise satisfied our seafood-famished appetites with homemade crawfish etouffee, seafood gumbo, shrimp- and crab-meat-stuffed mirliton and—best of all—boiled shrimp and crabs piled high on a kitchen table spread with the *Times Picayune*.

Sightseeing excursions to the French Quarter provided welcome opportunities to sample the regional cuisine, such as the time my cousin Barbara and I, ages ten and twelve respectively, downed a dozen raw oysters at the Acme Oyster Bar and asked for more; the pride in Daddy's grin was obvious as the astonished waiter fulfilled our request and gave us each a pearl to boot.

We were purists in some ways; guests who dared ask for catsup with which to douse their T-bones found themselves wincing under my father's disdainful glare. Daddy's dry mix for barbecue sauce was plain and simple—and a guarded secret. And Mother's jellies and preserves were by far the best.

Yet a flair for the unusual was well-cultivated in our kitchen, possibly because four-star restaurants and ethnic delicatessens were not exactly common occurrences in a town pushing 2,500 in population. We often laughed that the closest thing to a French restaurant was a greasy spoon a few miles outside of town that served "French" fried steak, French fries and French salad dressing.

Now, years later, I find myself the hostess, joining the others clinking glasses as we repeat the timeless Spanish phrase. What better words to begin a meal—they reflect a love of food and people and bringing the two together. Such was the prevailing philosophy in my childhood home, where sharing and enjoying food with family and friends was both a central focus and a matter of course.

I'm confident the tradition will continue. Despite the demands of a full-time job, two teenage sons and volunteer responsibilities, I still find myself planning for the next meal as I clean up after the last. I remember when the boys were little, they learned to "help" with Christmas cookies, their dad's world-class spaghetti sauce or their grandmother's fresh, hot biscuits—spreading her entire kitchen with a fine layer of flour in the process. Today they can pull their own weight in the kitchen, an accomplishment I hope someday my future daughters-in-law will thank me for. It's comforting to know that the spirit of Daddy's timeless toast will season our children's lives—and surely their children's lives—for many years to come.

Sarah Oliver Bonassin is a sustaining member of the League. Despite an often hectic schedule, Sarah says her family's love of enjoying good food together never goes on the back burner.

Beef Tenderloin with Green Peppercorns

1 (2-pound) beef
    tenderloin
Salt and freshly ground
    pepper to taste
1 tablespoon vegetable
    oil
1/2 cup minced shallots
1 cup dry red wine
1/2 cup beef broth
1/2 cup green
    peppercorns
2 teaspoons tomato paste
6 tablespoons butter
1/2 cup chopped fresh
    parsley

Season the beef with salt and pepper. Heat the oil in a skillet over high heat until hot. Add the beef. Cook for 3 minutes or until brown on all sides. Remove the beef with a slotted spoon to a roasting pan, reserving the pan drippings.

Bake at 350 degrees for 35 minutes or until a meat thermometer registers 135 degrees for rare. Remove to a serving platter with a slotted spoon. Let rest for 10 to 15 minutes; slice.

Sauté the shallots in the reserved pan drippings in the skillet for 2 minutes. Add the red wine and mix well. Cook until reduced by 1/2, stirring frequently. Deglaze the skillet with the broth. Stir in the peppercorns, tomato paste and any juices accumulated in the roasting pan. Cook until reduced by 1/2, stirring frequently. Add the butter, stirring until blended. Spoon over the sliced beef; sprinkle with the parsley. *Yield: 4 servings.*

Note: Do not make substitutions for the green peppercorns. The green peppercorns have the perfect flavor and degree of spice for this dish.

Always allow a roasted piece of meat to rest for 10 to 15 minutes before carving. This resting time allows the juices to retreat back into the meat.

Beef Bourguignon

2 1/2 **pounds boneless beef chuck, cut into 1-inch cubes**
8 **tablespoons butter**
2 **tablespoons brandy**
8 **ounces pearl onions**
8 **ounces fresh mushrooms**
2 **tablespoons potato starch**
2 **tablespoons tomato paste**
2 **teaspoons meat extract**
1 1/2 **cups burgundy**
1 1/4 **cups beef broth**
3/4 **cup dry sherry**
3/4 **cup ruby port**
1/8 **teaspoon freshly ground pepper**
1 **bay leaf**
1 **tablespoon brandy**

Garnish:
Chopped fresh parsley

Wipe the beef with a paper towel. Heat 2 tablespoons of the butter in a 5-quart Dutch oven with a tightfitting lid over high heat. Brown 1/3 of the beef on all sides in the butter. Remove to a bowl with a slotted spoon. Repeat the process 2 more times with the remaining beef and 4 tablespoons of the butter. Return the beef to the Dutch oven.

Heat 2 tablespoons brandy in a saucepan just until the vapors rise. Ignite and pour over the beef. Remove the beef to a bowl with a slotted spoon when the flames subside, reserving the pan drippings. Add the remaining 2 tablespoons butter to the pan drippings. Heat just until melted. Add the onions. Cook, covered, over low heat until light brown, stirring occasionally. Stir in the mushrooms. Cook for 3 minutes, stirring constantly. Remove from heat.

Remove the onions and mushrooms with a slotted spoon to a bowl, reserving the pan drippings. Stir the potato starch, tomato paste and meat extract into the reserved pan drippings and mix well. Add the burgundy, broth, sherry and port and mix well. Bring just to a boil, stirring constantly. Remove from heat. Stir in the beef, onion mixture, pepper, bay leaf and 1 tablespoon brandy.

Cover with waxed paper. Place the lid on top of the waxed paper. Bake at 350 degrees for 1 1/2 hours or until the beef is done to taste, stirring occasionally. Discard the waxed paper. Discard the bay leaf. Garnish with the parsley. *Yield: 6 servings.*

Note: Meat extract is a "beef-upper" available in most supermarkets.

This recipe is well worth the effort. Don't skimp on the liquor.

Oriental Pot Roast

2 tablespoons vegetable
   oil
1 (3-pound) beef chuck
   roast
2 tablespoons grated
   gingerroot
1/2 cup sherry
1/4 cup soy sauce
1/2 cup water
3 tablespoons chopped
   green bell pepper
3 whole green onions
1 teaspoon salt
1/2 teaspoon anise seeds,
   crushed

Heat the oil in a roasting pan until hot.
Add the chuck roast and gingerroot. Cook
until the roast is brown on all sides; drain.
Stir in the sherry and soy sauce. Cook for
5 minutes, stirring occasionally. Add the
water, green pepper, green onions, salt and
anise seeds and mix well. Cook, covered,
over low heat for 3 hours or until the roast
is done to taste, stirring occasionally.
Yield: 4 to 6 servings.

   Note: May substitute beef top or
bottom round roast for the beef chuck
roast.

*Anise seeds play an
important role in the
cooking in Southeast
Asia. The seeds
have a distinctive
sweet licorice flavor.*

Filetto al Barolo

2 ounces shiitake
   mushrooms, sliced
1 portobello mushroom,
   sliced
1 ounce sun-dried
   tomatoes, chopped
2 cloves of garlic, minced
1/4 cup butter
1 cup Barolo red wine
2 cups beef broth
2 tablespoons Kitchen
   Bouquet
Salt and freshly ground
   pepper to taste
1 tablespoon roux
2 (8-ounce) filet
   mignons

Sauté the mushrooms, sun-dried tomatoes
and garlic in the butter in a skillet for 3 to
4 minutes. Stir in the red wine. Cook for 5
minutes, stirring frequently. Add the broth
and Kitchen Bouquet. Season with salt
and pepper. Stir in the roux. Cook over
medium heat until the sauce is creamy,
stirring occasionally. Grill the filets over
hot coals until done to taste. Top each filet
with some of the mushroom sauce. Serve
immediately. *Yield: 2 servings.*

   Note: A roux is a mixture of flour and
fat that is cooked and stirred until it is
brown in color. The longer the roux is
cooked, the deeper brown and more
flavorful it becomes. The proportions are
equal amounts of flour and fat. The end
result should have the consistency of a
thin pudding. Do not let the roux burn! To
avoid this, simply stir constantly until of
the desired color.

*Opened in 1977,
Clementine's is one of
the first restaurants in
northwest Houston.
They serve a variety
of lovely dishes, such as
Filetto al Barolo, and
in keeping with the
nineties, added an
Aribica coffee bar.*

Filet of Beef with Gorgonzola Sauce

4 (8-ounce) filet mignons
Salt and pepper to taste
3 1/2 ounces enoki
    mushrooms, tough
    ends removed, sliced
1 tablespoon butter
2 tablespoons vegetable
    oil
1 tablespoon butter
1 tablespoon minced
    shallots
1/2 cup beef broth
1/4 cup port
2 tablespoons crumbled
    Gorgonzola cheese
1 tablespoon butter

Season the filets with salt and pepper. Sauté the mushrooms in 1 tablespoon butter in a saucepan for 1 minute. Remove from heat. Heat the oil in a skillet over high heat. Add the filets. Cook for 3 minutes; turn. Cook for 2 minutes longer; drain. Remove the filets to a heated serving platter. Heat 1 tablespoon butter in the same skillet. Add the shallots. Sauté for 1 minute. Deglaze with the broth and wine. Stir in the cheese. Cook until the cheese melts, stirring constantly. Cook until the sauce is reduced to 1/3 cup, stirring constantly. Add 1 tablespoon butter, stirring until melted. Spoon the sauce over the filets. Top with the sautéed enoki mushrooms. *Yield: 4 servings.*
    Note: May substitute shiitake mushrooms for the enoki mushrooms.

If mushrooms appear clean, wipe them with a damp towel. If there is a doubt, submerge the mushrooms in a bowl of cold water, swish around, remove immediately, and dry completely.

Stuffed Flank Steak

1 (2-pound) beef flank
    steak
Salt and freshly ground
    pepper to taste
8 ounces pork sausage
1 cup chopped onion
8 ounces fresh
    mushrooms, chopped
4 cloves of garlic, minced
1/4 cup butter
1/4 cup chopped fresh
    parsley
Vegetable oil
1/2 cup beef broth

Season the flank steak with salt and pepper. Brown the sausage in an oven-proof skillet, stirring until crumbly; drain. Remove to a platter. Sauté the onion, mushrooms and garlic in the butter in the same skillet for 2 to 3 minutes. Remove from heat. Stir in the sausage and parsley. Spoon the sausage mixture lengthwise down the center of the steak; roll as for a jelly roll to enclose the filling. Tie at 1 1/2-inch intervals with kitchen twine. Brown the beef roll on all sides in oil in the skillet. Add the broth. Braise, covered with foil, at 325 degrees for 2 hours. Let stand for 5 to 10 minutes. Cut diagonally into 1/2-inch slices. Arrange the slices on a serving platter. Drizzle with the pan drippings. *Yield: 4 servings.*

Mustard-Crusted Beef Ribs

5 pounds beef ribs
Salt and freshly ground
    pepper to taste
1/2 cup dry white wine
1/4 cup Dijon mustard
1 cup bread crumbs
2 tablespoons minced
    shallots
1/4 cup unsalted butter
1/4 cup flour
1/2 cup beef broth
1 tablespoon meat
    extract
1/2 cup whipping cream

Season the ribs on both sides with salt and pepper. Arrange in a single layer on a greased rack in a roasting pan. Bake at 450 degrees for 30 minutes; turn the ribs. Reduce the oven temperature to 300 degrees. Bake for 30 minutes. Remove the ribs from the oven. Reduce the oven temperature to 200 degrees. Coat the ribs on both sides with a mixture of the white wine and Dijon mustard; sprinkle with the bread crumbs. Bake for 1 hour. Sauté the shallots in the butter in a saucepan for 2 minutes. Add the flour, stirring until mixed. Stir in the broth and meat extract. Simmer just until thickened, stirring constantly. Add the whipping cream and mix well. Simmer just until heated through, stirring constantly. Spoon over the ribs. *Yield: 6 servings.*

Serve these ribs with plenty of napkins!

Grilled London Broil

1/4 cup packed light
    brown sugar
1/4 cup soy sauce
1/4 cup vegetable oil
1/4 cup grated gingerroot
4 cloves of garlic,
    crushed
Freshly ground pepper to
    taste
1 (1 1/2- to 2-pound)
    London broil, 2 inches
    thick

Combine the brown sugar, soy sauce, oil, gingerroot, garlic and pepper in a bowl and mix well. Pour over the beef in a shallow dish, turning to coat. Marinate, covered, in the refrigerator for 12 hours, turning occasionally. Sear quickly over hot coals. Grill over low heat until done to taste, turning occasionally. Slice against the grain into thin strips. Arrange on a serving platter. *Yield: 4 to 6 servings.*

Note: This beef will cook quicker than usual due to the marinating process.

White Lasagna

9 lasagna noodles
1 1/2 pounds fresh
   spinach
1 pound ground sirloin
1 cup chopped onion
1 cup chopped celery
1 clove of garlic, minced
2 cups half-and-half
3 ounces cream cheese,
   softened
2 teaspoons basil
1 teaspoon salt
1 teaspoon oregano
1/2 teaspoon white pepper
1/2 cup white wine
8 ounces Cheddar
   cheese, shredded
7 ounces Gouda cheese,
   shredded
15 ounces ricotta cheese
1 egg, lightly beaten
12 ounces mozzarella
   cheese, shredded

Cook the noodles using package directions; drain. Rinse the spinach; do not drain. Place the spinach in a saucepan with only the water clinging to the leaves left from the rinsing. Steam, covered, over medium heat for 2 to 3 minutes or until wilted; drain.

Brown the ground sirloin in a skillet. Stir in the onion, celery and garlic. Cook until the vegetables are tender, stirring constantly; drain. Add the half-and-half, cream cheese, basil, salt, oregano and white pepper.

Cook over low heat until the cream cheese melts, stirring constantly. Stir in the white wine. Add the Cheddar cheese and Gouda cheese gradually and mix well. Cook until the cheese melts, stirring frequently. Remove from heat. Combine the ricotta cheese and egg in a bowl and mix well.

Layer the noodles, meat mixture, ricotta cheese mixture and spinach 1/3 at a time in a 9x13-inch baking dish. Sprinkle with the mozzarella cheese.

Bake at 375 degrees for 30 to 35 minutes or until bubbly. Remove from oven. Let stand, covered with foil, for 10 minutes before serving. *Yield: 6 servings.*

Rack of Lamb with Herbs and Chèvre

2 lamb shanks
1 carrot, chopped
1 onion, chopped
12 unpeeled cloves of
    garlic, chopped
2 tablespoons olive oil
1¼ cups dry white wine
4 cups chicken broth
1 cup crumbled chèvre
¼ cup chopped fresh
    chervil, stems
    removed
¼ cup chopped fresh
    tarragon, stems
    removed
¼ cup chopped fresh
    parsley
¼ cup snipped fresh
    chives
2 tablespoons butter,
    softened
2 tablespoons fresh
    lemon juice
Salt and freshly ground
    pepper to taste
2 racks of lamb (8 chops
    per rack)
2 tablespoons olive oil

Sauté the lamb shanks, carrot, onion and garlic in 2 tablespoons olive oil in a saucepan over high heat until light brown. Stir in the white wine. Cook until most of the wine has been absorbed, stirring frequently. Add the broth and mix well.

Simmer for 20 minutes, stirring frequently. Strain, reserving the broth and discarding the lamb shanks and vegetables. Return the broth to the saucepan.

Combine the chèvre, chervil, tarragon, parsley, chives and butter in a blender or food processor container. Process until puréed.

Combine the chèvre mixture and 1 cup of the reserved broth in a saucepan, whisking until smooth and creamy. May add additional broth for a thinner consistency. Stir in the lemon juice, salt and pepper. Cook over low heat for 3 to 4 minutes or until of the desired consistency, stirring constantly.

Season the lamb with salt and pepper; rub with 2 tablespoons olive oil. Arrange the racks on a baking sheet. Roast at 500 degrees for 20 minutes for medium-rare, turning frequently. Slice the lamb into chops. Serve warm with the chèvre sauce.
Yield: 8 servings.

Chèvre is made from goat's milk, coming in a variety of shapes and flavors. Most chèvres are tangy in flavor and creamy in texture. Imported or domestic, chèvre is becoming widely available.

Grilled Leg of Lamb

1 (6-pound) leg of lamb,
  boned, butterflied
1 cup olive oil
3/4 cup fresh lemon juice
1/4 cup chopped fresh
  parsley
2 teaspoons salt
1 1/2 teaspoons sage
1 1/2 teaspoons rosemary
1 1/2 teaspoons thyme
1/2 teaspoon freshly
  ground pepper
4 cloves of garlic,
  crushed
2 bay leaves
Burgundy Sauce

Garnish:
Sprigs of parsley

1/2 cup beef broth
1/3 cup red burgundy
2 tablespoons chopped
  shallots
1 1/2 teaspoons sage
1 1/2 teaspoons rosemary
1 1/2 teaspoons thyme
3 tablespoons butter,
  softened
3 tablespoons chopped
  fresh parsley

Arrange the lamb in a nonmetallic dish. Combine the olive oil, lemon juice, parsley, salt, sage, rosemary, thyme, pepper, garlic and bay leaves in a bowl and mix well. Pour over the lamb, turning to coat. Marinate, covered, in the refrigerator for 24 hours, turning occasionally. Drain, reserving the marinade.

Sear the lamb on both sides over hot coals; reduce the heat to medium. Grill for 45 minutes, turning and basting with the reserved marinade frequently.

Remove the lamb to a heated serving platter; cover with foil. Let stand for 10 to 15 minutes; slice. Arrange on a serving platter; drizzle with the Burgundy Sauce. Garnish with parsley. *Yield: 8 servings.*

Burgundy Sauce

Combine the broth, burgundy, shallots, sage, rosemary and thyme in a saucepan and mix well. Bring to a boil. Boil until reduced by 1/2, stirring constantly. Remove from heat. Stir in the butter and parsley.

This is an excellent dish to prepare for your family on Easter. Serve with a fresh green vegetable and mashed potatoes. A family tradition may begin.

Tunisian Lamb

1 (2- to 3-pound) lamb
  loin, cut into 1¹/₂-inch
  pieces
1 tablespoon olive oil
1¹/₂ cups chicken broth
1 Spanish onion, chopped
¹/₂ teaspoon cinnamon
¹/₂ teaspoon salt
¹/₂ teaspoon ginger
¹/₄ teaspoon freshly
  ground pepper
2 Granny Smith apples,
  peeled, chopped
6 prunes, pitted, cut into
  halves
4 thick lemon slices, cut
  into halves
3 carrots, cut into
  ¹/₂-inch slices
3 tablespoons honey

Brown the lamb in the olive oil in a saucepan over high heat. Add the broth, onion, cinnamon, salt, ginger and pepper. Bring to a boil; reduce heat. Simmer, covered, for 1¹/₂ hours, stirring occasionally. Add the apples, prunes, lemon slices, carrots and honey and mix well. Simmer for 30 minutes. Serve with rice pilaf. *Yield: 4 to 6 servings.*

Here's an easy way to test the temperature of coals. Hold your hand, palm side down, just above the coals. Then start counting the seconds. When your hand gets too hot, move it. The number of seconds you count will give you the correct temperature.

2 seconds .... hot
3 seconds ...... medium-hot
4 seconds .... medium
5 seconds ...... medium-low
6 seconds .... low

Bourbon-Spiced Pork Tenderloins

2 (1-pound) pork
  tenderloins
¹/₄ cup bourbon
¹/₄ cup soy sauce
¹/₄ cup Dijon mustard
¹/₄ cup packed brown
  sugar
¹/₄ cup olive oil
2 tablespoons grated
  gingerroot
2 teaspoons
  Worcestershire sauce
4 cloves of garlic, minced

Arrange the pork tenderloins in a nonmetallic dish. Combine the bourbon, soy sauce, Dijon mustard, brown sugar, olive oil, gingerroot, Worcestershire sauce and garlic in a blender or food processor container. Process until blended. Pour over the pork tenderloins, turning to coat. Marinate, covered, in the refrigerator for 8 to 10 hours. Drain, reserving the marinade. Sear the tenderloins on all sides over hot coals; do not pierce the pork. Reduce the temperature to medium. Grill for 20 minutes or until cooked through, basting with the reserved marinade frequently. Let stand for 10 minutes before slicing. Cut into ¹/₂-inch slices. *Yield: 6 servings.*

Roasted Honey Pepper Pork

1 (2½-pound) boneless
  pork loin roast, tied
¼ cup honey
2 tablespoons Dijon
  mustard
2 tablespoons mixed
  peppercorns, crushed
½ teaspoon thyme
½ teaspoon salt

Garnish:
Sprigs of thyme

Score ½-inch-deep slits on all sides of the roast. Arrange the roast in a shallow dish. Combine the honey, Dijon mustard, peppercorns, thyme and salt in a bowl and mix well. Spoon or brush ⅔ of the honey mixture over the roast, coating all sides. Place the pork on a rack in a baking pan. Bake at 300 degrees for 1 hour. Brush with the remaining honey mixture. Bake for 45 to 60 minutes longer or until cooked through. Let stand, tented with foil, for 10 minutes. Cut into slices. Arrange on a serving platter. Garnish with thyme.
Yield: 8 servings.

French Quarter Pork Chops

6 center-cut pork chops,
  ¾ to 1 inch thick
2 tablespoons vegetable
  oil
¾ cup chicken broth
1 onion, chopped
1 green bell pepper,
  chopped
2 tablespoons butter
1 (15-ounce) can plum
  tomatoes, chopped
¼ cup chopped fresh
  parsley
1 tablespoon basil
¾ teaspoon sugar
¼ teaspoon oregano
Salt and freshly ground
  pepper to taste

Brown the pork chops in the oil in a skillet; drain. Arrange the chops in a shallow baking dish. Pour the broth over the chops. Braise at 350 degrees for 20 minutes. Sauté the onion and green pepper in the butter in a skillet for 5 minutes. Stir in the plum tomatoes, parsley, basil, sugar, oregano, salt and pepper. Simmer for 5 minutes, stirring frequently. Pour over the chops. Bake for 20 minutes longer or until the chops are cooked through. Serve immediately.
Yield: 6 servings.

Pork Chops with Herbed Oven Rice

4 center-cut pork chops,
  3/4 to 1 inch thick
2 tablespoons vegetable
  oil
1 onion, cut into thin
  slices
1/2 cup apple juice or
  apple cider
1 teaspoon Homemade
  Herb Blend (at right)
1 beef bouillon cube
2 teaspoons cornstarch
1 tablespoon water
Herbed Oven Rice
  (at right)

Brown the pork chops in the oil in a skillet; drain. Stir in the onion, apple juice and 1 teaspoon Homemade Herb Blend. Simmer, covered, for 30 minutes, stirring occasionally. Remove the chops with a slotted spoon to a heated serving platter; tent with foil to keep warm. Add the bouillon cube to the onion mixture. Bring to a boil. Boil until reduced by 1/2, stirring frequently. Stir in a mixture of the cornstarch and water. Cook over medium heat until thickened, stirring constantly. Spoon over the pork chops. Serve with the Herbed Oven Rice. *Yield: 4 servings.*

Prepare Homemade Herb Blend by combining 4 teaspoons basil, 1 tablespoon parsley flakes, 1 1/2 teaspoons dillweed and 1/2 teaspoon thyme. Store in an airtight container.

For Herbed Oven Rice, combine 1 3/4 cups boiling water and 1 tablespoon butter in a 1-quart baking dish, stirring until the butter melts. Add 3/4 cup white rice, 1 shredded carrot, 1 teaspoon Homemade Herb Blend and 1/2 teaspoon salt. Bake, covered, for 35 minutes; stir.

Gingered Ribs

2 (2-pound) racks of
  pork spareribs
1/2 cup soy sauce
1/2 cup catsup
1/4 cup chicken broth
3 tablespoons packed
  brown sugar
2 tablespoons grated
  gingerroot
2 tablespoons sugar
1/2 teaspoon salt
1/4 teaspoon paprika
1/4 teaspoon turmeric
1/4 teaspoon celery seeds
1/8 teaspoon dry mustard

Boil the spareribs in enough water to cover in a stockpot for 10 minutes; drain. Arrange the ribs in a single layer in a large nonmetallic dish. Combine the soy sauce, catsup, broth, brown sugar and gingerroot in a bowl and mix well. Pour over the ribs, turning to coat. Marinate, covered, in the refrigerator for 8 to 10 hours. Drain, reserving the marinade. Pat the ribs dry with a paper towel. Combine the sugar, salt, paprika, turmeric, celery seeds and dry mustard in a bowl and mix well. Coat both sides of the ribs with the sugar mixture. Grill over medium-hot coals for 45 minutes or until cooked through, turning and basting with the reserved marinade frequently. Cut into individual ribs to serve. *Yield: 4 servings.*

Veal Chops with Mustard Sage Butter

2 veal loin chops, 1^1/$_2$
   inches thick
1^1/$_2$ tablespoons chopped
   fresh sage
1 tablespoon olive oil
2 teaspoons balsamic
   vinegar
1 clove of garlic, minced
Ground pepper to taste
3 tablespoons butter,
   softened
1^1/$_2$ tablespoons chopped
   fresh sage
2 teaspoons Dijon
   mustard

Arrange the veal chops in a nonmetallic dish. Combine 1^1/$_2$ tablespoons sage, olive oil, balsamic vinegar, garlic and pepper in a bowl and mix well. Coat the veal on both sides with the sage mixture. Marinate in the refrigerator for 30 minutes to 2 hours. Combine the butter, 1^1/$_2$ tablespoons sage and Dijon mustard in a bowl and mix well. Season generously with pepper. Grill the chops over hot coals for 7 minutes per side or just until pink in the center. Serve immediately with a dollop of the mustard sage butter. *Yield: 2 servings.*

Chicken Cacciatore

12 boneless skinless
   chicken breast halves
Salt and pepper to taste
2 tablespoons olive oil
^{1}/$_2$ cup chopped green
   bell pepper
^{1}/$_2$ cup chopped onion
2 cloves of garlic, minced
1 (26- to 30-ounce) can
   plum tomatoes
1 (8-ounce) can tomato
   sauce
^{1}/$_2$ cup chianti
2 to 3 teaspoons salt
1 teaspoon oregano
^{1}/$_2$ teaspoon allspice
2 bay leaves
^{1}/$_8$ teaspoon cayenne
1 pound fresh
   mushrooms, sliced

Rinse the chicken and pat dry. Season with salt and pepper to taste. Brown the chicken in the olive oil in a 5-quart saucepan. Remove the chicken with a slotted spoon to a platter, reserving the pan drippings. Sauté the green pepper, onion and garlic in the reserved pan drippings for 2 minutes. Add the chicken, undrained tomatoes, tomato sauce, wine, 2 to 3 teaspoons salt, oregano, allspice, bay leaves and cayenne and mix well. Simmer for 30 minutes, stirring occasionally. Stir in the mushrooms. Simmer for 15 minutes longer, stirring occasionally. Discard the bay leaves. Serve over hot cooked linguini. *Yield: 6 servings.*

An authentic Italian dish with a robust flavor. Serve with a mixed green salad drizzled with a light vinaigrette dressing.

Flamed Chicken with Mushrooms

8 boneless skinless
    chicken breast halves
Salt and freshly ground
    pepper to taste
1/4 cup minced shallots
3 tablespoons butter
8 ounces fresh
    mushrooms, sliced
1/4 cup dry white wine
2 tablespoons snipped
    fresh chives
1 tablespoon chopped
    fresh marjoram
2 tablespoons butter
1/4 cup brandy, heated
2 tablespoons chopped
    fresh parsley

Rinse the chicken and pat dry. Pound 1/2 inch thick between sheets of waxed paper. Season with salt and pepper. Cook the shallots in 3 tablespoons butter in a skillet over low heat for 1 minute, stirring constantly. Add the mushrooms. Cook for 1 minute, stirring constantly. Stir in the white wine, chives, marjoram, salt and pepper. Cook until the wine has been reduced to an essence, stirring frequently. Remove the mushrooms with a slotted spoon to a heated platter, reserving the pan drippings. Cover to keep warm. Heat 2 tablespoons butter with the reserved pan drippings. Sauté the chicken in the butter mixture for 3 to 4 minutes or until light brown; turn. Cook over medium heat for 4 to 5 minutes longer or until cooked through. Return the mushrooms to the skillet. Pour the heated brandy over the chicken. Ignite the brandy; let the flame subside. Sprinkle with parsley.
Yield: 4 servings.

Grilled Jalapeño Chicken

6 chicken breasts,
    skinned, cut into
    halves
1/2 cup fresh lime juice
1/4 cup honey
2 tablespoons chopped
    fresh cilantro
2 tablespoons soy sauce
3 jalapeños, seeded,
    minced
3 cloves of garlic, minced
1/4 teaspoon salt
1/4 teaspoon freshly
    ground pepper

Rinse the chicken and pat dry. Arrange in a shallow nonmetallic dish. Process the lime juice, honey, cilantro, soy sauce, jalapeños, garlic, salt and pepper in a blender until smooth. Reserve 1/4 cup of the marinade and store, covered, in the refrigerator. Pour the remaining marinade over the chicken, turning to coat. Marinate, covered, in the refrigerator for 8 hours, turning occasionally; drain. Grill over medium-hot coals for 35 to 45 minutes or until cooked through, turning and basting with the reserved marinade frequently. *Yield: 6 servings.*

Marinated Chicken with Pineapple

6 to 8 boneless skinless
   chicken breast halves
1 cup packed brown
   sugar
1 cup fresh orange juice
1 cup red burgundy
3/4 cup Worcestershire
   sauce
3/4 cup soy sauce
3/4 teaspoon garlic salt
3/4 teaspoon onion salt
1 1/2 tablespoons
   rosemary
6 to 8 slices pineapple

Rinse the chicken and pat dry. Process the brown sugar, orange juice, burgundy, Worcestershire sauce, soy sauce, garlic salt and onion salt in a blender until smooth. Pour into a shallow nonmetallic dish. Stir in the rosemary. Add the chicken, turning to coat. Marinate, covered, in the refrigerator for 8 to 10 hours, turning occasionally; drain. Grill the chicken over medium-hot coals for 10 minutes or until cooked through, turning occasionally. Grill the pineapple slices just before serving. Top each chicken breast with a pineapple slice. Serve immediately.
Yield: 6 to 8 servings.

Marinate in the refrigerator, never at room temperature.

Pumpkin Seed-Crusted Chicken

4 boneless skinless
   chicken breast halves
Salt and freshly ground
   pepper to taste
5 1/3 ounces pumpkin
   seeds
1/4 cup butter
Wild Rice Sauté

Rinse the chicken and pat dry. Season with salt and pepper. Process the pumpkin seeds in a food processor until ground or grind using a mortar and pestle. Coat the chicken heavily with the pumpkin seeds. Sauté in the butter in a skillet for 20 minutes or until cooked through, turning occasionally. Serve over Wild Rice Sauté.
Yield: 4 servings.

Wild Rice Sauté

1/4 cup butter
1/2 cup chopped fresh
   mushrooms
1/4 cup chopped green
   onions
1/4 cup chopped onion
1/4 teaspoon garlic powder
1 cup wild rice
2 1/2 cups water

Heat the butter in a 2 1/2-quart saucepan until melted. Sauté the mushrooms, green onions, onion and garlic powder in the butter for 1 minute. Add the rice, stirring until coated. Add the water and mix well; reduce heat. Simmer, covered, for 45 to 60 minutes or until tender.

The Baroness' Chicken

4 boneless skinless
    chicken breasts, split
Salt and freshly ground
    pepper to taste
1 teaspoon fresh lemon
    juice
$1/2$ teaspoon paprika
$1/4$ cup butter
$1/4$ cup chicken broth
$1/4$ cup madeira
1 cup sour cream
$1^1/2$ teaspoons lemon
    juice
1 teaspoon paprika
2 tablespoons chopped
    fresh parsley

Rinse the chicken and pat dry. Pound $1/4$ inch thick between sheets of waxed paper. Season with salt and pepper. Drizzle with 1 teaspoon lemon juice; sprinkle with $1/2$ teaspoon paprika. Heat the butter in a skillet until melted. Add the chicken. Cook until light brown on both sides. Cook, covered, for 6 minutes or until cooked through. Remove the chicken with a slotted spoon to a heated serving platter; tent with foil. Stir the broth and madeira into the pan drippings. Bring to a boil. Boil until of a syrupy consistency, stirring frequently; reduce heat. Stir in the sour cream. Simmer until slightly thickened, stirring constantly. Remove from heat. Stir in $1^1/2$ teaspoons lemon juice and 1 teaspoon paprika. Season with salt and pepper. Pour over the chicken; sprinkle with the parsley. *Yield: 4 servings.*

Stuffed Chicken with Sweet Pepper Sauce

4 boneless skinless
    chicken breast halves
4 slices mozzarella cheese
1 egg, lightly beaten
$1/2$ cup fresh bread
    crumbs
2 tablespoons olive oil
$1/4$ cup thinly sliced
    green onions
1 teaspoon minced garlic
1 tablespoon olive oil
1 (7-ounce) jar roasted
    red peppers, drained,
    chopped
1 cup whipping cream
1 tablespoon chopped
    fresh basil

Rinse the chicken and pat dry. Pound $1/4$ inch thick between sheets of waxed paper. Place 1 slice of cheese in the center of each chicken breast; fold to enclose. Dip in the egg; coat with the bread crumbs. Arrange in a greased baking dish. Drizzle with 2 tablespoons olive oil. Bake at 350 degrees for 45 minutes or until cooked through. Slice the chicken and arrange on 2 dinner plates. Cover to keep warm. Sauté the green onions and garlic in 1 tablespoon olive oil in a skillet for 1 minute. Add the red peppers, whipping cream and basil and mix well. Simmer for 3 to 4 minutes, stirring constantly. Drizzle over the chicken. *Yield: 2 servings.*

This recipe is very easy to prepare, yet it is an elegant and colorful dish.

Southwestern Rigatoni

2 boneless skinless
  chicken breasts, split
Juice of 4 limes
3 ears of unhusked corn
1 tablespoon unsalted
  butter
3 slices bacon, chopped
5 cloves of garlic, minced
1 (15-ounce) can black
  beans, drained, rinsed
1 beefsteak tomato,
  chopped
1/2 cup white tequila
1/4 cup fresh lime juice
1 tablespoon chopped
  fresh thyme
1 teaspoon salt
1 teaspoon red pepper
  flakes
2 jalapeños, seeded,
  minced
2 cups whipping cream
16 ounces rigatoni
Salt to taste

Garnish:
Chopped fresh cilantro

Rinse the chicken and pat dry. Arrange in a shallow nonmetallic dish. Drizzle with the juice of 4 limes, turning to coat. Marinate, covered, in the refrigerator.

Place the corn on the oven rack. Roast at 400 degrees for 15 minutes. Husk the corn and remove the silk. Cut the corn kernels with a sharp knife into a bowl.

Heat the butter in a skillet until melted. Add the bacon and 3 cloves of the garlic and mix well. Sauté until the garlic is light brown. Stir in the remaining 2 cloves of garlic, corn, beans, tomato, tequila, 1/4 cup lime juice, thyme, 1 teaspoon salt, red pepper flakes and jalapeños. Cook for 3 minutes, stirring constantly. Add the whipping cream and mix well. Simmer for 30 minutes or until the sauce is reduced by 1/3, stirring frequently.

Grill the chicken over medium-hot coals for 20 minutes or until cooked through; slice. Cook the pasta in boiling salted water using package directions; drain.

Place the pasta in a heated serving bowl. Add the corn mixture, tossing to mix. Arrange the chicken over the pasta mixture. Garnish with cilantro. Serve immediately. *Yield: 4 servings.*

Good food and cookbooks make me think of my sweet grandmother, Mamaw. Upon entering her home, my mouth begins to water from the delicious aromas drifting from the kitchen. I was in a quandary about a gift for her eightieth birthday, so I went to a gourmet shop in search of a cookbook that she didn't already own. After explaining to the salesperson what I was looking for, she exclaimed, "Oh, my. Your grandmother still cooks and lives by herself?" I replied, "Oh, no. She lives with my ninety-year-old grandfather, and he loves her cooking."

Kaye Hill-Birkkolz

Cajun Deep-Fried Turkey

1 (10- to 12-pound) turkey
Creole seasoning to taste
1½ cups melted butter
¼ cup onion juice
¼ cup garlic juice
¼ cup celery juice
¼ cup lemon juice
¼ cup Worcestershire sauce
¼ cup Tabasco sauce
2 tablespoons liquid smoke
8 gallons peanut oil for deep-frying

Rinse the turkey and pat dry. Rub the turkey with Creole seasoning; wrap with plastic wrap. Marinate in the refrigerator for 24 hours.

Combine the butter, onion juice, garlic juice, celery juice, lemon juice, Worcestershire sauce, Tabasco sauce and liquid smoke in a saucepan 1 hour before the planned time for cooking the turkey. Cook over low heat just until heated through, stirring occasionally. Fill the syringe with the warm mixture. Inject the turkey all over until the turkey is bloated and can hold no more of the mixture; use all the mixture. Chill for 1 hour.

Heat the peanut oil in a 60-quart Cajun pot to 350 to 375 degrees. Place the turkey in a fryer basket. Submerge the basket slowly into the oil. Deep-fry for 3½ to 4 minutes per pound or until cooked through; drain. Wrap the turkey in parchment paper. Chill for 20 minutes before slicing. *Yield: 8 servings.*

Note: This is, without a doubt, the best turkey ever! The preparation is worth the mess as the turkey is extremely moist and flavorful. Do several at a time.

Cajun deep-fried turkey is a family favorite that my husband, Craig, cooks. My commitments often leave my family fending for themselves. One night, I returned home from a meeting to find my daughter Kelly, and a group of her friends, perched around the kitchen table happily visiting and eating Cajun deep-fried turkey, rice, beans, and bread... prepared and served by Craig. They were having a great time! Little did I realize that the turkey was to become a school-holiday tradition. Occasionally we disappoint the group, but usually we come through. I imagine that when Kelly comes home from college next year, the cooker will be cooking.

～ *Diane Brown* ～

Apricot-Glazed Cornish Game Hens

4 Cornish game hens
2 cups water
1 chicken bouillon cube
1 cup wild rice
1/4 cup chopped unpeeled
    red apple
1/4 cup chopped dried
    apricots
1/4 cup chopped pecans
1/4 cup chopped water
    chestnuts
1 1/2 teaspoons grated
    orange zest
1/2 teaspoon basil
1/2 teaspoon thyme
Salt and freshly ground
    pepper to taste
1/4 cup melted butter
Apricot Glaze

Rinse the game hens and pat dry. Bring the water to a boil in a saucepan. Add the bouillon cube, stirring until dissolved. Stir in the rice.

Bring to a boil; reduce heat. Simmer, covered, for 1 hour. Remove from heat; drain.

Combine the rice, apple, apricots, pecans, water chestnuts, orange zest, basil and thyme in a bowl and mix well. Season with salt and pepper.

Fill the cavities of the game hens with the rice mixture; truss. Place the game hens in a shallow roasting pan. Brush with the butter. Bake at 350 degrees for 2 hours, basting frequently with the Apricot Glaze. *Yield: 4 servings.*

Apricot Glaze

2 cups apricot nectar
2/3 cup sugar
2 tablespoons cornstarch
1 tablespoon fresh lemon
    juice
1/4 teaspoon ground
    cloves

Combine the apricot nectar, sugar, cornstarch, lemon juice and cloves in a saucepan and mix well. Cook over low heat until the sugar dissolves and the mixture is of the desired consistency, stirring constantly.

Roasted Duck with Hot-and-Sour Chutney

2 (4¹/2- to 5-pound)
   ducks
Salt and freshly ground
   pepper to taste
¹/2 lemon
Hot-and-Sour Chutney

Rinse the duck and pat dry. Season with salt and pepper outside and inside. Rub the inside of the duck cavities with the lemon. Arrange breast side up on a rack in a roasting pan.

Roast at 400 degrees for 30 minutes or until cooked through, basting occasionally with the accumulated juices and fat in the pan. The skin should be brown and crisp and the meat slightly pink when the duck is cooked through.

Remove from oven. Let stand, covered with foil, for 10 minutes. Cut the duck into quarters; remove the backbone. Serve with the Hot-and-Sour Chutney.

Yield: 4 to 6 servings.

Hot-and-Sour Chutney

1 tablespoon olive oil
¹/2 red onion, minced
1 jalapeño, minced
1 tablespoon minced
   gingerroot
1 clove of garlic, minced
¹/2 red pepper, minced
¹/2 cup currants
¹/4 cup packed light
   brown sugar
¹/4 cup white wine
   vinegar
¹/2 teaspoon cayenne
¹/2 teaspoon salt
¹/4 teaspoon turmeric
¹/4 teaspoon dry mustard
Grated peel of 1 lemon
2 Granny Smith apples,
   peeled, chopped
2 peaches, peeled,
   chopped
1 pear, peeled, chopped

Heat the olive oil in a saucepan over medium heat until hot. Stir in the onion, jalapeño, gingerroot, garlic and red pepper. Simmer for 6 minutes, stirring occasionally. Add the currants, brown sugar, wine vinegar, cayenne, salt, turmeric, dry mustard and lemon peel. Cook for 10 minutes, stirring occasionally. Stir in the apples, peaches and pear. Cook for 5 minutes longer, stirring frequently. Remove from heat.

Duck meat is rich and flavorful. There are many varieties. The most common, the Long Island duck or White Petin, can be purchased year-round at specialty meat markets. Wild ducks, such as the mallard or teal, are occasionally available for purchase, but can always be found in your neighborly hunter's freezer. Choose a fresh duck with a broad, plump breast with an elastic, not saggy, skin. Make sure the packaging is tight and unbroken if purchasing frozen duck.

Pheasant in Tarragon

1 (3-pound) pheasant,
    cut up, skinned
3 tablespoons butter
1/2 cup chopped onion
2 cloves of garlic, minced
2 tablespoons flour
2 tablespoons catsup
1 1/2 cups chicken broth
2 teaspoons tarragon
1 teaspoon salt
1/2 teaspoon freshly
    ground pepper
1/2 cup sour cream
2 tablespoons grated
    Parmesan cheese

Rinse the pheasant and pat dry. Brown in the butter in a skillet. Remove the pheasant with a slotted spoon to a platter, reserving the pan drippings. Stir the onion and garlic into the reserved pan drippings. Cook until tender, stirring constantly. Add the flour and catsup and mix well. Stir in the broth gradually. Bring to a boil, stirring constantly. Boil until slightly thickened, stirring constantly. Stir in the tarragon, salt and pepper. Return the pheasant to the skillet, turning to coat. Simmer, covered, for 45 minutes, stirring occasionally. Transfer the pheasant with a slotted spoon to a heated platter. Stir the sour cream into the sauce gradually. Add the pheasant, turning to coat. Sprinkle with the cheese. *Yield: 4 servings.*

Roasted Quail with Mushroom Gravy

6 quail
1/4 cup flour
1 teaspoon salt
1/2 teaspoon freshly
    ground pepper
8 ounces fresh
    mushrooms, sliced
2 tablespoons butter
1/2 cup butter
1/4 cup plus 1 tablespoon
    flour
2 cups chicken broth
1/2 cup sherry

Rinse the quail and pat dry. Mix 1/4 cup flour, salt and pepper in a bowl. Coat the quail with the flour mixture. Sauté the mushrooms in 2 tablespoons butter in a skillet for 4 minutes. Remove the mushrooms to a bowl. Heat 1/2 cup butter in the skillet over high heat until melted. Brown the quail on all sides in the butter. Remove the quail with a slotted spoon to a 1 1/2-quart baking dish, reserving the pan drippings. Stir 1/4 cup plus 1 tablespoon flour into the pan drippings. Cook for 1 minute, stirring constantly. Add the broth and sherry gradually. Cook over medium heat until thickened, stirring constantly. Stir in the mushrooms. Pour over the quail. Bake, covered, at 350 degrees for 1 hour. Let stand for 15 minutes before serving. *Yield: 6 servings.*

This recipe can be adapted to dove, goose, or pheasant. Double the gravy for larger birds. It may be necessary to split the larger birds to maintain the same cooking time.

Entrées

Steamed Striped Bass with Wilted Spinach

1 tablespoon chopped
    fresh parsley
1 tablespoon minced
    lemon zest
1 tablespoon minced
    orange zest
1 tablespoon chopped
    fresh chives
1 clove of garlic,
    poached, julienned
1 shallot, minced
1 tablespoon butter
2 red bell peppers,
    chopped
Juice of 1 lime
6 tablespoons unsalted
    butter
¼ cup chopped fresh
    cilantro
Salt and freshly ground
    pepper to taste
4 (7-ounce) bass fillets,
    with skin
2 tablespoons melted
    butter
1 to 2 shallots, minced
1 pound fresh spinach,
    stemmed
1 tablespoon butter

Combine the parsley, lemon zest, orange zest, chives and garlic in a bowl and mix well. Sauté 1 shallot in 1 tablespoon butter in a skillet until tender. Add the red peppers and mix well. Cook until tender, stirring frequently. Process the red pepper mixture in a blender or food processor until puréed.

Return the purée to the skillet. Add the lime juice and mix well. Add the unsalted butter 2 tablespoons at a time, mixing well after each addition. Cook over low heat just until blended. Stir in the cilantro, salt and pepper. Keep warm over low heat.

Rinse the fillets and pat dry. Arrange the fillets in a buttered baking dish. Brush with 2 tablespoons melted butter; sprinkle with 1 to 2 shallots. Bake, covered tightly with foil, at 400 degrees for 14 minutes.

Blanch the spinach in boiling salted water in a saucepan for 1 to 2 minutes; drain. Toss the spinach with 1 tablespoon butter, salt and pepper in a bowl.

Spoon a pool of the red pepper sauce in the centers of 4 dinner plates. Make a bed of spinach on top. Arrange the bass skin side up over the spinach. Sprinkle with the parsley mixture. *Yield: 4 servings.*

This recipe is submitted by Chez Nous. Located in a charming old home, Chez Nous has been chosen by the Zagart Survey as having the best food in Houston every year since 1992.

Catfish Meuniere

4 (4-ounce) catfish fillets
¹/4 cup milk
1 egg, lightly beaten
¹/3 cup flour
¹/2 teaspoon salt
¹/2 teaspoon cayenne
¹/2 cup butter
¹/4 cup vegetable oil
2 tablespoons lemon juice
1 teaspoon
 Worcestershire sauce

Garnish:
Sprigs of parsley
Lemon wedges

Rinse the fillets and pat dry. Mix the milk and egg in a bowl. Mix the flour, salt and cayenne in a shallow dish. Dip the fillets in the egg mixture. Coat with the flour mixture; shake off excess. Heat ¹/4 cup of the butter and the oil in a skillet. Sauté the fillets in the butter mixture for 2 minutes per side or until golden brown. Remove to a heated platter; cover loosely with foil. Melt the remaining butter in the skillet over high heat. Stir in the lemon juice and Worcestershire sauce. Cook just until heated through, stirring constantly. Pour over the fillets. Garnish with parsley and lemon wedges. *Yield: 4 servings.*

Crab-Stuffed Flounder

6 flounder fillets
3 green onions, chopped
1 rib celery, chopped
2 cloves of garlic, minced
¹/4 cup olive oil
8 ounces lump crab meat
1 cup fresh bread crumbs
¹/2 cup grated Parmesan
 cheese
1 plum tomato, chopped
1 egg, lightly beaten
2 tablespoons fresh
 lemon juice
1 tablespoon chopped
 fresh parsley
Salt and freshly ground
 pepper to taste
¹/2 cup butter

Garnish:
Lemon wedges

Rinse the fillets and pat dry. Sauté the green onions, celery and garlic in the olive oil in a skillet until tender. Remove from heat. Stir in the crab meat, bread crumbs, cheese, tomato, egg, lemon juice, parsley, salt and pepper. Heat the butter in a baking dish until melted. Coat the fillets with the butter. Spoon 1 heaping tablespoon of the crab meat mixture on each fillet; roll to enclose the filling. Arrange the fish rolls in the prepared baking dish. Top with the remaining crab meat mixture. Bake, covered with foil, at 375 degrees for 20 minutes; remove foil. Bake for 10 minutes longer or until the fish flakes easily. Garnish with lemon wedges. Serve immediately. *Yield: 6 servings.*

Orange Roughy with Herbed Citrus Sauce

1 pound orange roughy
   fillets
1/2 cup milk
1/4 teaspoon salt
1/3 cup flour
2 tablespoons olive oil
Herbed Citrus Sauce
   (at top right)

Rinse the fillets and pat dry. Soak the fish in the milk in a shallow dish for 10 minutes; drain. Sprinkle with salt; coat with flour. Heat the olive oil in a skillet until hot. Add the fish. Sauté for 3 to 4 minutes; turn. Sauté for 3 to 4 minutes longer or until the fish flakes easily. Remove the fillets to a heated serving platter; drizzle with the warm Herbed Citrus Sauce. *Yield: 2 servings.*

Note: To reduce fat grams broil the fish. Broil for approximately 3 minutes per side or until the fish flakes easily.

To prepare Herbed Citrus Sauce, cook 1 1/2 teaspoons minced garlic in 1 teaspoon olive oil in a skillet over low heat for 30 seconds. Add 3 tablespoons fresh lime juice, 2 tablespoons fresh lemon juice, 1 tablespoon fresh orange juice, 1 tablespoon chopped fresh parsley and 2 teaspoons snipped fresh chives. Cook for 2 minutes, stirring constantly. Add 1 tablespoon unsalted butter, swirling the skillet until the sauce is blended.

Grilled Grouper with Roasted Pecan Sauce

4 (6-ounce) grouper
   fillets
1 tablespoon white
   pepper
1 tablespoon freshly
   ground black pepper
1 teaspoon chili powder
1/2 teaspoon garlic
   powder
1/2 teaspoon salt
Roasted Pecan Sauce

Rinse the fillets and pat dry. Combine the white pepper, black pepper, chili powder, garlic powder and salt in a shallow dish and mix well. Coat the fillets with the spice mixture. Arrange the fillets on a greased grill rack. Grill over medium-hot coals for 4 minutes per side or until the fish flakes easily. Arrange on a serving platter; drizzle with the warm Roasted Pecan Sauce. Serve immediately. *Yield: 4 servings.*

Roasted Pecan Sauce

1 cup chopped pecans
6 tablespoons unsalted
   butter
3 tablespoons minced
   onion
1/2 teaspoon Tabasco
   sauce
1 clove of garlic, minced

Spread the pecans in a single layer on a baking sheet. Roast in a 350-degree oven for 4 minutes or until fragrant and golden brown, shaking the pan once or twice. Melt the butter in a saucepan over low heat. Stir in the pecans, onion, Tabasco sauce and garlic. Cook just until heated through. Keep warm over low heat.

Poached Pompano with Fresh Vegetables

2 (6- to 8-ounce)
  pompano fillets
1/2 cup dry white wine
2 tablespoons butter
2 plum tomatoes,
  chopped
3 green onions, minced
1 rib celery, chopped
1/3 cup chopped fresh
  parsley
1 clove of garlic, minced
2 tablespoons extra-
  virgin olive oil
Salt and freshly ground
  pepper to taste
4 lemon slices

Garnish:
Lemon wedges

Rinse the fillets and pat dry. Arrange in a shallow baking dish. Pour the white wine over the fish; dot with the butter. Combine the tomatoes, green onions, celery, parsley and garlic in a bowl and mix well. Spoon 1/2 of the mixture down the center of each fillet; drizzle with the olive oil. Sprinkle with salt and pepper. Place 2 lemon slices on top of each fillet. Bake, covered loosely with foil, at 350 degrees for 20 minutes. Remove the foil and lemon slices. Broil for 5 minutes. Serve immediately, garnished with lemon wedges. *Yield: 2 servings.*

A very flavorful, yet light entrée. Can easily be doubled or tripled according to the crowd.

Red Snapper Excelsior

4 (6-ounce) red snapper
  fillets, 3/4 inch thick
2 tablespoons flour
Salt and freshly ground
  pepper to taste
1/2 cup butter
1 1/2 cups sliced fresh
  mushrooms
3 artichoke bottoms,
  sliced
1/4 cup chopped fresh
  parsley
1/4 cup red wine
1 tablespoon fresh lemon
  juice

Rinse the fillets and pat dry. Coat with the flour; sprinkle with salt and pepper. Heat the butter in a skillet over medium heat until brown in color. Add the mushrooms and artichokes and mix well. Sauté for 2 minutes. Stir in the parsley and red wine. Add the fillets. Cook for 5 minutes or until the fish flakes easily. Drizzle with the lemon juice. Serve immediately. *Yield: 4 servings.*

Internationally known, Maxim's has been a Houston favorite since 1950. Prepare Red Snapper Excelsior, one of Maxim's favorites, at your next dinner party.

Red Snapper with Crawfish Cream Sauce

1 pound red snapper
    fillets
1/4 cup flour
Salt and freshly ground
    pepper to taste
1/2 cup butter
Crawfish Cream Sauce

Rinse the fillets and pat dry. Coat the fillets with a mixture of the flour, salt and pepper.

Sauté the fillets in the butter in a skillet for 3 to 4 minutes per side or until the fillets flake easily, turning once. Arrange on a serving platter.

Spoon the warm Crawfish Cream Sauce over the fillets. Serve immediately. *Yield: 4 servings.*

Crawfish Cream Sauce

1 pound crawfish tails,
    peeled
1/2 cup butter
1/2 green bell pepper,
    chopped
1 cup half-and-half
1 egg yolk, lightly beaten
1 bunch green onions,
    sliced
1 cup chopped fresh
    parsley
6 cloves of garlic, minced
1/4 cup dry sherry
1 teaspoon white pepper
1/2 teaspoon salt
1/2 teaspoon freshly
    ground black pepper
1/4 teaspoon thyme
1/4 teaspoon basil
1/4 teaspoon oregano

Rinse the crawfish and pat dry. Sauté the crawfish in the butter in a skillet for 2 minutes. Add the green pepper and mix well. Stir in a mixture of the half-and-half and egg yolk, reduce heat. Add the green onions, parsley, garlic, sherry, white pepper, salt, black pepper, thyme, basil and oregano and mix well. Cook for 5 minutes, stirring frequently.

Glazed Salmon

4 salmon steaks
$^1/_3$ cup olive oil
$^1/_3$ cup packed light
   brown sugar
$^1/_3$ cup Dijon mustard
2 tablespoons tarragon

Garnish:
Lemon wedges

Rinse the salmon and pat dry. Place in a shallow nonmetallic dish. Combine the olive oil, brown sugar, Dijon mustard and tarragon in a bowl and mix well. Pour over the salmon, turning to coat. Drain, reserving the glaze. Place the salmon on a greased grill rack. Grill over medium-hot coals for 5 minutes per side or until the salmon flakes easily, basting with the reserved glaze frequently. Garnish with lemon wedges. May broil if desired. May substitute two 10-inch salmon fillets for the salmon steaks. *Yield: 4 servings.*

Toss leftover salmon chunks with your favorite hot pasta, chopped fresh dillweed, and olive oil for a delicious entrée.

Roasted Salmon with Crisp Skin

$^1/_2$ bunch dillweed,
   minced
2 shallots, minced
6 sprigs of thyme
3 sprigs of rosemary
1 (2-pound) salmon
   fillet, scales removed,
   at room temperature
Extra-virgin olive oil to
   taste
Sea salt and freshly
   ground pepper to taste
$^1/_4$ cup dry vermouth
Fresh Citrus Sauce

Arrange the dillweed, shallots, thyme and rosemary in a broiler pan. Rinse the salmon and pat dry. Coat with olive oil; sprinkle with sea salt and pepper. Place the salmon skin side up over the prepared layer. Pour the vermouth into the bottom of the pan. Broil the salmon 5 to 6 inches from the heat source for 12 minutes or until the skin is charred and crisp. Remove to a heated serving platter. Serve with Fresh Citrus Sauce. *Yield: 2 servings.*

Fresh Citrus Sauce

Juice of 3 oranges
Juice of 1 lemon
Juice of 1 lime
Salt and freshly ground
   pepper to taste

Combine the orange juice, lemon juice and lime juice in a saucepan and mix well. Cook until reduced by $^1/_2$, stirring frequently. Season with salt and pepper.

Savory Baked Sole

1 1/2 pounds sole fillets
1 cup fresh bread crumbs
1/2 cup butter
1 tablespoon cider
  vinegar
1 tablespoon
  Worcestershire sauce
1 tablespoon fresh lemon
  juice
1 teaspoon Dijon
  mustard

Rinse the sole and pat dry. Coat with bread crumbs. Arrange the fillets in a single layer in a buttered 8x14-inch baking dish. Heat the butter in a saucepan until melted. Stir in the vinegar, Worcestershire sauce, lemon juice and Dijon mustard. Pour over the sole. Bake at 350 degrees for 20 minutes or until the fish fillets flake easily, basting with the pan drippings every 5 minutes. Serve immediately.
Yield: 4 servings.
   Note: May substitute flounder, haddock, scrod or orange roughy for the sole.

Escotovich Fish

4 (6- to 8-ounce)
  swordfish steaks
2 zucchini, julienned
2 carrots, peeled,
  julienned
1 onion, cut into paper-
  thin slices
1 yellow bell pepper,
  julienned
1 cup extra-virgin olive
  oil
1/2 cup cider vinegar
1 teaspoon salt
1/2 teaspoon freshly
  ground pepper
2 cloves of garlic, minced

Rinse the fish and pat dry. Arrange in a single layer in a shallow nonmetallic dish. Combine the zucchini, carrots, onion and yellow pepper in a bowl. Combine the olive oil, vinegar, salt, pepper and garlic in a bowl and mix well. Pour 1/2 of the olive oil mixture over the fish, turning to coat. Marinate, covered, in the refrigerator for 2 hours, turning occasionally. Pour the remaining olive oil mixture over the vegetables, tossing to coat. Marinate at room temperature for 2 hours, stirring occasionally. Spoon the undrained vegetables into a saucepan. Cook over low heat for 5 minutes, stirring occasionally. Cover to keep warm. Drain the fish, reserving the marinade. Grill the fish over medium-hot coals for 6 minutes per side or until the fish flakes easily, turning and basting with the reserved marinade frequently. Remove to a heated platter. Spoon the vegetables with a slotted spoon over the swordfish. Serve immediately. *Yield: 4 servings.*

Grilled Ahi

2 (6-ounce) tuna steaks
1/4 cup lemon juice
1 1/2 teaspoons snipped
    fresh dillweed
1 teaspoon minced fresh
    oregano
1 clove of garlic, minced

Garnish:
Lemon wedges

Rinse the tuna with cold water and pat dry. Arrange the steaks in a single layer in a shallow nonmetallic dish. Combine the lemon juice, dillweed, oregano and garlic in a bowl, whisking to mix. Pour over the tuna, turning to coat. Marinate at room temperature for 30 minutes. Drain, reserving the marinade. Place the steaks 2 inches apart on a lightly greased grill rack. Grill over hot coals for 5 minutes, basting with the reserved marinade once; turn. Grill for 5 minutes longer or until the tuna flakes easily, basting with the remaining marinade. Garnish with lemon wedges. Serve immediately. May broil if desired. *Yield: 2 servings.*

Make grilling clean-up easy by spraying cold barbecue racks with nonstick cooking spray before firing up the coals.

Fish Stock

2 tablespoons unsalted
    butter
2 leeks, chopped
1 fennel bulb, or 2 ribs
    celery, chopped
2 (2-inch) strips each
    orange and lemon peel
2 bay leaves
4 sprigs of rosemary
1 teaspoon each thyme
    and fennel seeds,
    crushed
1 tablespoon flour
1 pound fish trimmings
    (heads, tails, skin,
    bones)
4 cups water
1 cup dry white wine
1 teaspoon salt

Heat the butter in a saucepan until melted. Stir in the leeks, fennel, orange peel, lemon peel, bay leaves, rosemary, thyme and fennel seeds. Cook for 10 minutes, stirring occasionally. Stir in the flour. Cook for 1 minute, stirring constantly. Add the fish trimmings, water, white wine and salt and mix well. Bring to a boil; reduce heat. Simmer for 30 minutes, stirring occasionally; strain. Let stand until cool. Store, covered, in the refrigerator or freeze for future use. *Yield: 4 to 5 cups.*

Soft-Shell Crabs

4 large or 6 small soft-
    shell crabs, cleaned
1/2 cup flour
Salt and freshly ground
    pepper to taste
6 tablespoons olive oil
1/2 cup white wine
1/2 cup Quick and Easy
    Fish Stock
1 tablespoon chopped
    fresh tarragon
1 tablespoon chopped
    fresh parsley
2 tablespoons Ricard
    liqueur
3 tablespoons unsalted
    butter

Garnish:
Lemon wedges

Rinse the crabs and pat dry. Combine the flour, salt and pepper in a shallow dish and mix well. Coat the crabs with the flour mixture; shake off excess.

Heat 3 tablespoons of the olive oil in a skillet over high heat. Add half the crabs. Sauté for 3 minutes; turn. Sauté for 3 minutes longer. Remove the crabs with a slotted spoon to a heated serving platter. Repeat the process with the remaining olive oil and remaining crabs.

Deglaze the skillet with the white wine and stock. Stir in the tarragon and parsley. Cook until reduced by 1/2. Stir in the liqueur. Whisk in the butter 1 table-spoon at a time, whisking well after each addition.

Cook just until creamy, stirring constantly. Pour over the crabs. Garnish with lemon wedges. Serve immediately. *Yield: 2 servings.*

Quick and Easy Fish Stock

2 cups water
2 cups clam juice
1 cup dry white wine
1 cup chopped onion
3 sprigs of parsley
Salt and freshly ground
    pepper to taste

Combine the water, clam juice, white wine, onion and parsley in a saucepan and mix well. Simmer over low heat until reduced to 1 cup, stirring frequently; strain. Season with salt and pepper.

Deglazing refers to heating stock, wine, or any type of liquid in the pan in which the meat or seafood has been cooked, mixing with the pan juices and sediment to form a gravy or sauce base.

Gulf Coast Crab Cakes

1/4 cup minced red
  pepper
1/4 cup minced green
  onions
2 tablespoons chopped
  fresh cilantro
2 tablespoons
  mayonnaise
2 teaspoons Dijon
  mustard
1 teaspoon crab boil
1/2 teaspoon Tabasco
  sauce
1/2 teaspoon
  Worcestershire sauce
1 egg
1 pound fresh lump crab
  meat
1 1/4 cups fresh bread
  crumbs
1/4 teaspoon curry
  powder
Salt and freshly ground
  pepper to taste
4 teaspoons butter
Lemon wedges
Homemade Tartar Sauce

Combine the red pepper, green onions, cilantro, mayonnaise, Dijon mustard, crab boil, Tabasco sauce, Worcestershire sauce and egg in a bowl and mix well. Add the crab meat and 1/3 cup of the bread crumbs and mix gently. Shape by 1/3 cupfuls into 8 patties; patties should be 3/4 inch thick and 3 inches in diameter.

Combine the remaining bread crumbs, curry powder, salt and pepper in a shallow dish. Coat the patties with the crumb mixture, gently reshaping while pressing on the crumb mixture. Arrange on a baking sheet. Chill for 30 minutes.

Spray a nonstick skillet with nonstick cooking spray. Heat the skillet over medium heat until hot. Add 2 teaspoons of the butter, swirling the skillet until the butter melts. Add 4 of the patties. Cook for 4 minutes per side or until golden brown. Remove to a heated serving platter. Repeat the process with the remaining butter and remaining patties. Top with lemon wedges. Serve with Homemade Tartar Sauce. *Yield: 4 servings.*

Homemade Tartar Sauce

2 cups mayonnaise
1/2 cup minced sweet
  gherkins
1/4 cup finely chopped
  scallions
1 teaspoon dry mustard
1/2 teaspoon salt
1/2 teaspoon freshly
  ground pepper
1/2 teaspoon
  Worcestershire sauce

Combine the mayonnaise, gherkins, scallions, dry mustard, salt, pepper and Worcestershire sauce in a bowl and mix well. Chill, covered, until serving time.

Lobster with Scallions and Ginger

2 (1½-pound) live
   lobsters
8 scallions
3 tablespoons vegetable
   oil
8 slices peeled gingerroot
2 teaspoons minced
   garlic
3 tablespoons fish stock
   or water
2 tablespoons cooking
   wine or sherry
2 teaspoons oyster sauce
2 teaspoons sugar
⅓ teaspoon salt
Freshly ground pepper to
   taste
1½ tablespoons water
2 teaspoons cornstarch
1 teaspoon sesame oil
Hot cooked rice

Plunge the lobsters head first into boiling water in a stockpot. Boil for 3 minutes. Remove the lobsters. Let stand until cool.

Remove the meat from the tail and claws; cut into bite-size pieces. Cut the scallions diagonally into 2-inch slices; separate the green and white parts.

Heat a wok for 1 minute. Add the oil. Stir-fry the gingerroot, garlic and white part of the scallions in the oil for 2 minutes. Add the lobster and mix well. Stir in the fish stock, cooking wine, oyster sauce, sugar, salt and pepper.

Cook, covered, for 4 minutes. Add the green part of the scallions and mix well. Stir in a mixture of the water and cornstarch. Cook until thickened, stirring constantly. Sprinkle with the sesame oil. Spoon over hot cooked rice on a serving platter. Serve immediately.

Yield: 2 servings.

Serving many exotic and delicious Vietnamese dishes, such as Lobster with Scallions and Ginger, Saigon Palace was rated by the Houston Chronicle as the best Vietnamese restaurant in Houston.

Scallops with Lemon Coriander Sauce

1 1/2 teaspoons coriander
seeds
1/2 cup extra-virgin olive
oil
1/3 cup fresh lemon juice
3 plum tomatoes, peeled,
seeded, chopped
Salt and freshly ground
pepper to taste
1 pound fresh sea
scallops

Garnish:
Chives, cut into 1-inch
lengths

Spread the coriander seeds on a baking
sheet. Toast at 350 degrees for 10 minutes,
shaking the baking sheet once. Combine
the coriander seeds, olive oil, lemon juice,
tomatoes, salt and pepper in a saucepan
and mix well. Cook just until heated
through, stirring frequently. Keep warm
over low heat. Rinse the scallops and pat
dry. Arrange the scallops in a single layer
in a baking dish. Broil for 4 to 5 minutes;
turn. Broil for 3 minutes longer. Garnish
with chives. Serve immediately with the
lemon sauce. *Yield: 2 servings.*

*Fresh scallops should
be sweet-smelling,
firm, and have a moist
sheen. Scallops may be
stored in their liquid,
covered, in the
refrigerator for up
to two days.*

Baked Shrimp with Feta Cheese

6 tablespoons unsalted
butter
36 large shrimp, peeled,
deveined
3 cloves of garlic, minced
3/4 teaspoon oregano,
crushed
1/4 teaspoon red pepper
flakes
1/8 teaspoon salt
3/4 cup dry vermouth
6 fresh plum tomatoes,
seeded, chopped
3 ounces feta cheese,
crumbled
1/4 cup loosely packed
minced fresh parsley
Hot cooked angel hair
pasta

Heat the butter in a skillet over medium
heat until melted. Add the shrimp, garlic,
oregano, red pepper flakes and salt and
mix well. Cook for 3 minutes or until the
shrimp are almost pink, stirring frequently.
Spoon the shrimp with a slotted spoon
into a shallow baking dish or spoon into
four 6-inch gratin dishes; arrange the
shrimp in a single layer. Add the vermouth
to the pan drippings in the skillet. Bring to
a boil. Boil until reduced by 1/2, adding any
juices accumulated in the baking dish from
the shrimp. Add the tomatoes and mix
gently. Cook for 30 seconds or just until
heated through, stirring constantly. Spoon
over the shrimp. Top with the feta cheese.
Bake at 350 degrees for 8 to 10 minutes or
until bubbly. Sprinkle with the parsley.
Spoon over the pasta on a serving platter.
Yield: 4 servings.

*Feta mellows
wonderfully when
baked.*

Shrimp with Butter Chive Dipping Sauce

1 pound large shrimp,
  peeled, deveined
4 egg whites, lightly
  beaten
1/3 to 1/2 cup (about)
  flour
2 cups vegetable oil
Butter Chive Dipping
  Sauce (at top right)

Dip the shrimp in the egg whites. Coat with the flour, shaking off the excess. Heat the oil in a saucepan over medium heat until hot. Deep-fry the shrimp 6 at a time for 1 minute or until golden brown; drain. Arrange the shrimp in a shallow baking pan. Broil for 1 minute. Serve immediately with the Butter Chive Dipping Sauce. *Yield: 2 servings.*

For Butter Chive Dipping Sauce, combine 1 lightly beaten egg yolk and the juice of 1 lemon in a saucepan and mix well. Add 1/2 cup butter. Cook over medium heat until smooth, stirring constantly. Stir in 1 minced clove of garlic. Cook until thickened, stirring constantly. Add 2 tablespoons snipped fresh chives and mix well.

Cajun Barbecued Shrimp

1/2 cup butter
1 onion, chopped
2 cloves of garlic, minced
1 teaspoon
  Worcestershire sauce
1 teaspoon red pepper
  flakes
1 teaspoon freshly
  ground black pepper
1/2 teaspoon white pepper
1/2 teaspoon thyme
1/2 teaspoon rosemary
1/8 teaspoon oregano
2 pounds large shrimp,
  peeled, deveined
1/2 cup butter
1/2 cup chicken broth
1/4 cup beer
4 cups hot cooked white
  rice

Garnish:
Sprigs of parsley

Heat 1/2 cup butter in a skillet until melted. Add the onion, garlic, Worcestershire sauce, red pepper flakes, black pepper, white pepper, thyme, rosemary and oregano and mix well. Cook over medium heat for 2 minutes, stirring constantly. Add the shrimp and mix well. Cook for 2 minutes, stirring constantly. Stir in 1/2 cup butter and the broth. Cook for 5 minutes, stirring constantly. Add the beer and mix well. Cook for 1 minute, stirring constantly. Spoon the rice in the shape of a ring on 4 dinner plates; pour the shrimp and sauce into the center of the ring. Garnish with sprigs of parsley. Serve with crusty French bread. *Yield: 4 servings.*

Creole Black-Eyed Peas, Rice and Shrimp

1 pound dried black-eyed
    peas
8 ounces salt pork
2¹/₂ cups chopped onions
1¹/₂ cups chopped fresh
    parsley
2 bunches green onions,
    chopped
1 cup tomato sauce
1 cup chopped green bell
    pepper
3 cloves of garlic,
    crushed
1 tablespoon
    Worcestershire sauce
1 teaspoon salt
1 teaspoon red pepper
    flakes
1 teaspoon freshly
    ground black pepper
¹/₂ teaspoon oregano
¹/₂ teaspoon thyme
Hot sauce to taste
2 pounds smoked
    sausage, cut into
    ¹/₂-inch slices
1 pound large shrimp,
    peeled, deveined
Hot cooked rice

Sort and rinse the peas. Combine with enough water to cover in a bowl. Let stand for 8 to 10 hours; drain.

Combine the peas and salt pork with enough water to cover in a stockpot. Bring to a boil; reduce heat. Cook, covered, over low heat for 45 minutes, stirring occasionally.

Add the onions, parsley, green onions, tomato sauce, green pepper, garlic, Worcestershire sauce, salt, red pepper flakes, black pepper, oregano, thyme and hot sauce and mix well. Cook, covered, over low heat for 45 minutes, stirring occasionally. Add the sausage. Cook, uncovered, for 30 minutes.

Add the shrimp. Cook for 10 minutes longer or until the shrimp turn pink, stirring occasionally. Ladle over hot cooked rice. *Yield: 10 servings.*

Two to two-and-a-half pounds of shrimp in the shell yields one pound cooked, peeled shrimp, or two cups.

Spicy Shrimp Kabobs

2 pounds large unpeeled
  shrimp
$1/2$ cup unsalted butter
3 tablespoons olive oil
2 tablespoons chili sauce
1 tablespoon
  Worcestershire sauce
1 tablespoon fresh lemon
  juice
1 tablespoon minced
  fresh parsley
$3/4$ teaspoon red pepper
  flakes
$3/4$ teaspoon liquid smoke
$1/2$ teaspoon paprika
$1/2$ teaspoon oregano
$1/4$ teaspoon Tabasco
  sauce
2 cloves of garlic,
  crushed
$1/2$ lemon, thinly sliced
Salt and freshly ground
  black pepper to taste
Onions, cut into wedges
Red bell peppers, cut
  into chunks
Cherry tomatoes

Make a slit down the back of each shrimp and devein. Rinse the shrimp in cold water and pat dry. Arrange in a single layer in a shallow nonmetallic dish.

Combine the butter, olive oil, chili sauce, Worcestershire sauce, lemon juice, parsley, red pepper flakes, liquid smoke, paprika, oregano, Tabasco sauce, garlic, lemon slices, salt and black pepper in a saucepan and mix well. Simmer for 10 minutes, stirring occasionally.

Pour over the shrimp, turning to coat. Marinate, covered, in the refrigerator for 2 to 3 hours, turning occasionally. Drain, reserving the marinade.

Thread the shrimp, onions, red peppers and cherry tomatoes alternately on skewers.

Grill over hot coals or broil for 15 minutes or until the shrimp turn pink, turning and basting with the reserved marinade frequently. *Yield: 6 servings.*

Linguini with Shrimp

12 ounces linguini
Salt to taste
Olive oil to taste
1 cup sliced mushrooms
2 cloves of garlic, minced
3/4 teaspoon rosemary
2 tablespoons olive oil
2 pounds shrimp, peeled,
    deveined
1 cup clam juice
2/3 cup whipping cream
1/2 teaspoon freshly
    ground pepper

Cook the pasta in boiling salted water in a saucepan using package directions; drain. Toss with just enough olive oil to coat in a bowl. Sauté the mushrooms, garlic and rosemary in 2 tablespoons olive oil in a skillet for 2 minutes. Add the shrimp. Cook just until the shrimp turn pink, stirring constantly; do not overcook. Stir in the clam juice, whipping cream and pepper. Simmer until thickened and slightly reduced, stirring constantly. Pour over the pasta, tossing to mix. Serve immediately. *Yield: 4 servings.*

To butterfly shrimp before cooking, peel the shrimp to the tail, leaving the tail intact. Devein the shrimp. Holding so the underside faces up, slice down its length almost to the vein. Spread and flatten.

Scampi Primavera

1/2 cup butter
2 carrots, julienned
1 zucchini, julienned
1 red pepper, julienned
4 to 6 cloves of garlic,
    minced
3 tablespoons extra-
    virgin olive oil
1 1/2 pounds medium
    shrimp, peeled,
    deveined
2 tablespoons fresh
    lemon juice
2 tablespoons chopped
    fresh basil
2 tablespoons chopped
    fresh parsley
1/2 teaspoon salt
1/4 teaspoon freshly
    ground pepper

Heat the butter in a skillet over medium heat until melted. Add the carrots, zucchini, red pepper, garlic and olive oil and mix well. Cook for 1 minute, stirring constantly. Add the shrimp and mix well. Cook for 3 to 4 minutes or until the shrimp turn pink, stirring constantly. Remove from heat. Drizzle with the lemon juice; sprinkle with the basil, parsley, salt and pepper. Serve immediately.
Yield: 4 servings.

   Note: May serve over your favorite hot cooked pasta.

Beef Imperiale

2 pounds lean top sirloin
Salt and pepper to taste
1/2 cup flour
1/4 cup vegetable oil
1 1/2 cups chopped yellow
    onions
1 clove of garlic, minced
2 cups beef broth
1 teaspoon liquid beef
    extract
8 ounces mushrooms
1/4 cup chopped fresh
    parsley
3 tablespoons fresh
    lemon juice
1 tablespoon
    Worcestershire sauce
1/2 to 1 cup sour cream
    (optional)
Hot buttered noodles

Cut the beef into thin strips. Season with salt and pepper. Coat with the flour, shaking off the excess. Brown the beef on both sides in the oil in a skillet. Add the onions and garlic. Sauté for 1 minute. Remove beef and onions from pan. Deglaze with the beef broth and beef extract. Return beef and onions to pan and simmer for 30 minutes, stirring occasionally. Slice the mushrooms. Stir the mushrooms and parsley into the skillet. Simmer for 30 minutes, stirring occasionally. Add the lemon juice and Worcestershire sauce and mix well. Remove from heat. Stir in the sour cream. Serve with hot buttered noodles. *Yield: 4 servings.*

Linguini with Tomatoes, Feta and Olives

12 ounces linguini
Salt to taste
2 tablespoons extra-
    virgin olive oil
3 cloves of garlic, minced
6 to 8 plum tomatoes,
    peeled, seeded,
    chopped
1 tablespoon chopped
    fresh oregano
12 large kalamata olives,
    cut into quarters
6 ounces feta cheese,
    crumbled
Juice of 1/2 lemon
Pepper to taste

Cook the linguini in boiling salted water in a saucepan using package directions; drain. Cover to keep warm. Heat the olive oil in a skillet until hot. Add the garlic. Sauté for 20 seconds; reduce the heat. Stir in the tomatoes and oregano. Simmer for 6 to 8 minutes, stirring frequently. Add the hot pasta, tossing to coat. Add the olives, feta cheese, lemon juice, salt and pepper, tossing to mix. Serve immediately.
Yield: 4 servings.
    Note: May substitute 1 teaspoon dried oregano for the chopped fresh oregano.

Kalamata olives are Greek in origin. They are purple-black in color and are considered superior in quality. They can be found in gourmet specialty shops and at the deli counter of some supermarkets. Any large black Greek or Italian olive may be substituted.

Penne with Prosciutto and Peas

1/4 cup butter
6 plum tomatoes, peeled,
  cut into halves
1 clove of garlic, cut
  lengthwise into halves
1/4 cup butter
2 tablespoons flour
1 cup whipping cream
6 ounces prosciutto,
  julienned
1 cup fresh peas,
  blanched
2 tablespoons grated
  Parmesan cheese
1 tablespoon chopped
  fresh Italian parsley
1 teaspoon freshly
  ground pepper
1 pound penne
Salt to taste

Heat 1/4 cup butter in a skillet until melted. Arrange the tomatoes and garlic cut side down in a single layer in the skillet. Cook over medium heat for 10 minutes. Process the tomato mixture in a blender or food processor until smooth. Heat 1/4 cup butter in the same skillet. Add the flour, stirring until blended. Add the whipping cream gradually, stirring constantly. Cook until thickened, stirring constantly. Stir in the prosciutto, peas, cheese, parsley and pepper. Bring to a simmer, stirring constantly. Stir in the tomato mixture. Cover to keep warm. Cook the pasta in boiling salted water in a saucepan using package directions; drain. Combine the pasta and tomato mixture in a bowl, tossing to mix. Serve immediately. *Yield: 4 servings.*

Cheese Ravioli with Sun-Dried Tomatoes

9 ounces fresh cheese
  ravioli
1/2 cup butter
4 cloves of garlic, minced
2 cups light cream
1 cup freshly grated
  Parmesan cheese
1/2 cup oil-pack sun-dried
  tomatoes
Freshly ground pepper to
  taste
1/4 cup vodka (optional)

Cook the ravioli using package directions; drain. Cover to keep warm. Heat the butter in a skillet over medium heat until melted. Add the garlic. Cook until light golden brown, stirring constantly. Add the light cream, whisking constantly. Bring to a simmer, whisking constantly; do not boil. Remove from heat. Add the cheese, tomatoes and pepper and mix well. Cook until thickened, stirring constantly. Stir in the vodka. Cook just until heated through. Remove from heat. Add the ravioli, tossing to coat. Serve immediately. *Yield: 2 servings.*

Tagliatelle with Fresh Tomatoes and Basil

8 ripe firm beefsteak
  tomatoes
1/2 cup chopped fresh
  Italian parsley
1/2 cup chopped fresh
  basil
1/4 cup extra-virgin olive
  oil
1/2 teaspoon sugar
2 cloves of garlic, minced
Salt and freshly ground
  pepper to taste
12 ounces tagliatelle
Grated Parmesan cheese

Plunge the tomatoes in boiling water in a saucepan for 30 seconds; drain. Peel and chop the tomatoes. Place in a nonmetallic bowl. Stir in the parsley, basil, olive oil, sugar, garlic, salt and pepper. Let stand at room temperature for several hours, stirring occasionally. Cook the pasta in boiling salted water in a saucepan using package directions; drain. Add the hot pasta to the tomato mixture, tossing to mix. Serve immediately with Parmesan cheese and pepper. *Yield: 4 servings.*

This is a summertime meal! The tomatoes make this dish and can only be found at certain times of the year. There are no substitutes for beefsteak tomatoes. When buying tomatoes for this recipe, select the ripest, unbruised ones. Let them ripen several more days in your windowsill.

Three-Pepper Pasta with Goat Cheese

16 ounces farfalle
Salt to taste
1 (7-ounce) can
  artichoke hearts
1/2 cup chopped red
  onion
2 cloves of garlic, minced
1/4 cup extra-virgin olive
  oil
1 pound fresh
  mushrooms, sliced
1/2 cup each julienned
  green, red and yellow
  bell pepper
3 plum tomatoes,
  chopped
1 teaspoon basil
1 teaspoon oregano
Pepper to taste
8 ounces goat cheese
1/4 cup chopped fresh basil

Cook the pasta in boiling salted water in a saucepan until al dente; drain. Cover to keep warm. Drain the artichoke hearts and cut into quarters. Sauté the red onion and garlic in the olive oil in a skillet for 2 minutes. Stir in the mushrooms, artichokes, green pepper, red pepper, yellow pepper, tomatoes, basil and oregano. Sauté for 5 minutes. Season with salt and pepper. Toss the pasta and pepper mixture in a heated pasta bowl. Crumble the goat cheese. Sprinkle the goat cheese and basil over the top. Serve immediately.
Yield: 4 servings.

Summer Squash Enchiladas

3/4 cup chopped onion
2 cloves of garlic, minced
1 tablespoon olive oil
3 cups chopped zucchini
    or yellow squash
2 ounces green chile
    peppers, chopped
2 tablespoons butter
2 tablespoons flour
2 teaspoons cumin
1 1/2 teaspoons chili
    powder
1/4 teaspoon salt
1/8 teaspoon white pepper
1 cup milk
1 cup shredded
    Monterey Jack cheese
8 (6- or 7-inch) flour
    tortillas
1/2 cup shredded Cheddar
    cheese
5 plum tomatoes,
    chopped
Mango Salsa

Sauté the onion and garlic in the olive oil in a skillet for 2 minutes. Stir in the zucchini. Cook, covered, for 3 to 5 minutes or until tender, stirring occasionally; drain. Stir in the chile peppers.

Heat the butter in a saucepan until melted. Add the flour and mix well. Stir in the cumin, chili powder, salt and white pepper. Add the milk gradually, stirring constantly. Cook until thickened, stirring constantly. Add the Monterey Jack cheese and mix well. Cook just until the cheese melts, stirring constantly.

Stir 1/3 of the cheese mixture into the zucchini mixture. Spoon 1/3 cup of the mixture onto each tortilla; roll to enclose the filling. Arrange the tortillas seam side down in a buttered 9x12-inch baking dish. Top with the remaining cheese mixture. Sprinkle with the Cheddar cheese.

Bake, covered, for 25 minutes. Sprinkle with the tomatoes. Bake for 5 minutes longer. Serve with Mango Salsa. *Yield: 6 servings.*

Mango Salsa

1 large tomato or 3 plum
    tomatoes, chopped
1 mango, chopped
1 avocado, chopped
1/4 cup chopped red
    onion
1/3 cup loosely packed
    chopped fresh cilantro
Juice of 1 lime
1 jalapeño, seeded,
    minced (optional)
Salt and freshly ground
    pepper to taste

Combine the tomato, mango, avocado, red onion, cilantro, lime juice, jalapeño, salt and pepper in a bowl and mix gently.

During the winter months, this dish is excellent served with tortilla soup and an avocado salad. Serve with grilled chicken and Mango Salsa during the summer months.

Complements

Fort Tomato

by Julie S. Miracle

There's been some construction at my parents' home lately. Dad's a general contractor, so the sights and sounds of construction projects around the house are a fairly common occurrence, though muddy trucks and hard-hatted crews aren't part of the scene on this particular job. It's rather small and personal. Honestly, it's not even very professional, but it reflects passion.

Passion, because it shelters something precious: a most-loved fruit (or is it a vegetable?) which has been prized, imported, preserved, even feared, by populations across time. Medieval Europeans shunned this exotic commodity and labeled it the Devil's Apple. Thomas Jefferson named it the Love Fruit. In recent history, southerners have incorporated this culinary gem into every conceivable meal through all seasons of the year.

When I reflect on the importance of these gorgeous ruby orbs to cooks and diners everywhere, Dad's efforts only make sense. In case there's any doubt about the beloved entity

sheltered behind Dad's newly constructed edifice, he's posted a sign on the gate. It reads: Fort Tomato.

The taste and beauty of tomatoes on the table is essential to good southern cooking. In my life, tomatoes are an ingredient that open the door to family images and memories and help me connect, through taste buds, to people and times that I love—like dinner at Gran's.

I can't imagine a summer dinner at Gran's without a plate of sliced tomatoes, seasoned simply with salt and pepper, present on the table. Red slices of tang ready to layer onto a ham biscuit or fork next to string beans. And besides tasting wonderful, those tomatoes generated conversation along the lines of vegetable "fish stories": their size, taste and this season's bumper crop. Or, maybe, there'd be a genetic mutation sliced on the table that would keep the kids guessing its shape like they do with clouds floating by on a clear day.

Often Gran would serve a dish of sliced tomatoes, cucumbers and onions in a weakened cider vinegar. My mother dishes up this salad in her blue-and-white antique bowl with sprigs of dill from her garden. The quirky thing about this side dish is that both women always place ice cubes on the top. I guess it's a holdover from the days of limited refrigeration, or perhaps just to keep those crunchy veggies cold while the family talks and eats through the evening. Many times, as I prepare that particular salad years and miles away from summer dinners on the porch at Gran's, I, without thinking, put my automatic ice maker cubes on the top. It's strange how those cubes connect me from now to then.

Hot stewed tomatoes enjoyed in a winter meal connect me to another memory—the tomato explosion. It occurred in my mother's kitchen when I was about ten. My family had recently left their suburban subdivision home for a turn-of-the-century farmhouse and acreage just outside the city sprawl. My parents, the urbanites, started to work on their "Green Acres." Dad grew a beard and planted a garden. Mom took up canning everything from green beans to raspberry jam, everything, including tomatoes.

Thank God, none of us was in the kitchen when the boiling bath in the canner caused the jars to explode. We probably would have shrapnel wounds in addition to burns. *Attack of the Killer Tomatoes* really happened in that kitchen. Red blobs clung to the wallpaper, juice pooled on the floor, splatters were everywhere: on windows, baseboards, even on the baskets hanging from the beamed ceiling. The only thing missing was the crime scene tape and the body.

Those tomatoes that survived the canning ordeal ended up as wintertime stewed tomatoes. That side dish always gave me a twinge of embarrassment if company stayed for dinner. Mom had an eccentric habit of adding bits of torn bread to the liquid. Of course, Gran did this, too, and, I admit it tastes wonderful, but it looks so soppy. Once, while visiting Monticello in Charlottesville, Virginia, my husband I enjoyed a colonial period meal that included, yes, stewed tomatoes with that soppy bread. To think that Jefferson himself most likely relished his stewed tomatoes this way gives me impetus to continue the tasty tradition.

Tomatoes are traditional. Eating them matches us to the seasons of the year and patterns of our culture. Nothing says summer more than a tomato sandwich. Some might ask, "Uh, tomato and what?" Well, just tomato: spread with a little mayonnaise and eaten on the back porch steps. Make a tall glass of lemonade to sip on, too. Tomatoes say fall to us when they're hastily picked before a frost, dipped in cornmeal batter and fried in a cast-iron skillet. Why, it's worth making a movie about.

Southerners love their tomatoes. And we won't accept less than the generous, flavorful garden-grown variety. God forbid to have to resort to pale, pithy, grocery-counter substitutes. Like my Dad, many go to great lengths to grow their own tomatoes. At my first apartment there was hardly a blade of grass in sight and certainly no prospects of a garden. Solution: pots with cherry tomato plants! And a connection to heart and home, as well.

Truly the tradition of the tomato that endures and grows in our family kitchens deserves preserving and celebrating. In fact, there are no lengths too great to protect what Thomas Jefferson named the love fruit. Long live Fort Tomato!

Julie S. Miracle is an active member of The Junior League of North Harris County. She writes, cooks and endeavors each summer to grow the perfect tomato.

Scalloped Asparagus

1 pound fresh asparagus
Salt to taste
1 tablespoon butter
1 tablespoon flour
1 cup milk
2 hard-cooked eggs,
   finely chopped
3 tablespoons butter
$^1/_2$ teaspoon salt
$^1/_2$ teaspoon cayenne
$^1/_4$ cup fine bread crumbs
$^1/_4$ cup shredded Swiss
   cheese

Rinse the asparagus. Discard the tough ends; remove the scales. Bring enough salted water to cover the asparagus to a boil in a saucepan. Add the asparagus; reduce heat. Simmer, covered, for 10 minutes or until tender-crisp. Drain on paper towels.

Heat 1 tablespoon butter in a saucepan until melted. Add the flour and mix well. Cook for 1 minute, stirring constantly. Add the milk gradually, stirring constantly. Cook for 3 minutes or until thickened, stirring constantly. Remove from heat.

Layer $^1/_2$ of the asparagus in a $1^1/_2$-quart shallow baking dish. Sprinkle with $^1/_2$ of the egg; dot with 1 tablespoon of the butter. Season with $^1/_2$ teaspoon salt and cayenne. Top with the remaining asparagus. Sprinkle the remaining egg along the center portion of the asparagus. Pour the cream sauce down the middle of the baking dish. Sprinkle with the bread crumbs and cheese. Dot uncovered portions of the asparagus with the remaining 2 tablespoons butter.

Bake, covered, at 400 degrees for 15 minutes; remove the cover. Bake for 3 minutes longer or until brown. Serve immediately. *Yield: 4 to 6 servings.*

Asparagus stalks should be tender and firm and tips should be close and compact. The most tender stalks have very little white on them. Remember to use fresh asparagus immediately, since it toughens rapidly.

Asparagus Caesar

1 pound fresh asparagus
1/4 cup melted butter
3 tablespoons fresh
    lemon juice
1/2 cup freshly grated
    Parmesan cheese
Paprika to taste

Steam the asparagus in a steamer until tender-crisp. Arrange the asparagus in an 8x8-inch baking dish. Combine the butter and lemon juice in a bowl and mix well. Drizzle over the asparagus. Sprinkle with the cheese and paprika. Bake at 425 degrees until bubbly. Serve immediately. *Yield: 4 servings.*

Use a vegetable peeler to remove the scales on asparagus stalks.

Green Beans and Peppers

24 fresh pearl onions
1 1/2 pounds fresh green
    beans, sliced
    diagonally
3 tablespoons extra-
    virgin olive oil
1 medium red bell
    pepper, thinly sliced
1 medium yellow bell
    pepper, thinly sliced
1 medium green bell
    pepper, thinly sliced
1/4 cup balsamic vinegar
2 cloves of garlic, minced
Salt and freshly ground
    pepper to taste

Garnish:
Freshly grated Parmesan
    cheese

Blanch the onions and drain; remove the skins. Blanch the green beans; drain. Heat the olive oil in a skillet until hot. Add the bell peppers. Sauté just until tender. Stir in the green beans, onions, balsamic vinegar, garlic, salt and pepper. Cook just until heated through. Spoon into a serving bowl. Garnish with freshly grated Parmesan cheese. Serve immediately. *Yield: 6 servings.*

Green Beans Wrapped in Sweet Peppers

1 quart water
1 1/2 pounds fresh green
   beans, trimmed,
   strings removed
2 yellow or red bell
   peppers, cut into 8
   strips
3/4 cup coarsely chopped
   cashews
1/2 cup butter
2 tablespoons chopped
   fresh parsley
2 tablespoons sliced
   green onions
2 teaspoons fresh lemon
   juice
1 teaspoon grated lemon
   zest

Garnish:
Whole cashews

Bring the water to a boil in a saucepan. Add the green beans. Cook for 5 minutes or until tender-crisp. Drain and plunge into ice water in a bowl; drain. Divide the beans into 8 equal portions. Wrap 1 bell pepper slice around each portion. Arrange in a shallow dish. Chill, covered, for 8 to 10 hours. Sauté the cashews in the butter in a saucepan until light brown. Remove from heat. Stir in the parsley, green onions, lemon juice and lemon zest. Chill, covered, for up to 24 hours. Let the green beans and cashew butter stand at room temperature for 45 minutes before baking. Spoon the cashew butter over the beans. Bake, covered, at 350 degrees for 12 minutes or until heated through. Garnish with whole cashews. Serve immediately. *Yield: 8 servings.*

Gourmet Baked Beans

2 cups kidney beans
2 cups butter beans or
   Great Northern beans
2 cups pork and beans
1/2 cup catsup
1/2 cup packed brown
   sugar
1/8 teaspoon garlic
   powder
8 ounces bacon, chopped
1 cup chopped onion

Combine the kidney beans, butter beans and pork and beans in a bowl, stirring gently. Stir in a mixture of the catsup, brown sugar and garlic powder. Brown the bacon and onion in a skillet; drain. Add to the bean mixture and mix gently. Spoon into a 2-quart baking dish. Bake at 350 degrees for 1 hour. *Yield: 8 to 10 servings.*

Broccoli Mousse with Mushroom Sauce

1 pound broccoli florets
1/2 cup whipping cream
Juice of 1/2 lemon
1 teaspoon salt
1/2 teaspoon freshly
  ground pepper
1/8 teaspoon nutmeg
4 eggs
Mushroom Sauce

Cook the broccoli in boiling water in a saucepan until tender-crisp; drain. Plunge into ice water in a bowl; drain.

Bring the whipping cream to a boil in a saucepan. Stir in the broccoli, lemon juice, salt, pepper and nutmeg. Cook until the cream is absorbed, stirring occasionally.

Process the broccoli mixture in a blender or food processor until puréed. Add the eggs 1 at a time, processing well after each addition. Spoon the purée into 8 buttered ramekins.

Arrange the ramekins in a baking pan. Add enough hot water to the baking pan to reach halfway up the sides of the ramekins. Cover with buttered foil. Bake at 375 degrees for 30 minutes or until set. Invert onto a serving platter. Serve immediately with the warm Mushroom Sauce. *Yield: 8 servings.*

My grandmother once told me, "When cooking vegetables, remember to boil vegetables that grow above ground without a cover."

∼ Karen Cate ∼

Mushroom Sauce

1 cup butter, chilled
18 dried mushrooms,
  rehydrated, chopped
1 shallot, minced
1/2 cup dry vermouth
1 cup whipping cream
Salt and freshly ground
  pepper to taste
Lemon juice to taste

Heat 1 tablespoon of the butter in a saucepan over medium heat until melted. Add the mushrooms and shallot and mix well. Cook until all the liquid has been absorbed, stirring frequently. Crumble the remaining chilled butter into a bowl. Stir the vermouth into the mushroom mixture. Cook over medium heat, stirring frequently. Stir in the whipping cream. Cook until slightly thickened, stirring constantly. Remove from heat. Add the butter a little at a time, stirring until blended after each addition. Season with salt, pepper and lemon juice.

Bleu Cheese Broccoli

1¹/₂ pounds fresh
  broccoli
3 ounces cream cheese,
  softened
¹/₄ cup crumbled bleu
  cheese
2 tablespoons butter
2 tablespoons flour
¹/₄ teaspoon salt
1 cup milk
¹/₃ cup finely crushed
  butter crackers

Steam the broccoli in a steamer until
tender-crisp; drain. Combine the cream
cheese, bleu cheese, butter, flour and salt
in a saucepan and mix well. Add the milk.
Cook until the mixture comes to a boil,
stirring constantly. Stir in the broccoli
gently. Spoon into a 1-quart baking dish.
Sprinkle with the cracker crumbs. Bake at
350 degrees for 30 minutes.
Yield: 6 to 8 servings.

Red Cabbage with Apples

1 (2-pound) head red
  cabbage, cut into
  quarters
2 onions, chopped
2 teaspoons salt
¹/₂ teaspoon nutmeg
Freshly ground pepper to
  taste
¹/₄ cup butter
2 cups water
2 tablespoons cider
  vinegar
4 Granny Smith apples,
  peeled, sliced
3 tablespoons fresh
  lemon juice

Shred the cabbage, discarding the core.
Sauté the onions, salt, nutmeg and pepper
in the butter in a large saucepan until the
onions are golden brown. Add the water
and vinegar and mix well. Stir in the
cabbage. Cook, covered, over medium
heat for 30 minutes. Add the apples and
mix well. Cook for 30 minutes longer,
stirring occasionally. May add additional
water if the cabbage appears dry. Stir in
the lemon juice. Serve immediately.
Yield: 8 servings.

Carrots Baked in Apple Orange Sauce

5 tablespoons sugar
2 tablespoons flour
5 Rome apples, peeled,
  thinly sliced
2 cups cooked sliced
  fresh carrots
1/2 cup fresh orange juice
1/4 cup pecan pieces
2 tablespoons butter
Cinnamon to taste

Combine the sugar and flour in a bowl and mix well. Layer 1/2 of the apples and 1/2 of the carrots in a shallow 1-quart baking dish. Sprinkle with some of the sugar mixture. Repeat the layers with the remaining apples, carrots and sugar mixture. Pour the orange juice over the top; sprinkle with the pecans. Dot with the butter. Bake at 350 degrees for 45 minutes or until the apples are tender. Sprinkle with cinnamon just before serving.
Yield: 6 servings.

Avoid storing carrots near apples. This will give the carrots a bitter taste.

Fresh Corn and Zucchini

1 1/2 cups chopped yellow
  bell pepper
3/4 cup chopped onion
2 tablespoons butter
2 1/2 cups fresh corn
  kernels
2 cups chopped zucchini
1/4 cup whipping cream
Salt and freshly ground
  pepper to taste
1/3 cup chopped fresh
  basil

Sauté the yellow pepper and onion in the butter in a skillet for 2 minutes. Add the corn and zucchini and mix well. Cook for 1 minute, stirring constantly. Stir in the whipping cream, salt and pepper. Cook, covered, until heated through, stirring occasionally. Add the basil and mix well. Serve immediately. *Yield: 6 to 8 servings.*

Black Beans, Corn and Tomatoes

1/3 cup vegetable oil
1/4 cup fresh lemon juice
1 1/2 teaspoons salt
1 teaspoon
    Worcestershire sauce
1/2 teaspoon dry mustard
1/2 teaspoon celery salt
1/4 teaspoon red pepper
1/4 teaspoon black pepper
1/4 teaspoon white pepper
2 cups rinsed drained
    black beans
2 cups drained white
    Shoe Peg corn
1 cup chopped green
    onions
1/3 cup chopped fresh
    cilantro
3 cups chopped tomatoes

Combine the oil, lemon juice, salt, Worcestershire sauce, dry mustard, celery salt, red pepper, black pepper and white pepper in a bowl and mix well. Chill, covered, in the refrigerator. Combine the black beans, corn, green onions, cilantro and tomatoes in a bowl and mix gently. Pour the chilled oil mixture over the bean mixture, tossing to coat. Marinate, covered, in the refrigerator for 8 to 10 hours, stirring occasionally. May serve with salsa and sour cream. *Yield: 12 servings.*

Grilled Wild Mushrooms

1 pound large fresh
    shiitake or portobello
    mushrooms
1/2 cup melted butter
1/4 cup chopped fresh
    parsley
3 cloves of garlic, minced
1/2 teaspoon salt
1/4 teaspoon freshly
    ground pepper

Remove the stems from the mushrooms. Combine the butter, parsley, garlic, salt and pepper in a bowl and mix well. Drizzle the butter mixture over both sides of the mushrooms. Grill over medium-hot coals for 8 minutes, turning once. Serve immediately with grilled steaks or toss with hot cooked pasta. *Yield: 4 servings.*

One of my fondest childhood memories was of my grand-mother preparing fresh corn. "Reach in the drawer and hand me the shoehorn," she stated, very matter-of-factly. Convinced that senility had set in, I politely asked, "Wouldn't you rather have a knife?" "Heavens no!" she replied. "Shoehorns are just perfect for shearing off kernels in a jiffy!" It wasn't until many years later that I sadly discovered this was not the reason they named a certain variety of corn Shoe Peg.

⌐ Karen Cate ⌐

Grilled Okra and Sweet Peppers

1 pound fresh okra
1¼ cups spicy hot
   vegetable juice
   cocktail
2 red bell peppers, cut
   into 2-inch pieces
½ teaspoon whole thyme
1 tablespoon olive oil
Lemon wedges

Combine the okra, vegetable juice cock-tail, red peppers and thyme in a bowl and mix gently. Marinate at room temperature for 1 hour, stirring frequently. Drain, reserving the marinade. Thread the okra and red peppers alternately on six 9-inch skewers; brush with the olive oil. Place the skewers on a greased grill rack. Grill over medium-hot coals for 7 minutes per side, basting frequently with the reserved marinade. Serve immediately with lemon wedges. *Yield: 6 servings.*

To blanch food, immerse it in boiling water briefly to inactivate enzymes, loosen skin, or soak away excess salt. Then immerse in cold water to stop the cooking process.

Onions Parmesan

2 pounds sweet yellow
   onions
1 tablespoon butter
½ cup freshly grated
   Parmesan cheese
1 cup light cream
2 tablespoons flour
2 teaspoons salt
¼ teaspoon
   Worcestershire sauce
⅛ teaspoon freshly
   ground pepper
Paprika to taste

Blanch the onions; remove the skins. Cut the onions into ¼-inch slices. Butter a 10-inch electric skillet. Arrange ½ of the onions in 3 rows. Sprinkle with ½ of the cheese. Layer with the remaining onions and cheese. Combine the light cream, flour, salt, Worcestershire sauce and pepper in a bowl and mix well. Spoon over the prepared layers. Cook, covered, at 275 degrees for 12 minutes or until the onions are tender. Sprinkle with paprika. Serve immediately. *Yield: 6 servings.*

   Note: Sweet yellow onions may be Vidalia onions or Texas 1015 onions.

Three-Onion Casserole

1 tablespoon butter
2 cups thinly sliced
  yellow onions
2 cups thinly sliced red
  onions
2 cups thinly sliced leeks
1 teaspoon salt
1/2 teaspoon freshly
  ground pepper
1 1/2 cups shredded
  Havarti cheese
1 1/2 cups crumbled
  boursin cheese with
  herbs
1 1/2 cups grated Gruyère
  cheese
2 tablespoons butter
2/3 cup dry white wine

Grease a 2-quart baking dish with 1 table-spoon butter. Layer 1/3 of the yellow onions, 1/3 of the red onions and 1/3 of the leeks in the prepared dish. Sprinkle with 1/3 of the salt and 1/3 of the pepper. Top with the Havarti cheese. Layer with 1/2 of the remaining yellow onions, 1/2 of the remaining red onions, 1/2 of the remaining leeks, 1/2 of the remaining salt and 1/2 of the remaining pepper. Sprinkle with the boursin cheese. Top with the remaining yellow onions, remaining red onions, remaining leeks, remaining salt and remaining pepper. Sprinkle with the Gruyère cheese. Dot with 2 tablespoons butter. Pour the wine over the top. Bake at 350 degrees for 1 hour. *Yield: 6 to 8 servings*

Note: Cover with foil if needed to prevent overbrowning.

*Place onions in the
freezer fifteen minutes
before slicing to
eliminate the odor.*

New Potatoes with Balsamic Vinegar

6 large new potatoes, cut
  into halves
3 tablespoons olive oil
1 tablespoon balsamic
  vinegar
1/2 teaspoon tarragon
1/2 teaspoon thyme
Salt and freshly ground
  pepper to taste

Arrange the potatoes in a baking pan. Bake at 350 degrees for 25 minutes or until tender. Combine the olive oil, balsamic vinegar, tarragon, thyme, salt and pepper in a bowl and mix well. Pour over the potatoes. Bake for 5 to 10 minutes longer. Serve immediately. *Yield: 6 to 8 servings.*

Jalapeño Potatoes au Gratin

8 unpeeled potatoes
Salt and freshly ground
 black pepper to taste
1 cup each chopped red
 and green bell pepper
$^1/_2$ cup chopped green
 onions
1 jalapeño, minced
$^1/_2$ teaspoon garlic
$^3/_4$ cup butter
2 tablespoons flour
2 cups milk
6 ounces Pepper Havarti
 cheese, cubed
6 ounces White Double
 Gloucester cheese,
 cubed
2 ounces pimento,
 chopped
$^1/_2$ teaspoon garlic powder
$^1/_4$ teaspoon white pepper

Combine the potatoes with enough water to cover in a saucepan. Bring to a boil. Boil just until tender; drain. Peel and slice. Layer the potatoes in a buttered 3-quart baking dish, sprinkling with salt and black pepper between each layer. Sauté the red pepper, green pepper, green onions, jalapeño and $^1/_2$ teaspoon garlic in $^1/_4$ cup of the butter in a saucepan until the vegetables are tender; drain. Heat the remaining $^1/_2$ cup butter in a saucepan until melted. Add the flour and mix well. Cook until bubbly, stirring constantly. Stir in the milk and cheeses. Cook over medium heat until the cheese melts, stirring constantly. Add the pepper mixture, pimento, garlic powder and white pepper and mix well. Pour over the potatoes. Bake at 350 degrees for 45 minutes. *Yield: 8 servings.*

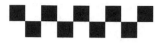

Keep boiled potatoes white by adding a teaspoon of lemon juice or vinegar to the cooking water.

Seasoned Potato Bake

6 cups chopped, peeled
 boiled potatoes
1 cup chopped green bell
 pepper
1 cup chopped onion
1 cup shredded Cheddar
 cheese
1 tablespoon flour
2 teaspoons salt
1 teaspoon black pepper
$^1/_4$ teaspoon cayenne
1 cup milk
$^1/_2$ cup butter
Paprika to taste

Combine the potatoes, green pepper, onion, cheese, flour, salt, black pepper and cayenne in a bowl and mix gently. Heat the milk and butter in a saucepan until the butter melts, stirring occasionally. Pour over the potatoes and mix gently. Spoon into a $2^1/_2$-quart baking dish. Sprinkle with paprika. Bake at 325 degrees for 45 minutes. *Yield: 6 to 8 servings.*

Amaretto Sweet Potatoes

2 pounds sweet potatoes
3/4 cup sugar
2/3 cup buttermilk
1/2 cup butter, softened
2 eggs
2 tablespoons amaretto
1 1/4 teaspoons vanilla
   extract
1 teaspoon cinnamon
1 teaspoon baking soda
2/3 cup chopped pecans

Combine the sweet potatoes with enough water to cover in a saucepan. Bring to a boil. Boil until tender; drain. Remove the skins of the sweet potatoes. Arrange the sweet potatoes in a greased 2-quart baking dish. Process the sugar, buttermilk, butter, eggs, amaretto, vanilla, cinnamon and baking soda in a blender until smooth. Stir in the pecans. Spoon over the sweet potatoes. Bake at 350 degrees for 30 minutes. *Yield: 8 servings.*

Honeyed Sweet Potatoes with Pecans

6 sweet potatoes
3/4 cup honey
6 tablespoons butter,
   softened
1/3 cup packed brown
   sugar
1 tablespoon nutmeg
1 tablespoon ginger
1/8 teaspoon salt
Freshly ground pepper to
   taste
1 1/4 cups chopped pecans

Combine the sweet potatoes with enough cold water to cover in a saucepan. Bring to a boil; reduce heat. Simmer, covered, for 45 minutes or until tender; drain. Cool slightly. Peel the potatoes. Mash the potatoes with a potato masher in a bowl until smooth. Stir in the honey, butter, brown sugar, nutmeg, ginger, salt, pepper and pecans. Serve immediately.
Yield: 8 servings.

Cashew Rice

1 cup chopped onion
8 ounces mushrooms,
  sliced
1/2 cup cashews
1/2 cup sliced celery
5 tablespoons butter
2 cups water
1 cup white rice
2 chicken bouillon cubes
1/2 teaspoon salt
1/4 teaspoon freshly
  ground pepper
1/2 teaspoon thyme

Sauté the onion, mushrooms, cashews and celery in 2 tablespoons of the butter in a skillet for 5 minutes. Stir in the remaining 3 tablespoons butter, water, rice, bouillon cubes, salt, pepper and thyme. Bring to a boil, cooking until the bouillon cubes dissolve, stirring occasionally; reduce heat. Simmer, covered, for 15 minutes or until the rice is tender and the liquid is absorbed. *Yield: 4 servings.*

Soaking nuts in milk for about an hour will rehydrate the nuts and enhance their flavor.

Pecan Wild Rice

3 cups cooked wild rice
1 cup pecan halves
1 cup golden raisins
1/3 cup fresh orange juice
1/4 cup olive oil
4 scallions, sliced
1 1/2 teaspoons salt
Zest of 1 orange
Freshly ground pepper to
  taste

Combine the wild rice, pecans, raisins, orange juice, olive oil, scallions, salt, orange zest and pepper in a bowl, tossing gently to mix. Let stand, covered, at room temperature for 2 hours before serving. *Yield: 8 servings.*

Creamy Spinach and Artichokes

4 cups fresh spinach
1/2 cup chopped green
   onions
6 tablespoons butter
2 cups chopped
   artichoke hearts
2 cups sour cream
1/4 cup grated Parmesan
   cheese
2 tablespoons fresh
   lemon juice
1/4 teaspoon garlic salt
1/2 cup bread crumbs
2 tablespoons melted
   butter

Combine the spinach with a small amount of water in a saucepan. Cook over medium heat until tender; drain well. Sauté the green onions in 6 tablespoons butter in a saucepan until tender. Combine the green onion mixture with the spinach in a bowl and mix well. Stir in the artichoke hearts, sour cream, cheese, lemon juice and garlic salt. Spoon into a 2-quart baking dish. Sprinkle with a mixture of the bread crumbs and 2 tablespoons butter. Bake at 350 degrees for 25 minutes or until bubbly.
Yield: 8 servings.

Splendid Squash and Carrots

3 pounds yellow squash,
   sliced
1/4 cup butter
1/4 cup flour
1 cup milk
1 teaspoon salt
1/2 teaspoon pepper
1/4 teaspoon nutmeg
1 1/2 cups shredded
   carrots
1 cup sour cream
1/2 cup chopped pimentos
1/2 cup chopped onion
2 cups herb stuffing mix
1 tablespoon plus 1
   teaspoon melted butter

Steam the squash in a steamer for 8 minutes. Drain in a colander. Mash with the back of a spoon to remove excess liquid; drain. Heat 1/4 cup butter in a saucepan until melted. Add the flour and mix well. Cook for 1 minute, stirring constantly. Add the milk gradually, stirring constantly. Bring to a boil. Boil for 1 minute, stirring constantly. Stir in the salt, pepper and nutmeg. Remove from heat. Add the squash, carrots, sour cream, pimentos and onion and mix well. Toss the stuffing mix with the melted butter in a bowl. Spread 1/2 of the stuffing mixture in a 9x13-inch baking dish. Spoon the squash mixture over the prepared layer. Top with the remaining stuffing mixture. Bake at 350 degrees for 30 to 40 minutes or until bubbly. Serve immediately.
Yield: 12 servings.

Yellow Squash with Red Pepper

2 teaspoons olive oil
2 teaspoons butter
1/2 cup thinly sliced red
    onion
1 red bell pepper, cut
    into 1/2-inch strips
3 yellow squash, cut into
    diagonal slices
1 tablespoon minced
    fresh basil
1/4 teaspoon salt
1/4 teaspoon freshly
    ground pepper

Garnish:
Sprigs of parsley

Heat the olive oil and butter in a skillet over low heat. Add the red onion and mix well. Cook, partially covered, until tender, stirring frequently. Stir in the red pepper. Cook, covered, until tender-crisp. Add the squash. Cook, covered, for 3 minutes or just until the squash is tender-crisp. Increase the heat to high. Cook, uncovered, for 2 minutes or until the squash is tender, stirring constantly. Add the basil and mix well. Season with the salt and pepper. Spoon into a serving bowl. Garnish with parsley. *Yield: 4 servings.*

My grandmother always kept a jar of pennies on her kitchen shelf. She felt this brought luck to everything she prepared. There surely was truth to this as everything she made was the best!

~ *Linda Martens* ~

Southern Succotash

6 cups fresh lima beans
6 cups fresh corn kernels
1 1/2 cups chopped red
    bell peppers
3 tablespoons butter,
    softened
1 cup plus 2 tablespoons
    whipping cream
3/4 teaspoon sugar
Salt and freshly ground
    pepper to taste
3 tablespoons minced
    fresh parsley

Combine the lima beans with enough water to cover in a saucepan. Bring to a boil; reduce heat. Cook until tender-crisp. Stir in the corn. Simmer for 2 minutes, stirring occasionally. Add the red peppers and mix well. Cook for 3 minutes, stirring occasionally; drain. Add the butter, tossing to coat. May be prepared to this point 1 day in advance, covered and stored in the refrigerator until just before serving. Stir in the whipping cream. Cook over medium heat until thickened, stirring occasionally. Add the sugar and mix well. Season with salt and pepper. Spoon into a serving bowl. Sprinkle with the minced parsley. Serve immediately. *Yield: 10 servings.*

Scalloped Fresh Tomatoes

1 cup fine bread crumbs
1/4 cup grated Parmesan
   cheese
1 cup chopped onion
1 tablespoon butter
6 tomatoes, peeled, sliced
Sugar to taste
Salt and freshly ground
   pepper to taste
1 tablespoon butter

Combine the bread crumbs and cheese in a bowl and mix well. Sauté the onion in 1 tablespoon butter in a skillet until tender. Let stand until cool. Layer the tomatoes, sugar, salt, pepper, onion mixture and bread crumb mixture alternately in a buttered 1¹/₂-quart baking dish until all the ingredients are used, ending with the bread crumb mixture. Dot with 1 tablespoon butter. Bake at 400 degrees for 35 minutes. *Yield: 6 to 8 servings.*

Spinach- and Artichoke-Stuffed Tomatoes

8 medium tomatoes
2 pounds fresh spinach
2 cups artichoke hearts,
   drained, cut into
   quarters, chopped
1 cup sour cream
1 teaspoon
   Worcestershire sauce
1/2 teaspoon salt
1/2 teaspoon hot sauce
1/2 cup freshly grated
   Parmesan cheese
1/2 cup chopped green
   onions
1/2 cup butter
1/4 cup freshly grated
   Parmesan cheese
3 tablespoons butter

Cut a slice off the top of each tomato, discarding the top. Remove the pulp carefully and discard. Invert the shells onto paper towels to drain. Cook the spinach in a small amount of water in a saucepan until tender; drain well. Combine the spinach, artichokes, sour cream, Worcestershire sauce, salt and hot sauce in a bowl and mix well. Stir in 1/2 cup Parmesan cheese. Sauté the green onions in 1/2 cup butter in a skillet over medium heat. Add to the spinach mixture and mix well. Spoon the spinach mixture into the tomato shells. Arrange the stuffed shells in a lightly greased 9x13-inch baking dish. Sprinkle with 1/4 cup Parmesan cheese. Dot with 3 tablespoons butter. Bake at 350 degrees for 20 minutes or until heated through. Serve immediately. *Yield: 8 servings.*

Garden Vegetable Medley

1 pound zucchini, thinly
 sliced
1 pound carrots, thinly
 sliced
1 pound yellow squash,
 thinly sliced
2 onions, thinly sliced
1 tablespoon butter
1 pound fresh
 mushrooms, thinly
 sliced
Salt and freshly ground
 pepper to taste
1 cup snipped fresh
 parsley
2¹/4 cups shredded
 Jarlsberg cheese
³/4 cup grated Parmesan
 cheese
12 cherry tomatoes, cut
 into halves
Grated Parmesan cheese
 to taste

Cook the zucchini, carrots and yellow
squash in enough water to cover in
separate saucepans until tender-crisp;
drain. Sauté the onions in the butter until
tender. Remove with a slotted spoon to a
bowl. Add the mushrooms to the pan
drippings. Sauté until tender. Remove
with a slotted spoon to a bowl. Layer the
zucchini, carrots, yellow squash, onions
and mushrooms in a 3-quart baking dish,
sprinkling portions of the salt, pepper,
parsley, Jarlsberg cheese and the ³/4 cup
Parmesan cheese between each layer. Top
with the cherry tomatoes; sprinkle with
Parmesan cheese to taste. Bake at 350
degrees for 30 minutes. Serve immediately.
Yield: 12 servings.

*Prepare Toasted
Hazelnut Butter by
mixing ³/4 cup chopped
toasted hazelnuts,
¹/2 cup softened butter
and 2 teaspoons honey
in a bowl. Toss with
your favorite steamed
vegetables. Store,
covered, in the
refrigerator. Bring to
room temperature
before tossing with
vegetables.*

Gingered Butter

¹/2 cup orange marmalade
¹/2 cup butter, softened
1 tablespoon balsamic
 vinegar
1 tablespoon minced
 crystallized ginger
2 teaspoons grated
 orange zest

Heat the marmalade in a saucepan just
until melted, stirring frequently. Beat the
butter in a mixer bowl until light and
fluffy. Add the marmalade gradually,
beating until mixed. Add the balsamic
vinegar, ginger and orange zest. Beat until
mixed, scraping the bowl occasionally.
Chill, covered, until serving time.
Yield: 1 cup.

 Note: Serve Gingered Butter with
steamed green vegetables, such as green
beans or asparagus.

Brunch and Breads

Breaking Bread Together

by Martha Maxfield Cottingham

Breaking bread together...what an odd phrase. Yet, the concept of sharing a meal is a time-honored tradition. It brings to mind a host of images ranging from the Biblical "last supper" to state dinners at the White House. Closer to home, I think of holiday meals and how some things have changed and some remain the same.

My mother has a table in her dining room, a trestle-style table fourteen feet long. As the story goes, it was made for the Library of Congress but somehow it didn't meet government specifications. My father found it in an unclaimed-freight warehouse years ago. He was a real scrounger. A friend who worked at the warehouse would call when anything interesting turned up. Dad had to get the table, you see, because he already had a tablecloth just the right size. My father had begun scrounging when he was in Europe during World War II. He sent an interesting assortment of items back home. Included in these treasures were a linen tablecloth and a set of silver salt cellars. Luckily things worked out. He met and married my mom, who shared his love of entertaining. Several years later, they built a house and adapted the plans to make room for the dining table.

As you may suspect, a table that size causes tremendous repercussions. When my sister was on the high school yearbook staff, layout was always done at our house. There were frequent after-prom parties, bridal showers and such. But most importantly, there were the family dinners. We always hosted large gatherings for holidays and special occasions. In addition to family members, friends were included and, occasionally, strangers.

Our family is probably no different from any other. We have our share of black sheep and scalawags. I have noticed that we often tend to assume that our family traditions are widely accepted by others. What a shock it was when I discovered that scalloped oysters are not normally considered holiday fare.

It should have occurred to me since I have never seen scalloped oysters served anywhere outside my family. Occasionally you will find the recipe in cookbooks. Yet when I was growing up, no holiday meal was complete without them. In fact, there were years when both of my grandmothers would bring scalloped oysters to Christmas dinner. Thankfully, some things change.

As an adult, the scope of my holidays has broadened. Some years ago, when I was working as a flight attendant, I spent my first Christmas away from home. Our 747 crew, composed of three pilots and fourteen flight attendants, celebrated with a potluck dinner in San Juan, Puerto Rico. Each of us brought something to share. We feasted on the aircraft during the short turnaround time between flights. Although I was dreading it, that holiday has become one of my most memorable.

Over the years, there have been further variations to our holiday concept. One year, our first year of marriage, my husband I were adopted by our next-door neighbors. Since then the tables have turned. It is not unusual for us to host large gatherings. Several times, when immediate family was not readily available, we have combined our holiday celebrations with friends.

Whatever we do, each year is special. Friends or family gathered around a table sharing a meal is a constant in our lives. That is the tradition we are passing on to our children. We no longer stick to prescribed menus. Some years we have turkey, sometimes spaghetti or whatever strikes our fancy.

Maybe next year I will make scalloped oysters.

Martha Maxfield Cottingham began her Junior League career in Honolulu, Hawaii. Now a sustaining member, she was active in The Junior League of North Harris County for many years. She is still not sure what she wants to be when she grows up.

Cozy Apple Cider

1 gallon apple cider
1 cup fresh orange juice
³/4 cup sugar
6 tablespoons fresh
  lemon juice
4 teaspoons whole
  allspice
4 sticks cinnamon,
  broken into thirds
48 whole cloves

Combine the apple cider, orange juice, sugar, lemon juice, allspice, cinnamon sticks and cloves in a saucepan. Bring to a boil; reduce heat. Simmer for 10 minutes; strain. Serve hot. *Yield: 15 to 20 servings.*

Note: May store, covered, in the refrigerator for up to one week.

Good Morning Granola

2 (14-ounce) cans
  sweetened condensed
  milk
3 cups wheat germ
3 cups quick-cooking
  oats
1 cup chopped dried
  apples
1 cup dried blueberries
1 cup dried cherries
1 cup shredded coconut
1 cup sunflower kernels
¹/2 cup vegetable oil
2 teaspoons cinnamon

Combine the condensed milk, wheat germ, oats, apples, blueberries, cherries, coconut, sunflower kernels, oil and cinnamon in a bowl and mix well. Spread in an 11x17-inch baking pan. Bake at 300 degrees for 45 to 50 minutes, stirring occasionally. Cool to room temperature. Store in an airtight container. *Yield: 6 cups.*

Note: Any combination of dried fruits and seeds may be substituted for the apples, blueberries, cherries and sunflower kernels.

Prepare Sweetened Condensed Milk by combining 1 cup confectioners' sugar, ¹/3 cup boiling water, ²/3 cup granulated sugar and 3 tablespoons butter in a blender container. Process until the sugars are dissolved. Store in a jar with a tightfitting lid in the refrigerator.

Pear Granola with Lemon Cream

12 medium pears
3 cups granola
1/4 cup raisins
1/4 cup packed brown
   sugar
2 tablespoons peanut
   butter
1 1/2 teaspoons nutmeg
1 1/2 teaspoons cinnamon
1 1/2 cups Lemon Cream

Slice the top off each pear and discard the top. Scoop out the pulp, leaving a 1/2-inch shell. Reserve the pulp, discarding the seeds.

Combine the reserved pulp, granola, raisins, brown sugar, peanut butter, nutmeg and cinnamon in a bowl and mix well. Fill each pear shell with some of the granola mixture. Place the pears bottom side down in a baking dish. Add water to a depth of 1 inch. Bake at 400 degrees for 10 minutes.

Arrange the pears on a serving platter. Top each pear with 2 tablespoons of the Lemon Cream. *Yield: 12 servings.*

Lemon Cream

1 cup lemon yogurt
4 ounces cream cheese,
   softened
1 1/4 tablespoons fresh
   lemon juice

Combine the lemon yogurt, cream cheese and fresh lemon juice in a mixer bowl. Beat until smooth, scraping the bowl occasionally.

When coring a pear, make sure to remove all the gritty flesh around the core.

All-In-One Brunch Strata

20 slices white sandwich
  bread, crusts removed
2 cups chopped ham
10 ounces sharp
  Cheddar cheese,
  shredded
10 ounces Swiss cheese,
  shredded
3 cups milk
6 eggs, lightly beaten
1/2 teaspoon onion salt
1/2 teaspoon dry mustard
3 cups crushed
  cornflakes
1/2 cup melted butter

Layer the bread, ham, Cheddar cheese and
Swiss cheese 1/2 at a time in a 9x13-inch
baking pan. Combine the milk, eggs,
onion salt and dry mustard in a bowl and
mix well. Pour over the prepared layers.
Chill, covered with foil, for 8 to 10 hours.
Sprinkle with the cornflakes; drizzle with
the butter. Bake at 375 degrees for 50 to 60
minutes or until set. Let stand for 10
minutes before serving. *Yield: 12 servings.*

Note: May substitute chopped
Canadian bacon, crumbled crisp-fried
bacon or crumbled cooked sausage for
the ham.

*A strata is a great
make-ahead entrée for
a brunch. The dish is
assembled one day in
advance and chilled
overnight to allow
time for the bread
to moisten.*

Company Brunch

5 sourdough English
  muffins, split
1 cup shredded Cheddar
  cheese
1 cup shredded Swiss
  cheese
1 pound breakfast
  sausage, cooked,
  drained, crumbled
12 eggs, lightly beaten
2 cups milk
1/3 cup chopped fresh
  parsley
1/3 cup chopped green
  onions with tops
1 cup sliced fresh
  mushrooms

Arrange the English muffins in a buttered
9x13-inch baking dish. Sprinkle with the
Cheddar cheese, Swiss cheese and sausage.
Beat the eggs, milk, parsley and green
onions in a bowl until mixed. Pour over
the prepared layers. Chill, covered with
foil, for 8 to 10 hours. Sprinkle with the
mushrooms. Bake at 350 degrees for 50
minutes or until set. Let stand for 10
minutes before serving. *Yield: 8 servings.*

Note: May substitute crisp-fried bacon
or chopped ham for the sausage.

Buttercrust Corn Pie with Tomato Salsa

1 1/4 cups finely crushed
  saltine crackers
1/3 cup freshly grated
  Parmesan cheese
1/2 cup melted butter
2 cups fresh corn kernels
1 cup milk
1 teaspoon salt
1/2 teaspoon white pepper
1/4 cup milk
2 tablespoons flour
1/2 cup sliced green
  onions
1/4 cup chopped green
  olives
2 eggs, lightly beaten
Paprika to taste
Tomato Salsa

Combine the crackers, cheese and butter in a bowl and mix well. Reserve 2 tablespoons of the cracker mixture. Press the remaining cracker mixture over the bottom and up the side of a 9-inch pie plate.

Combine the corn, 1 cup milk, salt and white pepper in a saucepan. Bring to a boil over medium heat; reduce heat. Simmer for 3 minutes, stirring frequently.

Combine 1/4 cup milk and flour in a bowl and mix well. Add to the corn mixture gradually, stirring constantly. Cook for 1 minute or until thickened, stirring constantly. Remove from heat.

Stir in the green onions and green olives. Stir 1/4 of the hot mixture into the eggs; stir the eggs into the hot mixture. Spoon into the prepared pie plate. Top with the reserved crumb mixture. Sprinkle with paprika. Bake at 400 degrees for 20 minutes or until set. Cut into wedges. Serve with Tomato Salsa. *Yield: 6 servings.*

Tomato Salsa

2 cups chopped peeled
  tomatoes
1 jalapeño, seeded,
  minced
1/4 cup thinly sliced
  green onions
2 tablespoons fresh
  lemon juice
1/2 teaspoon salt
1/2 teaspoon oregano
1/8 teaspoon freshly
  ground pepper

Combine the tomatoes, jalapeño, green onions, lemon juice, salt, oregano and pepper in a bowl and mix gently. Chill, covered, for 3 hours or longer.

Plunge tomatoes into boiling water for 20 seconds. Using a slotted spoon, drain and immerse tomatoes in ice water until cooled. Skins will slide right off. This also works well with peaches and pears.

Breakfast Chiles Rellenos Bake

1 cup half-and-half or
    milk
2 eggs
$1/2$ cup flour
12 ounces whole green
    chiles
1 pound Monterey Jack
    cheese, shredded
1 cup tomato sauce

Beat the half-and-half, eggs and flour in a bowl until smooth. Split and rinse the chiles. Dip the chiles in the flour mixture. Layer $1/2$ of the chiles and $1/3$ of the cheese in a buttered 8x8-inch baking pan. Repeat the layers. Top with the remaining flour mixture. Pour the tomato sauce over the prepared layers. Sprinkle with the remaining cheese. Bake at 350 degrees for 45 minutes. Let stand for 10 minutes before serving. *Yield: 6 servings.*

Chile and Cheese Breakfast

3 English muffins, split
2 tablespoons butter,
    softened
1 pound hot pork
    sausage
1 (4-ounce) can green
    chiles, drained,
    chopped
3 cups shredded Cheddar
    cheese
$1^1/2$ cups sour cream
12 eggs, beaten

Spread the cut side of each muffin with 1 teaspoon butter. Arrange cut side down in a buttered 9x13-inch baking pan. Brown the sausage in a skillet, stirring until crumbly; drain. Rinse with hot water; drain. Layer $1/2$ of the sausage, $1/2$ of the chiles and $1/2$ of the cheese over the muffins. Spread with a mixture of the sour cream and eggs. Layer with the remaining sausage, remaining chiles and remaining cheese. Chill, covered, for 8 to 10 hours. Let stand at room temperature for 30 minutes. Bake, uncovered, at 350 degrees for 30 to 45 minutes or until brown and bubbly. *Yield: 8 servings.*

Farm Cheese Quiche

2²/₃ cups flour
1¹/₄ teaspoons salt
1 cup shortening
6 to 7 tablespoons ice
    water
1¹/₂ cups shredded
    Jarlsberg cheese
1¹/₂ cups grated Gruyère
    cheese
8 ounces cream cheese,
    softened
12 eggs
4 cups milk
¹/₃ cup freshly grated
    Parmesan cheese
2 tablespoons chopped
    green onions
2¹/₂ teaspoons salt
¹/₂ teaspoon oregano
¹/₄ teaspoon freshly
    ground pepper

Combine the flour and salt in a bowl and mix well. Cut in the shortening until crumbly. Add the water, stirring until the mixture forms a ball.

Roll the dough on a lightly floured surface to fit a 9x13-inch baking pan. Fit into the baking pan. Sprinkle with the Jarlsberg cheese and Gruyère cheese.

Beat the cream cheese in a mixer bowl until smooth. Add the eggs 1 at a time, beating well after each addition. Add the milk, Parmesan cheese, green onions, salt, oregano and pepper, beating until mixed. Spoon into the prepared baking pan. Bake at 375 degrees for 45 minutes or until set. *Yield: 12 servings.*

Easy Cheese Soufflé

8 slices white bread,
    crusts removed, cubed
1 pound sharp Cheddar
    cheese, shredded
6 eggs
2 cups milk
1/2 cup melted butter
1/2 teaspoon salt
1/4 teaspoon freshly
    ground pepper

Layer the bread and cheese 1/3 at a time in a 2-quart baking pan. Beat the eggs in a mixer bowl until frothy. Add the milk, butter, salt and pepper, beating until blended. Pour over the bread. Chill, covered, for 6 to 10 hours. Bake at 350 degrees for 1 1/4 hours or until bubbly. *Yield: 4 servings.*

Note: This recipe may be doubled and baked in a 9x13-inch baking pan.

Honey Puff

3 ounces cream cheese,
    cubed, softened
1 cup flour
1 cup milk
6 eggs
3 tablespoons honey
1 teaspoon vanilla
    extract
1/2 teaspoon salt
1/2 teaspoon baking
    powder
3 tablespoons butter
2 tablespoons
    confectioners' sugar

Garnish:
Fresh seasonal fruit

Combine the cream cheese, flour, milk, eggs, honey, vanilla, salt and baking powder in a blender container. Process on High for 2 to 4 minutes or until blended. Heat the butter in a 10-inch ovenproof skillet or baking pan at 375 degrees until melted. Pour the cream cheese mixture into the prepared skillet or baking pan. Bake for 25 to 30 minutes or until a knife inserted in the middle comes out clean. Sprinkle with the confectioners' sugar. Garnish with seasonal fruit. *Yield: 6 servings.*

Note: The puff will rise and fall like a soufflé.

When using natural cheeses, finely shred to increase melting times. A well-chilled cheese will shred more easily than a cheese that has been sitting at room temperature.

Sweet Noodle Pudding

12 ounces egg noodles
3/4 cup sugar
6 eggs
2 cups sour cream
11/2 cups cottage cheese
8 ounces cream cheese,
    softened
1/2 cup milk
1 cup golden raisins
1/2 cup melted butter
Graham Cracker
    Topping

2 cups crushed graham
    crackers
1/4 cup melted butter
1/4 cup cinnamon-sugar

Cook the noodles using package directions; drain. Beat the sugar and eggs in a mixer bowl until blended. Add the sour cream, cottage cheese and cream cheese, beating until smooth. Beat in the milk until blended. Stir in the raisins and noodles. Spoon into a buttered and floured 9x13-inch baking pan. Drizzle with the butter. Sprinkle with the Graham Cracker Topping. Bake at 350 degrees for 45 to 60 minutes or until bubbly. Serve warm.
Yield: 12 servings.

Graham Cracker Topping

Combine the graham crackers, butter and cinnamon-sugar in a bowl and mix well.

My mother's Sweet Noodle Pudding was a holiday treat. When I was growing up, I would often ask why she prepared it only for special occasions since it was such a favorite. I make it now, and my children ask the same question. I can only tell them that it is a delicious treat that adds something extra to the holidays . . . and for me, it brings back wonderful memories.

⌁ Sheila Jortner ⌁

Baked Apples and Cranberries

3 cups fresh cranberries
3 cups chopped Rome
    apples
1 cup sugar
1/2 cup quick-cooking
    oats
1/2 cup packed brown
    sugar
1/2 cup chopped pecans
1/2 cup melted butter

Arrange the cranberries and apples in a greased 2-quart baking dish. Sprinkle with the sugar. Combine the oats, brown sugar and pecans in a bowl and mix well. Add the butter, stirring until mixed. Sprinkle the oat mixture over the prepared layers. Bake at 325 degrees for 45 minutes.
Yield: 6 servings.

   Note: Great accompaniment to Cajun Deep-Fried Turkey, found on page 89.

Green Chile Cheese Grits

4 cups water
1 cup quick-cooking
   grits
2 teaspoons salt
6 ounces Cheddar
   cheese, shredded
2 tablespoons butter
4 eggs, beaten
1 (4-ounce) can green
   chiles, drained,
   chopped
1/2 teaspoon garlic
   powder

Combine the water, grits and salt in a saucepan. Cook for 10 minutes or until the water is absorbed. Stir in the cheese and butter. Add the eggs and mix well. Stir in the chiles and garlic powder. Spoon into a buttered 2-quart baking dish. Bake at 400 degrees for 30 minutes. *Yield: 8 servings.*

Great served for brunch with ham or as an accompaniment for brisket. It is equally as good made without the chiles.

Rice-Crusted Broccoli Bake

1 tablespoon butter
2 pounds fresh broccoli,
   chopped
1/2 cup chopped onion
3 cups hot cooked rice
3/4 cup shredded sharp
   Cheddar cheese
2 eggs, lightly beaten
1/2 teaspoon salt
1/2 cup milk
1/2 cup sliced fresh
   mushrooms
4 eggs, lightly beaten
1 teaspoon salt
1/4 teaspoon freshly
   ground pepper
3/4 cup shredded sharp
   Cheddar cheese

Heat the butter in a saucepan until melted. Add the broccoli and onion. Cook until tender, stirring frequently. Combine the rice, 3/4 cup cheese, 2 eggs and 1/2 teaspoon salt in a bowl and mix well. Pat over the bottom and up the sides of 2 buttered 9-inch pie plates. Combine the milk, mushrooms, eggs, 1 teaspoon salt and pepper in a bowl and mix well. Add to the broccoli mixture and mix well. Spoon into the prepared pie plates. Bake at 375 degrees for 20 minutes. Sprinkle with 3/4 cup cheese. Bake for 10 minutes longer. Let stand for 5 minutes before cutting into wedges. *Yield: 12 servings.*

Sherried Watermelon

1 red or yellow
    watermelon, chilled
Sherry to taste

Cut 2 round holes 2 inches in diameter, 5 inches deep and 6 inches apart in the watermelon. Pull out the plugs. Pour the sherry into the holes gradually, adding as much as the watermelon will absorb. Cover the holes with foil. Chill for several hours before serving. *Yield: 15 servings.*

Mango Curd

³/4 cup sugar
2 tablespoons cornstarch
1 cup puréed mango
¹/4 cup butter
2 tablespoons fresh
    lemon juice
1 tablespoon orange zest
6 egg yolks, beaten

Combine the sugar and cornstarch in a saucepan. Stir in the mango, butter, lemon juice and orange zest. Cook over medium heat until thickened, stirring constantly. Stir ¹/2 of the hot mixture into the egg yolks; stir the egg yolks into the hot mixture. Bring just to a boil. Cook for 2 minutes, stirring constantly. Spoon into a bowl; cover the surface with plastic wrap. Chill until serving time. *Yield: 2 cups.*

During the summers when I was a child, I remember that my grandfather would always have a watermelon or two on hand just waiting for the grandchildren to come over and eat with him. He would sprinkle on a little salt to make it tasty.

~ *Susan Schatz* ~

Apple Nut Coffee Cake

2 cups flour
1 teaspoon baking
    powder
1 teaspoon baking soda
1/4 teaspoon salt
1 cup sugar
1/2 cup butter, softened
2 eggs
1 teaspoon vanilla
    extract
1 cup sour cream
2 cups finely chopped
    Granny Smith apples
Brown Sugar Topping

Sift the flour, baking powder, baking soda and salt into a bowl and mix well.

Beat the sugar and butter in a mixer bowl until light and fluffy, scraping the bowl occasionally. Add the eggs and vanilla. Beat until smooth. Add the flour mixture alternately with the sour cream, mixing well after each addition. Fold in the apples.

Spread in a buttered 9x13-inch baking pan. Sprinkle with the Brown Sugar Topping. Bake at 350 degrees for 40 minutes. Cool in the pan on a wire rack for 10 minutes before removing.
Yield: 15 servings.

Brown Sugar Topping

1/2 cup packed brown
    sugar
2 tablespoons melted
    butter
1 teaspoon cinnamon
1/2 cup chopped pecans

Combine the brown sugar, butter and cinnamon in a bowl and mix well. Stir in the pecans.

Chocolate Chip Coffee Cake

1 cup sugar
1/2 cup butter, softened
1 cup sour cream
2 eggs
1 teaspoon baking
  powder
1 teaspoon baking soda
1 teaspoon salt
2 teaspoons vanilla
  extract
2 cups flour
Chocolate Chip Topping

Beat the sugar and butter in a mixer bowl until smooth, scraping the bowl occasionally. Add the sour cream and eggs. Beat until blended. Beat in the baking powder, baking soda, salt and vanilla. Add the flour gradually, beating constantly until blended.

Place 1/3 of the Chocolate Chip Topping in a buttered and floured 9-inch bundt pan. Layer the batter and remaining Chocolate Chip Topping 1/2 at a time in the prepared pan.

Bake at 350 degrees for 45 minutes or until the coffee cake tests done.
Yield: 12 servings.

Chocolate Chip Topping

1/3 cup packed brown
  sugar
1/4 cup sugar
1 teaspoon cinnamon
1 cup chopped nuts
1 cup semisweet
  chocolate chips

Combine the brown sugar, sugar and cinnamon in a bowl and mix well. Stir in the nuts and chocolate chips.

Brown sugar won't harden if an apple slice is placed in the container. But if your brown sugar is already brick-hard, put your cheese grater to work and grate the amount you need.

Raspberry Crumble

2¹/4 cups flour

- 2¹/4 cups flour
- ³/4 cup sugar
- ³/4 cup butter
- ³/4 cup sour cream
- 1 egg
- 1 teaspoon almond extract
- ³/4 teaspoon baking powder
- ¹/2 teaspoon baking soda
- ¹/8 teaspoon salt
- 8 ounces cream cheese, softened
- ¹/4 cup sugar
- 1 egg
- ²/3 cup raspberry preserves
- ¹/2 cup sliced almonds, toasted

Combine the flour and ³/4 cup sugar in a bowl and mix well. Cut in the butter with a pastry cutter or fork until crumbly. Reserve 1 cup of the crumb mixture.

Add the sour cream, 1 egg, almond extract, baking powder, baking soda and salt to the remaining crumb mixture and mix well. Spread approximately ¹/4 inch thick over the bottom and 2 inches up the side of a buttered and floured 9- or 10-inch springform pan.

Beat the cream cheese, ¹/4 cup sugar and 1 egg in a mixer bowl until blended. Spread over the prepared layer. Spoon the preserves evenly over the top.

Combine the reserved crumb mixture and almonds in a bowl and mix well. Sprinkle over the top. Bake at 350 degrees for 45 to 55 minutes or until set and the crust is a golden brown.

Cool in the pan on a wire rack for 15 minutes. Remove the side of the pan. Cut into wedges. Serve warm or cold. Store, covered, in the refrigerator.
Yield: 16 servings.

Cheese Blinis

2 large loaves thinly
   sliced white bread,
   crusts removed
16 ounces cream cheese,
   softened
1/4 cup sugar
2 egg yolks
1 cup melted butter
Cinnamon-sugar to taste

Flatten the bread with a rolling pin. Beat the cream cheese, sugar and egg yolks in a mixer bowl until blended. Spread over 1 side of each slice of bread; roll to enclose the filling. Roll the blinis in the butter; coat with the cinnamon-sugar. Arrange on a baking sheet. Freeze until firm. Place in sealable plastic freezer bags. Return to the freezer. Remove the desired number of blinis from the freezer just prior to serving. Arrange on a baking sheet. Bake at 400 degrees for 15 minutes; watch carefully, being sure not to overbrown. Serve with confectioners' sugar, sour cream and/or your favorite jam or jelly. *Yield: 60 servings.*

Note: Cheese Blinis may be stored in the freezer for several weeks.

It is not necessary to always use a loaf pan when baking breads. A round 1¹/₂-quart baking dish may be substituted for a 4x8-inch loaf pan, and a 2-quart baking dish may be used in place of a 5x9-inch loaf pan.

Apple Cheddar Walnut Bread

2 cups self-rising flour
²/₃ cup sugar
1/2 teaspoon cinnamon
1/2 cup coarsely chopped
   walnuts
1¹/₂ cups chopped peeled
   Granny Smith apples
1/2 cup melted butter
1/2 cup shredded sharp
   Cheddar cheese
1/4 cup milk
2 eggs, lightly beaten

Combine the self-rising flour, sugar and cinnamon in a bowl and mix well. Stir in the walnuts. Combine the apples, butter, cheese, milk and eggs in a bowl and mix well. Add to the flour mixture, stirring until mixed; batter will be lumpy. Spoon into a buttered and floured 5x9-inch loaf pan. Bake at 350 degrees for 60 to 70 minutes or until the loaf tests done, covering with foil during the last 15 minutes of the baking time if needed to prevent overbrowning. Invert onto a wire rack to cool. *Yield: 1 loaf.*

Banana Blueberry Bread

1 cup sugar
$^{1}/_{2}$ cup butter
1$^{1}/_{2}$ cups mashed ripe
   bananas
2 eggs, beaten
1 teaspoon baking soda
2 tablespoons milk
$^{2}/_{3}$ cup orange marmalade
2 cups flour
1 cup fresh blueberries
Crumb Topping

Beat the sugar and butter in a mixer bowl until creamy. Add the bananas and eggs gradually, beating until blended.

Dissolve the baking soda in the milk and mix well. Add to the banana mixture. Add the marmalade, beating until mixed. Add the flour gradually, stirring until mixed. Fold in the blueberries.

Spoon into 2 buttered and floured miniature loaf pans. Sprinkle with the Crumb Topping.

Bake at 325 degrees for 1 hour or until the loaves test done.
Yield: 2 miniature loaves.

Crumb Topping

1 cup flour
$^{1}/_{2}$ cup sugar
$^{1}/_{2}$ cup butter, chilled

Combine the flour and sugar in a bowl and mix well. Cut in the butter with a pastry cutter until crumbly.

Banana Apricot Nut Bread

1 cup all-purpose flour
1 cup whole wheat flour
1/2 teaspoon salt
1/2 teaspoon baking soda
1/2 cup butter, softened
1/3 cup packed brown
  sugar
1/3 cup sugar
2 eggs
1 1/2 cups mashed ripe
  bananas
1 cup minced dried
  apricots
1/2 cup chopped walnuts
  or pecans

Sift the all-purpose flour, whole wheat flour, salt and baking soda together. Beat the butter, brown sugar and sugar in a mixer bowl until creamy, scraping the bowl occasionally. Add the eggs, mixing until blended. Add the bananas and flour mixture alternately, mixing well after each addition. Stir in the apricots and walnuts. Spoon into a buttered and floured 5x9-inch glass loaf pan. Let stand for 20 minutes. Bake at 350 degrees for 70 minutes. Invert onto a wire rack to cool. *Yield: 1 loaf.*

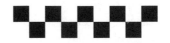

Cranapple Bread

1 cup finely chopped
  fresh cranberries
1/4 cup sugar
1 3/4 cups flour
1/3 cup sugar
1 tablespoon baking
  powder
3/4 teaspoon cinnamon
1/2 teaspoon salt
1/4 teaspoon allspice
1 cup applesauce
1/3 cup vegetable oil
1 egg, beaten
1/4 cup chopped pecans
  or walnuts

Toss the cranberries with 1/4 cup sugar in a bowl. Combine the flour, 1/3 cup sugar, baking powder, cinnamon, salt and allspice in a bowl and mix well. Combine the applesauce, oil and egg in a bowl and mix well. Add to the dry ingredients, stirring until blended. Fold in the cranberries and pecans. Spoon into a buttered and floured 5x9-inch loaf pan. Bake at 350 degrees for 35 minutes. *Yield: 1 loaf.*

Earth Bread

2 cups sugar
1 cup vegetable oil
3 eggs
1 teaspoon vanilla
 extract
2 cups whole wheat flour
1 cup all-purpose flour
1 teaspoon baking soda
1 teaspoon salt
3/4 teaspoon pumpkin pie
 spice
1/2 teaspoon baking
 powder
1/4 teaspoon cinnamon
1 cup finely grated
 zucchini
1/2 cup finely grated
 carrot
1/2 cup mashed ripe
 banana
1/2 cup chopped nuts

Combine the sugar, oil, eggs and vanilla in a bowl and mix well.

Sift the whole wheat flour, all-purpose flour, baking soda, salt, pumpkin pie spice, baking powder and cinnamon into a bowl and mix well. Add to the oil mixture, stirring until blended. Stir in the zucchini, carrot, banana and nuts.

Spoon the batter into 2 buttered and floured 5x9-inch loaf pans. Bake at 375 degrees for 55 to 60 minutes. Invert onto a wire rack to cool. *Yield: 2 loaves.*

Remove bread loaves from the pans as soon as baked. If allowed to cool in the pans, the bread may continue to cook and the bottom may become soggy. Cool on wire racks for best results.

Poppy Seed Bread with Almonds

3 cups flour
2¼ cups sugar
1½ cups milk
1¼ cups vegetable oil
3 eggs
1½ tablespoons poppy
  seeds
1½ teaspoons baking
  powder
1½ teaspoons salt
1½ teaspoons vanilla
  extract
1½ teaspoons almond
  extract
1½ teaspoons butter
  flavoring
Orange Glaze

³/4 cup superfine sugar
¼ cup orange juice
½ teaspoon butter
  flavoring
½ teaspoon almond
  extract
½ teaspoon vanilla
  extract
³/4 cup sliced almonds

Combine the flour, sugar, milk, oil, eggs, poppy seeds, baking powder, salt and flavorings in a mixer bowl. Beat for 2 minutes, scraping the bowl occasionally. Spoon into three 4x8-inch buttered and floured loaf pans. Bake at 350 degrees for 1 hour.

    Pierce the top of the hot loaves with a fork. Pour the Orange Glaze over the top. Cool in the pans on a wire rack before removing. *Yield: 3 loaves.*

Orange Glaze

Combine the sugar, orange juice and flavorings in a bowl and mix well. Stir in the almonds.

Use ingredients at room temperature for both yeast and quick breads to speed rising and baking times.

Traditional Pumpkin Bread

3 1/2 cups flour
3 cups sugar
2 teaspoons baking soda
1 1/2 teaspoons salt
1 teaspoon ginger
1 teaspoon nutmeg
1 teaspoon allspice
1 teaspoon cinnamon
2 cups solid-pack
  pumpkin
1 cup vegetable oil
1/2 cup water
4 eggs
1 cup chopped nuts
  (optional)

Combine the flour, sugar, baking soda, salt, ginger, nutmeg, allspice and cinnamon in a bowl and mix well. Make a well in the center of the dry ingredients. Combine the pumpkin, oil, water and eggs in a bowl and mix well. Spoon the pumpkin mixture into the well and mix well. Add the nuts, stirring just until mixed. Spoon into 2 buttered and floured 5x9-inch loaf pans. Bake at 350 degrees for 1 hour. *Yield: 2 loaves.*

Zucchini and Pineapple Bread

1 1/2 cups flour
1 1/2 teaspoons cinnamon
1/2 teaspoon baking soda
1/2 teaspoon baking
  powder
1/2 teaspoon salt
1/2 teaspoon allspice
1/2 teaspoon ground
  cloves
2 eggs, beaten
1 cup sugar
1/2 cup vegetable oil
1 teaspoon vanilla
  extract
1 cup grated zucchini
4 ounces crushed
  pineapple, drained

Combine the flour, cinnamon, baking soda, baking powder, salt, allspice and cloves in a bowl and mix well. Stir in the eggs. Add the sugar, oil and vanilla and mix well. Fold in the zucchini and pineapple. Spoon into a buttered and floured 5x9-inch loaf pan. Bake at 325 degrees for 1 hour. Cool in the pan on a wire rack for 10 minutes. Invert onto the wire rack to cool completely. *Yield: 1 loaf.*

Fresh Raspberry Cheesecake Muffins

3 ounces cream cheese,
  softened
1 egg
$^1/_4$ cup sugar
$^1/_4$ teaspoon vanilla
  extract
1 cup milk
6 tablespoons butter
1 teaspoon vanilla
  extract
2 eggs
2 cups flour
2$^3/_4$ teaspoons baking
  powder
$^1/_4$ teaspoon salt
$^3/_4$ cup sugar
1 cup fresh raspberries

Beat the cream cheese, 1 egg, $^1/_4$ cup sugar and $^1/_4$ teaspoon vanilla in a mixer bowl until smooth, scraping the bowl occasionally.

Combine the milk, butter and 1 teaspoon vanilla in a saucepan. Cook over medium heat until the butter melts, stirring constantly. Cool until lukewarm. Add 2 eggs, beating until blended.

Combine the flour, baking powder, salt and $^3/_4$ cup sugar in a bowl and mix well. Add the milk mixture, stirring just until moistened. Fold in the raspberries.

Spoon the batter evenly into 12 buttered and floured or paper-lined muffin cups; top each with approximately 2 teaspoons of the cream cheese mixture. Swirl the cream cheese mixture slightly through the batter with a knife. Bake at 400 degrees for 20 minutes.
Yield: 12 muffins.

Strawberry Streusel Muffins

2/3 cup sugar
1/2 cup butter, softened
3/4 cup milk
2 eggs
1 1/4 teaspoons vanilla
   extract
1 3/4 cups flour
1/4 teaspoon salt
2 3/4 teaspoons baking
   powder
1 1/2 cups chopped firm
   strawberries
Streusel Topping

1/2 cup butter, chilled
1/2 cup packed brown
   sugar
1/2 teaspoon cinnamon
1/8 teaspoon salt
2/3 cup flour

Beat the sugar and butter in a mixer bowl until light and fluffy, scraping the bowl occasionally. Add the milk, eggs and vanilla. Beat until smooth.

Combine the flour, salt and baking powder in a bowl and mix well. Add to the creamed mixture, stirring just until moistened. Fold in the strawberries.

Spoon into 12 buttered and floured or paper-lined muffin cups. Sprinkle with the Streusel Topping.

Bake at 375 degrees for 25 minutes. Cool in the pan on a wire rack for 10 minutes before removing muffins.
Yield: 12 muffins.

Streusel Topping

Cut the butter into the brown sugar in a bowl. Add the cinnamon and salt and mix well. Add the flour, mixing with a pastry cutter until crumbly.

Note: The Streusel Topping may be prepared up to one week in advance and stored, covered, in the refrigerator.

When choosing berries, select plump, solid berries that have good color. Avoid containers with stains, as this may indicate wet or leaky berries. Raspberries and blackberries with caps intact may be underripe. Strawberries without caps are usually too ripe.

Poppin' Popovers

1 cup flour
1/2 teaspoon salt
1/2 cup milk
1/2 cup water
3 eggs
2/3 cup shredded Cheddar
   cheese (optional)
8 teaspoons butter

Combine the flour and salt in a bowl and mix well. Add the milk and water gradually, mixing well after each addition. Add the eggs, beating until blended. Fold in the cheese. Place 1 teaspoon butter in the bottom of eight 6-ounce ovenproof custard cups. Arrange the custard cups on a baking sheet. Heat in a 375-degree oven until the butter melts and the cups are heated. Fill the custard cups 1/2 to 2/3 full; all cups may not be used. Bake at 375 degrees for 45 minutes or until brown and puffed. Do not open the oven door during the baking process. Serve immediately with butter and your favorite preserves. *Yield: 8 popovers.*

Unlike most breads, popovers are leavened by eggs and steam. They are easy to prepare and bake.

Macadamia Streusel Topping

1/3 cup packed brown
   sugar
1/4 cup flour
2 tablespoons butter
1/3 cup chopped
   macadamia nuts

Combine the brown sugar and flour in a bowl and mix well. Cut in the butter with a pastry cutter until crumbly. Stir in the macadamia nuts. Store, covered, in the refrigerator. *Yield: 1 cup.*

   Note: Use to complement your favorite muffin or coffee cake recipe.

Kahlúa Cinnamon Rolls

1 envelope dry yeast
$1/4$ cup lukewarm water
$1/2$ cup milk
$1/3$ cup sugar
$1/4$ cup shortening
$1/4$ teaspoon salt
$2^{1}/2$ to $2^{3}/4$ cups flour
1 egg, beaten
Brown Sugar Filling
Kahlúa Syrup (at right)

Combine the yeast and lukewarm water in a bowl and mix well. Let stand until softened.

Bring the milk to a boil in a saucepan. Stir in the sugar, shortening and salt. Remove from heat. Stir in 1 cup of the flour. Add the egg, yeast mixture and enough of the remaining flour to form a stiff dough and mix well. Knead on a lightly floured surface for 6 minutes. Place the dough in a greased bowl, turning to coat the surface. Let rise, covered, for 1 hour.

Roll the dough into a 12x15-inch rectangle on a lightly floured surface. Spread with the Brown Sugar Filling. Roll as for a jelly roll; cut into 12 slices. Reserve $1/3$ cup of the Kahlúa Syrup. Pour the remaining syrup into a 9-inch round baking pan. Arrange the slices cut side down in the prepared pan, pressing each slice to flatten. Let stand for 25 minutes or until doubled in bulk.

Bake at 375 degrees for 20 to 25 minutes or until brown. Let stand for 5 minutes. Invert onto a serving platter. Drizzle with the reserved Kahlúa Syrup. *Yield: 12 rolls.*

Brown Sugar Filling

$2/3$ cup packed brown
   sugar
$1/2$ cup chopped raisins
$4^{1}/2$ tablespoons butter,
   softened
$1^{1}/4$ tablespoons
   cinnamon
$1^{1}/4$ tablespoons Kahlúa

Combine the brown sugar, chopped raisins, butter, cinnamon and Kahlúa in a bowl and mix well.

To prepare Kahlúa Syrup, combine $1/3$ cup packed brown sugar, $1/4$ cup Kahlúa, $1/4$ cup butter and $1^{1}/8$ tablespoons light corn syrup in a saucepan. Simmer until blended, stirring constantly.

Spoon Bread Rolls

1 envelope dry yeast
2 cups lukewarm water
$1/4$ cup sugar
$3/4$ cup vegetable oil
1 egg
4 cups self-rising flour

Spray 18 muffin cups with nonstick cooking spray. Soften the yeast in the lukewarm water in a measuring cup and mix well. Combine the yeast mixture and sugar in a bowl and mix well. Add the oil and egg, beating until blended. Stir in the flour. Fill the prepared muffin cups $1/2$ full. Bake at 400 degrees for 15 to 20 minutes or until light brown. *Yield: 18 rolls.*

Note: This recipe may be prepared in advance and stored in the refrigerator for three to four days. If you choose not to make all eighteen rolls at once, store the remaining batter in the refrigerator for several days.

Fresh Broccoli Corn Bread

1 pound broccoli florets, finely chopped
1 (16-ounce) package corn bread mix
$1^{1}/2$ cups small curd cottage cheese
1 cup melted butter
1 (5-ounce) can mild green chiles, drained, chopped
4 eggs

Combine the broccoli, corn bread mix, cottage cheese, butter, chiles and eggs in a bowl and mix well. Spoon into a 9x13-inch baking pan. Bake at 350 degrees for 45 to 50 minutes. *Yield: 12 servings.*

Focaccia or Italian Flat Bread

2 envelopes dry yeast
$1/2$ cup lukewarm water
8 cups flour
2 tablespoons olive oil
1 tablespoon salt
$2^1/2$ cups warm water
$1/4$ cup chopped fresh
    parsley
Olive oil to taste
Herb Dipping Sauce

Combine the yeast and $1/2$ cup lukewarm water in a bowl. Let stand until bubbly and mix well.

Combine the flour, 2 tablespoons olive oil and salt in a bowl and mix well. Add the yeast mixture, $2^1/2$ cups water and parsley. Knead by hand or in a food processor until smooth and elastic. Place the dough in a buttered bowl, turning to coat the surface.

Let stand, covered, in a warm place for 1 to 2 hours or until doubled in bulk.

Punch the dough down. Shape into a $1/2$-inch-thick circle on a baking sheet. Make indentations on the top with your thumb. Brush with olive oil to taste. Bake at 400 degrees for 20 to 25 minutes or until golden brown. Remove to a wire rack to cool. Serve with the Herb Dipping Sauce. *Yield: 12 servings.*

Note: Allow guests to pull sections of the bread and dip into the Herb Dipping Sauce as desired.

Herb Dipping Sauce

$1/2$ cup olive oil
1 teaspoon Italian herb
    seasoning

Combine the olive oil and Italian herb seasoning in a bowl and mix well.

An unheated oven is an ideal spot to proof a yeast dough. Press fingers about $1/2$ inch into dough to determine if it has risen enough. If the indentation remains, the dough is ready to shape.

161

Whole Wheat Bread

2 cups whole wheat flour
1/4 cup sugar
1 tablespoon salt
2 envelopes dry yeast
2¼ cups milk
1/4 cup vegetable oil
1 egg, beaten
3½ cups all-purpose
    flour
1 cup whole wheat flour

Grease two 5x9- or 4x8-inch loaf pans with vegetable shortening.

Combine 2 cups whole wheat flour, sugar, salt and yeast in a mixer bowl and mix well. Heat the milk and oil in a saucepan to 130 degrees, stirring frequently. Stir a small amount of the hot mixture into the egg; stir the egg into the hot mixture. Add to the flour mixture. Beat at low speed for 30 seconds. Beat at medium speed for 3 minutes, scraping the bowl occasionally. Stir in the all-purpose flour and 1 cup whole wheat flour. Knead for 1 minute or until smooth.

Place the dough in a greased 2½-quart bowl, turning to coat the surface. Let stand, covered, in a warm place (80 to 85 degrees) for 45 to 60 minutes or until light and doubled in bulk. Punch the dough down. Shape into 2 loaves in the prepared loaf pans.

Let rise, covered, in a warm place for 30 to 45 minutes or until light and doubled in bulk.

Bake at 350 degrees for 40 to 45 minutes or until the loaves sound hollow when tapped lightly. Invert onto a wire rack to cool. *Yield: 2 loaves.*

Overnight French Toast

16 ounces cream cheese,
   cubed
12 eggs, beaten
2 cups milk
1/3 cup maple syrup
1 1/2 teaspoons cinnamon
8 slices white bread,
   crusts removed, cubed

Combine the cream cheese, eggs, milk, maple syrup and cinnamon in a bowl and mix well. Add the bread and mix gently. Spoon into a 9x13-inch baking pan. Chill, covered, for 8 to 10 hours. Bake, uncovered, at 375 degrees for 40 minutes. Serve with additional maple syrup. *Yield: 15 servings.*

Reduce the oven temperature by twenty-five degrees when baking in glass containers.

Stuffed French Toast

1 loaf French bread, cut
   into 1 1/2-inch slices
1 (16-ounce) jar apricot
   preserves
8 ounces cream cheese,
   softened
1 cup milk
6 eggs, beaten
2 teaspoons cinnamon
1/2 cup chopped pecans
Confectioners' sugar to
   taste

Slit the top of each slice of bread to make a 2-inch-deep pocket. Beat 3 tablespoons of the preserves and the cream cheese in a mixer bowl until mixed. Spoon some of the mixture into the pocket of each bread slice. Beat the milk, eggs and cinnamon in a mixer bowl until blended. Dip the bread slices in the egg mixture. Brown both sides of the bread on a hot griddle, pressing down lightly when turning. Heat the remaining preserves in a saucepan until hot. Arrange the stuffed French toast on a platter; sprinkle with the pecans and confectioners' sugar. Serve with the warm apricot preserves. *Yield: 6 servings.*

Note: Your favorite preserves may be substituted for the apricot preserves.

Lighter-Than-Air Pancakes

1 cup sifted flour
1 tablespoon baking
   powder
3/4 tablespoon sugar
1/8 teaspoon salt
1 cup milk
2 tablespoons (rounded)
   sour cream
1 egg
2 tablespoons melted
   butter

Garnish:
Whipped cream
Fresh berries

Sift the flour, baking powder, sugar and salt into a bowl and mix well. Beat the milk, sour cream and egg in a bowl. Stir into the flour mixture. Add the butter, whisking until blended. May add additional milk 1 tablespoon at a time until of the desired consistency. Drop by small spoonfuls onto a hot buttered griddle. Bake until brown on both sides, turning once. Garnish with whipped cream and fresh berries. *Yield: 12 pancakes.*

Note: This is a favorite recipe for weekend guests. The recipe is easily doubled and stores well overnight.

Bake pancakes until bubbles appear on the surface and the underside is golden brown. Turn the pancakes over and bake just until golden brown.

Blueberry Pecan Scones

3 cups flour
3/4 cup sugar
1 tablespoon baking
   powder
1/2 teaspoon baking soda
1/2 teaspoon salt
3/4 cup butter, finely
   chopped
1 cup dried blueberries
1/2 cup chopped pecans
2 teaspoons orange zest
1 cup buttermilk
1 tablespoon sugar

Sift the flour, 3/4 cup sugar, baking powder, baking soda and salt into a bowl and mix well. Cut in the butter until crumbly. Stir in the blueberries, pecans and orange zest. Add the buttermilk, stirring with a fork just until moistened. Pat the dough into a 3/4-inch-thick circle on a lightly floured surface. Cut with a 2 1/2-inch cutter. Arrange on a buttered baking sheet. Sprinkle with 1 tablespoon sugar. Place the baking sheet on the lower oven rack. Bake at 400 degrees for 14 to 16 minutes or until light brown. Serve warm.
Yield: 15 scones.

Perfect Waffles

1³/4 cups flour
1 tablespoon baking
  powder
1/4 teaspoon salt
2 egg yolks
1³/4 cups milk
1/2 cup vegetable oil
2 egg whites

Combine the flour, baking powder and salt in a bowl and mix well. Beat the egg yolks in a bowl until frothy. Add the milk and oil and mix well. Add to the flour mixture and mix. Process the batter in a blender; the mixture will be lumpy. Pour into a bowl. Beat the egg whites in a mixer bowl until stiff peaks form. Fold into the batter, leaving a few fluffs of egg white; do not overmix. Butter the waffle iron. Pour the batter over the hot grids of the waffle iron. Bake on medium using the manufacturer's instructions; do not open the waffle iron while baking. *Yield: 3 (9-inch) waffles.*

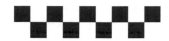

These are a great morning treat for a children's sleepover. Keep waffles hot by placing on a wire rack on top of a baking sheet in a warm oven.

Banana Pecan Waffles

2 cups flour
2 tablespoons sugar
1 tablespoon baking
  powder
1 teaspoon salt
1¹/2 cups milk
6 tablespoons vegetable
  oil
2 egg yolks
2 egg whites
2 bananas, mashed
³/4 cup chopped pecans

Sift the flour, sugar, baking powder and salt into a bowl and mix well. Whisk the milk, oil and egg yolks in a bowl until blended. Add to the flour mixture, stirring just until moistened. Beat the egg whites in a mixer bowl until stiff but moist peaks form. Fold into the batter. Fold in the bananas and pecans. Bake in a waffle iron using the manufacturer's instructions.
Yield: 16 (4-square) waffles.

  Note: Freeze leftover waffles between sheets of waxed paper in sealable freezer bags. Pop frozen waffles in the toaster for a special treat on a busy morning.

Beau Monde Bread

1 loaf French bread
12 ounces Swiss cheese,
 thinly sliced
1 cup butter
2 tablespoons prepared
 mustard
2 tablespoons lemon
 juice
1 tablespoon dried onion
1/2 teaspoon Beau Monde
 spice
1 tablespoon poppy seeds

Make crisscross slices 3/4 of the way through the loaf across the top of the bread. Place on a baking sheet. Stuff the cheese into the slices. Heat the butter in a saucepan over low heat until melted. Stir in the mustard, lemon juice, onion and Beau Monde spice. Pour over the loaf. Sprinkle with the poppy seeds. Bake at 400 degrees for 20 minutes. Serve immediately. *Yield: 8 servings.*

A foil lining placed under the cloth in a bread basket helps to keep breads warm.

Feta Basil Bread

1 large loaf Italian bread
1/3 cup (about) olive oil
1/3 cup chopped fresh
 basil
1 large tomato, seeded,
 chopped
1 cup crumbled feta
 cheese

Cut the loaf lengthwise into halves. Brush the cut sides with the olive oil. Layer the basil, tomato and feta cheese in the order listed over the olive oil. Arrange cut side up on a baking sheet. Broil until the edges of the bread are dark brown. Cut into 2-inch slices. Serve immediately. *Yield: 12 servings.*

Stuffed Crawfish Bread

2 cups chopped onions
1/4 cup butter
1 cup chopped green bell
  pepper
2 cloves of garlic, minced
1 pound crawfish tails,
  peeled
1/3 cup chopped green
  onions
2 tablespoons hot red
  pepper sauce
1/2 teaspoon freshly
  ground pepper
1 (48-ounce) package
  frozen bread dough
  (3 loaves), thawed
1 cup shredded Cheddar
  cheese
1 cup shredded
  mozzarella cheese
Melted butter

Sauté the onions in 1/4 cup butter in a skillet until tender. Stir in the green pepper and garlic. Sauté until the green pepper is tender. Add the crawfish tails, green onions, pepper sauce and pepper and mix well. Simmer, covered, for 5 minutes, stirring occasionally. Remove from heat.

Roll each bread loaf into a 5x20-inch rectangle on a lightly floured surface. Cut each rectangle into four 5-inch squares.

Spoon 1/4 cup of the crawfish mixture in the center of each square; sprinkle with 4 teaspoons of the Cheddar cheese and 4 teaspoons of the mozzarella cheese. Moisten the edges with water. Fold to enclose the filling; pinch to seal. Shape into 5-inch loaves. Arrange on a buttered baking sheet. Brush with melted butter.

Bake at 350 degrees for 25 minutes or until golden brown. Brush with melted butter. Serve warm. *Yield: 12 servings.*

Fresh Garlic and Herb Bread

2 tablespoons minced
   garlic
3 tablespoons olive oil
2 tablespoons chopped
   fresh rosemary
3 tablespoons butter
1/8 teaspoon salt
1/8 teaspoon freshly
   ground pepper
1 large loaf French bread
3 tablespoons grated
   Parmesan cheese
2 tablespoons chopped
   fresh Italian parsley

Garnish:
Sprigs of rosemary

Sauté the garlic in the olive oil over medium heat until fragrant. Remove from heat. Let stand until cool. Stir in the rosemary and butter. Season with the salt and pepper. Cut the bread lengthwise into halves. Brush the cut sides of the bread with the butter mixture; sprinkle with the cheese. Arrange on a foil-lined baking sheet. Bake at 375 degrees for 5 minutes or until hot and crisp. Sprinkle with the parsley. Cut into 2-inch slices. Arrange on a serving platter. Garnish with rosemary. *Yield: 8 servings.*

Brush bread loaves with butter for a soft, shiny crust. Use milk, water, or beaten egg for glossy, crisp crusts.

Stuffed Sausage Bread

1 (1-pound) loaf frozen
   bread dough
1 pound sausage with
   sage
1 cup chopped onion
1 cup chopped green bell
   pepper
1/2 cup chopped fresh
   mushrooms
1 cup shredded Cheddar
   cheese
1 cup shredded
   mozzarella cheese
1 egg, beaten

Thaw the bread and let rise using package directions. Brown the sausage with the onion, green pepper and mushrooms in a skillet, stirring until the sausage is crumbly; drain. Roll the bread dough flat with a floured rolling pin on a lightly floured surface. Arrange on a lightly buttered baking sheet. Spread 1/2 of the sausage mixture down the center of the dough; sprinkle with 1/2 of the Cheddar cheese and 1/2 of the mozzarella cheese. Repeat the layers with the remaining sausage mixture, remaining Cheddar cheese and remaining mozzarella cheese. Fold the dough over to enclose the filling; tuck ends under. Brush with the egg. Bake at 375 degrees for 20 minutes or until golden brown. *Yield: 8 servings.*

Desserts

Grandma's Apron

by Vickie Johnson Hamley

Hanging just inside my pantry is an apron. I see it every time I open the door—the blue and white calico has faded and the fabric is thin from use and washing. This apron belonged to my grandmother. It is a reminder of the years we shared, a tangible connection to a special woman who taught me a lot about sharing.

I was about twenty years old when Grandma died. Each of the seven granddaughters chose something of hers as a keepsake. While looking through her dresser with its delicate hand-kerchiefs, simple nightgowns and embroidered pillowcases, I came across the apron. There was nothing particularly remarkable about it, but seeing the apron reminded me of a story my dad once told about being sent to the store for sugar. Kitchen staples such as flour and sugar used to be bagged in calico fabrics. Since the fabric was often used to make clothes and quilts when the bags were emptied, the instructions to my dad about which calico bag of sugar to buy were very specific.

I like to think that the apron was made from the one my dad brought home—something pretty for Grandma to wear as she went about the routine of her daily work.

I did not choose the apron for its usefulness. I chose it because, in my memory picture of Grandma, she is always wearing it. When we arrived for a visit, Grandma would wipe her hands on her apron as she met us at the screen door. I could wrap my arms around her ample waist, lay my cheek on her apron and smell what she was preparing in the kitchen. Then, hiding her face behind the apron, she would tell my sister and me where to find the green dish with some special treats she had cooked just for us. Grandma's apron truly had many uses—it could keep her dress clean, polish an apple, dry wet hands or fan a heat-flushed face. Grandma always wore an apron when she was at home because she was never far from the kitchen.

As a young child, I thought Grandma lived in the kitchen. She was there in the morning to greet me with hot chocolate in my favorite Roy Rogers mug and still there cleaning up when I went to bed. She made biscuits from scratch, and I remember watching her sure movements as she mixed the ingredients and worked the dough. I spent a lot of time underfoot in the kitchen just so I could watch Grandma. There was a confidence in the way she prepared food using no measuring spoons or cups that I could only sense at the time. When no amount of "shoo-ing" would keep me out of the way, Grandma would tie an apron high around my chest and find something for me to do, whether it was cutting out biscuits, pour-ing the right amount of chocolate chips into the cookie dough or placing slices of bananas on each wafer for banana pudding. I would help, not because I was especially interested in cooking, but because I could spend time with Grandma.

Grandma lived on a farm and had a big garden. Behind

the house, she raised everything from corn to fruit trees. After breakfast, before it got too hot, Grandma would tie on her gardening apron with the big pockets, pull on her gloves and rubber boots, tie on her straw hat and tend to the plants and their daily harvest. During the summer and early fall, dinner and supper always included something fresh from the garden. Although she preferred working alone in the garden, Grandma would enlist some extra hands to help shell peas, snap beans or shuck corn. For my sister and me, sneaking cherry tomatoes from the pan where they were rinsing outside became a ritual. We would sneak just enough so that the missing ones would not be noticed. It was years before we found out that Grandma knew just what we were up to and only left out as many as she could spare.

Unaided by food processors, microwave ovens and dishwashers, Grandma prepared and cleaned up after three full meals each day for my grandfather, two bachelor uncles and whatever extra company was around at the time. As I saw it, this was the routine of her days. When I grew into my teens, I began to view Grandma's life as an endless monotony of kitchen and household chores. The delicious biscuits were still made from scratch and cookies still filled the green dish for our visits, but the appreciation for her efforts that I had as a child was replaced by the cynical view that I would never live my days like that. Unlike the women of my grandmother's generation, my life had too many exciting choices available and, to me, learning to cook was synonymous with aspiring to be a housewife. Grandma died before I had the chance to ask her if she was happy with the way her life turned out—if she derived pleasure from her daily routine or felt a sense of accomplishment at the end of the day.

It has taken years and the addition of a home and family of my own, but I have come full circle in appreciating and understanding that Grandma's efforts in the kitchen were her way of sharing with the people she loved. Although my labors in the kitchen are aided by numerous appliances and convenience foods, they are no less an expression of love. When my own children beg to help in the kitchen, I remember how important I felt when Grandma found something for me to do, and I take the opportunity to do the same. Tying tea-towel aprons around their waists, I have a true sense that the more things change, the more they stay the same. Grandma taught me that sharing food is a way of sharing yourself, and I am reminded of this each time I see her apron hanging in my pantry.

Vickie Johnson Hamley joined the League six years ago. In her free time, she enjoys writing and cooking and hopes one day to try all of the recipes handed down by her grandmother.

Grand Marnier Strawberry Cheesecake

32 ounces cream cheese, softened
1 cup packed light brown sugar
1/4 cup Grand Marnier
1/4 cup whipping cream
2 teaspoons vanilla extract
3 eggs, at room temperature, beaten
2 egg yolks
Macadamia Nut Crust (at right)
2 cups sour cream
1/4 cup packed brown sugar
4 teaspoons Grand Marnier
1 teaspoon vanilla extract
4 cups fresh strawberries, hulled
1/4 cup red currant jelly
5 1/2 teaspoons Grand Marnier
1/2 cup whipping cream
2 teaspoons confectioners' sugar

Garnish:
Fresh mint leaves

Beat the cream cheese in a mixer bowl until smooth. Add 1 cup brown sugar, 1/4 cup Grand Marnier, 1/4 cup whipping cream and 2 teaspoons vanilla. Beat until blended. Add the eggs and egg yolks, beating until smooth. Spoon over the Macadamia Nut Crust.

Bake at 350 degrees for 50 minutes or until the top puffs and is golden brown. Cool in the pan on a wire rack for 15 minutes. The cheesecake will fall as it cools.

Combine the sour cream, 1/4 cup brown sugar, 4 teaspoons Grand Marnier and 1 teaspoon vanilla in a bowl and mix well. Spread over the baked layer with the back of a spoon.

Bake at 350 degrees for 5 minutes. Let stand on a wire rack until cool. Chill, covered, for 8 to 10 hours.

Run a sharp knife around the edge of the cheesecake 2 hours before serving. Release the side of the pan. Place the cheesecake on a cake plate. Arrange the strawberries pointed ends up around the outer edge of the cheesecake, leaving a 1-inch border at the plate edge.

Heat the currant jelly in a saucepan over low heat until melted, stirring frequently. Add 4 of the 5 1/2 teaspoons Grand Marnier and mix well. Brush over the strawberries.

Beat 1/2 cup whipping cream in a mixer bowl until soft peaks form. Fold in the remaining 1 1/2 teaspoons Grand Marnier and confectioners' sugar. Spoon into a pastry bag fitted with a large star tip.

Pipe the whipped cream mixture decoratively around the outer 1-inch border of the cheesecake. Garnish with mint leaves. Chill until serving time.
Yield: 12 servings.

For Macadamia Nut Crust, combine 1 1/2 cups graham cracker crumbs, 1 cup roasted chopped macadamia nuts, 5 tablespoons butter, 2 tablespoons light brown sugar and 2 teaspoons orange zest in a bowl and mix well. Pat over the bottom and up the side to within 1/2 inch of the top of a buttered 10-inch springform pan. Place the pan on the center oven rack. Bake at 350 degrees for 10 minutes. Let stand on a wire rack until cool.

173

Lemon Cheesecake Blueberry Tarts

24 ounces cream cheese,
  softened
$3/4$ cup sugar
2 eggs
1 tablespoon vanilla
  extract
$1^1/4$ teaspoons lemon
  extract
1 recipe Sweet Pastry
  Shells (see page 204)
6 cups fresh blueberries
2 cups quick-cooking
  oats
1 cup sugar
1 cup melted butter

Beat the cream cheese, $3/4$ cup sugar, eggs and flavorings in a mixer bowl until smooth. Spoon into the Sweet Pastry Shells. Bake at 350 degrees for 15 minutes or until slightly firm. Remove from oven. Mound the blueberries on top of the baked layer.

Combine the oats, 1 cup sugar and butter in a bowl and mix well. Spoon over the blueberries. Bake for 20 minutes longer or until bubbly. *Yield: 12 servings.*

Note: This recipe may be varied according to personal taste. Fresh seasonal fruits would include strawberries, peaches, pears, raspberries, blackberries, or apples. A combination of fruits also works well. Extracts and/or liqueur flavorings would include almond, mint, orange, Frangelico, Godiva, Grand Marnier, brandy, or others of your choice. May bake in a tart pan.

Opened in 1985, Amedeo's is a family-owned and family-operated restaurant featuring Italian food as well as continental and seafood dishes. These tarts are a favorite of the restaurant's patrons.

Cheesecake with Fruit and Berries

3/4 cup graham cracker
crumbs
1/2 cup crushed pecans
3 tablespoons melted
butter
32 ounces cream cheese,
softened
3 cups sugar
5 eggs
Juice of 1 lemon
1/4 cup sugar
1 cup sour cream
Fresh fruit and/or
seasonal berries

Combine the graham cracker crumbs, pecans and butter in a bowl and mix well. Pat over the bottom of a 9x12-inch baking pan.

Beat the cream cheese, 3 cups sugar, eggs and lemon juice in a mixer bowl until smooth. Spread over the prepared layer.

Bake at 350 degrees for 30 to 35 minutes or until set. Remove to a wire rack. Let stand for 30 minutes.

Combine 1/4 cup sugar and sour cream in a bowl and mix well. Spread over the baked layer.

Bake for 2 to 3 minutes longer. Cool on a wire rack for 15 minutes.

Chill for 2 hours or longer before slicing into squares or rectangles. Serve with fresh fruit and/or berries.
Yield: 16 servings.

Since 1969, Houstonians have enjoyed many traditional Italian meals at Michelangelo's, the first sidewalk cafe in Houston. An often-requested dessert is this cheesecake.

Figs and Berries

8 fresh sonoma figs, cut
  into halves
1 cup raspberries
1 cup blackberries
1/2 cup red or black
  currants
Sabayon
Cookies
Key Lime Sorbet

Garnish:
Sprigs of mint

Arrange the figs cut side up around the inside rim of 4 ovenproof plates. Sprinkle with 1/2 of the raspberries, 1/2 of the blackberries and 1/2 of the currants. Spoon the Sabayon over the fruits.

Broil until brown. Sprinkle with the remaining raspberries, blackberries and currants. Place a cookie of your choice in the center of each plate. Mound a scoop of the Key Lime Sorbet over each cookie. Garnish with a sprig of mint.
Yield: 4 servings.

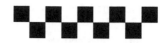

A specialty of Chez Nous in Houston is Figs and Berries with Sabayon and Key Lime Sorbet.

Sabayon

3 tablespoons sugar
3 egg yolks
6 tablespoons sauterne
1/4 cup whipping cream,
  whipped

Combine the sugar, egg yolks and sauterne in a stainless steel bowl over hot water. Simmer until thickened and doubled in volume, whisking constantly. Remove from heat. Whisk over ice water until cool. Fold in the whipped cream.

Key Lime Sorbet

3/4 cup water
1/2 cup sugar
1/4 cup Key lime juice
1/4 cup Key lime zest

Combine the water, sugar, Key lime juice and Key lime zest in a saucepan. Bring to a boil over medium heat, stirring frequently; reduce heat. Simmer for 5 minutes, stirring occasionally. Remove from heat. Let stand for 1 hour. Strain, chill and freeze in an ice cream freezer using manufacturer's instructions.

Desserts

Blackberry Dumplings

2 cups flour
3 tablespoons sugar
3¹/₂ teaspoons baking
   powder
1 teaspoon salt
1 egg
Milk
3 pints fresh blackberries
1 cup sugar
³/₄ cup water
1¹/₂ tablespoons butter

Sift the flour, 3 tablespoons sugar, baking powder and salt into a bowl and mix well. Add the egg, stirring until blended. Add just enough milk to make a stiff batter and mix well.

Combine the blackberries, 1 cup sugar, water and butter in a saucepan. Bring to a boil, stirring occasionally.

Drop the batter 1 spoonful at a time into the boiling blackberry mixture. Cook, covered, for 15 to 20 minutes. Serve with ice cream or whipped cream.

Yield: 6 servings.

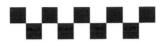

Teddi's Tea Room is the perfect place for showers and teas with its quaint private rooms serving homemade soups and salads. Teddi's is also known for its evening fare featuring a hearty Northern Italian cuisine in a family-friendly atmosphere. Their Blackberry Dumplings are the perfect finish to any meal.

Fresh Lemon Mousse

3 egg yolks
1/2 cup sugar
Juice and zest of
   2 lemons
3 egg whites
1/8 teaspoon salt
1/2 cup whipping cream

Combine the egg yolks and sugar in a mixer bowl. Beat until thickened. Stir in the lemon juice and lemon zest. Pour into a double boiler. Simmer for 10 minutes or until thickened and of a pudding consistency, whisking constantly. Let stand until cool. Beat the egg whites and salt in a chilled mixer bowl until stiff peaks form. Fold into the lemon mixture. Chill for 2 hours. Beat the whipping cream in a chilled mixer bowl until soft peaks form. Fold into the lemon mixture. Chill until serving time. Spoon the mousse into individual dessert bowls or chilled wine glasses. *Yield: 6 servings.*

For a wonderful, spicy aroma, toss dried orange, lemon, or lime peels into your fireplace.

Melon in Rum Lime Sauce

Melon balls of
   1/2 watermelon
Melon balls of
   2 honeydew melons
Melon balls of
   2 cantaloupes
1 cup blueberries
1 cup raspberries
1 cup sugar
1/2 cup water
2 teaspoons lime zest
2/3 cup light rum
6 tablespoons fresh lime
   juice

Garnish:
Sprigs of mint

Combine the watermelon, honeydew melons, cantaloupes, blueberries and raspberries in a bowl and mix gently. Chill, covered, in the refrigerator. Combine the sugar and water in a saucepan and mix well. Bring to a boil; reduce heat. Simmer for 5 minutes, stirring occasionally. Stir in the lime zest. Remove from heat. Let stand until cool. Add the rum and lime juice and mix well. Pour over the chilled fruit. Chill, covered, for 3 hours. Garnish with sprigs of mint. *Yield: 12 servings.*

Pears Pernod

1/4 cup Pernod
1/2 cup butter
1/4 cup sugar
8 fresh pear halves
4 scoops vanilla ice
  cream

Heat the Pernod in a saucepan. Cover to keep warm. Combine the butter and sugar in a skillet. Cook over high heat until blended, stirring constantly; do not brown. Add the pears. Cook for 2 minutes or until the pears are hot, spooning the sauce over the pears constantly. Stir in the warm Pernod. Ignite the mixture. Shake the skillet until the flames subside. Arrange 2 pear halves on each dessert plate. Top with a scoop of vanilla ice cream. Drizzle with the sauce. *Yield: 4 servings.*

Note: Canned pears may be substituted for the fresh pears, but they should be drained prior to using.

Hot Fudge Pudding

3/4 cup flour
1/2 cup sugar
1 1/2 tablespoons baking
  cocoa
1 1/2 teaspoons baking
  powder
1/8 teaspoon salt
2 tablespoons butter
1/3 cup half-and-half
2 ounces bittersweet
  chocolate, grated
3/4 teaspoon vanilla
  extract
1 cup packed dark brown
  sugar
1/4 cup baking cocoa
1 1/2 cups strong coffee
Whipped cream

Garnish:
Grated chocolate

Sift the flour, sugar, 1 1/2 tablespoons baking cocoa, baking powder and salt together 2 to 3 times. Heat the butter in a saucepan until melted. Combine the flour mixture, half-and-half, chocolate and vanilla in a bowl, stirring just until moistened. Add the butter, stirring just until combined; do not overmix. Spoon into a buttered 8x8-inch baking pan. Sift the brown sugar and 1/4 cup baking cocoa into a bowl and mix well. Sprinkle over the prepared layer. Pour the coffee over the top; do not stir. Bake at 350 degrees for 20 to 25 minutes. Serve warm topped with whipped cream. Garnish with grated chocolate. *Yield: 8 servings.*

Bread Pudding with Whiskey Sauce

4 cups half-and-half
2 cups sugar
1/2 cup melted butter
3 eggs, beaten
2 tablespoons vanilla
   extract
1 1/2 teaspoons cinnamon
1/2 teaspoon nutmeg
1 (10-ounce) loaf dry
   French bread, torn
   into bite-size pieces
1 cup raisins
1 cup shredded coconut
1 cup chopped pecans
Whiskey Sauce

1 1/3 cups confectioners'
   sugar
1/2 cup butter
1 egg yolk
1/4 cup whiskey

Combine the half-and-half, sugar, butter, eggs, vanilla, cinnamon and nutmeg in a bowl and mix well. Stir in the bread, raisins, coconut and pecans. Spoon into a buttered 9x13-inch baking pan.

Bake at 350 degrees for 1 1/4 hours or until golden brown; do not overbake.

Spoon into dessert bowls. Drizzle with the warm Whiskey Sauce.
Yield: 15 servings.

Whiskey Sauce

Combine the confectioners' sugar and butter in a saucepan. Cook over medium heat until smooth, stirring constantly. Remove from heat. Stir a small amount of the hot mixture into the egg yolk; stir the egg yolk into the hot mixture. Add the whiskey gradually, stirring constantly. The sauce will thicken as it cools.

Orange Caramel Flan

1/2 cup sugar
1/4 cup water
2 cups milk
1 (1-inch) cinnamon
 stick
Peel of 1 orange
3 eggs
2 egg yolks
1/2 cup sugar
1 teaspoon orange
 liqueur

Garnish:
Fresh orange slices

Combine 1/2 cup sugar and water in a saucepan and mix well. Bring to a boil. Boil until the mixture is dark and amber in color; do not stir. Pour into 6 ovenproof custard cups. Let stand until cool.

Combine the milk, cinnamon stick and orange peel in a saucepan. Bring to a boil gradually. Remove from heat. Let stand for 10 minutes or until cool. Strain, discarding the cinnamon stick and orange peel.

Beat the eggs, egg yolks, 1/2 cup sugar and liqueur in a bowl until blended. Whisk into the milk mixture and strain. Spoon into the prepared custard cups. Cover with foil.

Place the custard cups in a large baking pan. Add enough hot water to the baking pan to come halfway up the sides of the cups. Bake at 350 degrees for 30 minutes or until set. Remove to a wire rack to cool.

Unmold onto individual dessert plates, allowing the caramel to run over the top. Garnish with orange slices.
Yield: 6 servings.

Stick cinnamon has a more intense flavor than that of commercially ground cinnamon. Use as swizzle sticks for hot drinks such as hot buttered rum, coffee, and mulled wine.

Tiramisù

4 cups espresso, cooled
16 ladyfingers
8 egg yolks
1/2 cup sugar
12 ounces mascarpone
  cheese
2 tablespoons dark rum
1 1/2 cups whipping cream
8 ladyfingers
2 tablespoons baking
  cocoa

Pour the coffee into a shallow dish. Dip 16 ladyfingers in the coffee. Line a 12-inch round decorative glass pie plate or trifle bowl with the ladyfingers. Beat the egg yolks and sugar in a mixer bowl until frothy. Add the mascarpone cheese and rum. Beat until smooth, scraping the bowl occasionally. Fold in the whipping cream. Spoon 2/3 of the mascarpone mixture over the ladyfingers in the prepared plate. Dip 8 ladyfingers in the remaining coffee. Arrange over the prepared layers. Top with the remaining mascarpone mixture. Chill, covered, for 6 hours. Sift the baking cocoa over the top just before serving. *Yield: 8 servings.*

Keep a new powder puff in the flour canister for dusting greased cake pans.

Fresh Apple Cake

3 cups flour
1 1/2 teaspoons baking
  soda
1 teaspoon salt
1 teaspoon cinnamon
1 teaspoon baking
  powder
2 cups sugar
3 eggs
1 1/2 cups vegetable oil
1 teaspoon vanilla
  extract
3 cups chopped peeled
  Red Delicious apples
1 1/2 cups chopped pecans
Confectioners' sugar to
  taste

Sift the flour, baking soda, salt, cinnamon and baking powder together. Beat the sugar and eggs in a mixer bowl until creamy. Add the oil and vanilla, beating until blended. Add the dry ingredients gradually and mix well. Stir in the apples and pecans. Spoon into a buttered bundt pan. Bake at 300 degrees for 1 1/2 hours. Cool in the pan on a wire rack. Invert onto a serving platter. Sprinkle with confectioners' sugar. *Yield: 12 servings.*

  Note: Excellent served warm with coffee.

Carrot Cake

2 cups sugar
2 cups flour
2 teaspoons baking soda
2 teaspoons cinnamon
2 cups grated carrots
1½ cups vegetable oil
1 cup crushed pineapple
  with juice
1 cup flaked coconut
1 cup pecan pieces
4 eggs, beaten
2 teaspoons vanilla
  extract
1 teaspoon salt
Lemon Cream Cheese
  Frosting

Sift the sugar, flour, baking soda and cinnamon into a bowl and mix well.

Combine the carrots, oil, pineapple, coconut, pecans, eggs, vanilla and salt in a mixer bowl. Beat until mixed, scraping the bowl occasionally. Add the flour mixture gradually and mix well. Spoon into 2 buttered and floured 8-inch cake pans.

Bake at 350 degrees for 30 to 35 minutes or until the layers test done. Cool in the pans on a wire rack.

Spread the Lemon Cream Cheese Frosting between the layers and over the top and side of the cake. *Yield: 12 servings.*

Lemon Cream Cheese Frosting

12 ounces cream cheese,
  softened
1 cup butter, softened
2 teaspoons fresh lemon
  juice
2 cups sifted
  confectioners' sugar

Beat the cream cheese, butter and lemon juice in a mixer bowl until smooth. Add the confectioners' sugar gradually, beating constantly until of spreading consistency.

Chocolate Applesauce Cake

2 cups flour
1¹/₂ cups sugar
2 tablespoons baking
  cocoa
1¹/₂ teaspoons baking
  soda
¹/₄ teaspoon salt
¹/₂ cup butter, softened
2 eggs
2 cups applesauce
1 cup chocolate chips
¹/₂ cup chopped nuts
2 tablespoons sugar

Sift the flour, 1¹/₂ cups sugar, baking cocoa, baking soda and salt into a bowl and mix well. Blend in the butter and eggs. Stir in the applesauce. Spoon into a buttered and floured 9x13-inch cake pan. Sprinkle with the chocolate chips, nuts and 2 tablespoons sugar. Bake at 350 degrees for 35 minutes. *Yield: 15 servings.*

Chocolate Mousse Cake

12 ounces semisweet
  chocolate
³/₄ cup unsalted butter
9 egg yolks
1 cup sugar
2 tablespoons Grand
  Marnier
9 egg whites
1 cup whipping cream
4 ounces semisweet
  chocolate

Heat 12 ounces chocolate and the butter in a double boiler until blended, stirring frequently. Beat the egg yolks and sugar in a mixer bowl until pale yellow. Add the chocolate mixture and Grand Marnier and mix well. Beat the egg whites in a mixer bowl until stiff peaks form. Fold 1 cup of the egg whites into the chocolate mixture. Fold the chocolate mixture into the egg whites. Spoon ¹/₂ of the chocolate mixture into an 8-inch springform pan. Chill the remaining chocolate mixture. Bake at 350 degrees for 26 minutes or until the cake puffs in the center. Remove from oven. Cool for 30 minutes. The cake will sink in the middle. Beat the whipping cream in a mixer bowl until thick. Fold into the chilled chocolate mixture. Spread over the baked layer. Make chocolate curls from 4 ounces chocolate. Decorate the top of the cake with the curls. Freeze, covered, until firm. Let stand in the refrigerator for 2 to 3 hours before serving. *Yield: 10 servings.*

Chocolate Raspberry Cake

1 1/4 cups flour, sifted
1/3 cup baking cocoa
2 teaspoons baking
    powder
1/2 cup butter, softened
1 1/4 cups sugar
2 egg yolks
2/3 cup milk
1 1/4 teaspoons vanilla
    extract
2 egg whites
2 tablespoons seedless
    raspberry jam
2 tablespoons Chambord
    or raspberry liqueur
2 cups whipping cream
1/4 cup confectioners'
    sugar, sifted
3 cups fresh raspberries

Garnish:
Mint leaves

Butter two 9-inch round cake pans. Line with waxed paper; butter the waxed paper. Combine the flour, baking cocoa and baking powder in a bowl and mix well.

Beat the butter in a mixer bowl until creamy. Add the sugar and egg yolks gradually, beating well after each addition. Add the flour mixture alternately with the milk, beginning and ending with the flour mixture. Beat at low speed until blended. Stir in the vanilla.

Place the egg whites in a chilled mixer bowl. Beat at high speed until stiff peaks form. Fold into the cake batter. Spoon into the prepared cake pans.

Bake at 350 degrees for 18 minutes or until the layers test done. Cool in the pans on a wire rack for 10 minutes. Invert onto the wire rack to cool completely.

Heat the raspberry jam in a saucepan until melted. Stir in the Chambord. Remove from heat.

Beat the whipping cream in a chilled mixer bowl until stiff peaks form. Fold in the confectioners' sugar.

Arrange 1 cake layer on a cake plate. Brush with 1/2 of the jam mixture. Sprinkle with 1/2 of the raspberries; spread with 1/2 of the whipped cream. Top with the remaining cake layer. Brush with the remaining jam mixture; spread with the remaining whipped cream. Arrange the remaining raspberries over the top. Garnish with mint leaves.
Yield: 12 servings.

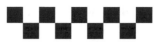

I remember that right before I was married, my grandmother gave me a gift that included an old cast-iron skillet and cake pans with wire cooling racks—two necessities for a well-equipped kitchen. Although I was delighted to receive such a gift, I didn't understand why I needed so many wire racks. My grandmother explained the secret of the perfect layer cake. Each layer of the cake requires one rack plus one extra for flipping the cake layers right side up. By cooling the cakes this way, the layers will not split or crack. Now, I always have perfect layers for my cakes . . . but my icing could still use a little help!

⤳ *Ellen Kirkwood* ⤳

Death by Chocolate

2 cups butter
1 cup sugar
1 cup water
2²/₃ cups semisweet
   chocolate chips
8 eggs
Raspberry Coulis

Garnish:
Chocolate shavings

Line a 9-inch springform pan with foil.
   Bring the butter, sugar and water to a
boil in a saucepan. Remove from heat.
Add the chocolate chips, stirring until
blended. Add the eggs 1 at a time, beating
well after each addition. The batter will be
very thin. Pour into the prepared pan.
   Bake at 350 degrees for 1 hour. Chill
for several hours before serving. Garnish
each serving with chocolate shavings.
Serve with Raspberry Coulis.
Yield: 8 servings.

Raspberry Coulis

3 pints fresh raspberries
1¹/₂ cups red currant
   jelly
1¹/₂ cups sugar
1¹/₂ teaspoons cornstarch
Salt to taste

Bring the raspberries and jelly to a boil in
a saucepan, stirring occasionally; reduce
heat. Stir in the sugar, cornstarch and salt.
Cook over low heat until thickened and
clear, stirring constantly. Remove from
heat and strain. Let stand until cool. Chill,
covered, until serving time.
   Note: Great served over ice cream or
pound cake.

German Chocolate Cake

2¹/₂ cups cake flour, sifted
1 teaspoon baking soda
¹/₂ teaspoon salt
4 ounces German's chocolate
¹/₂ cup boiling water
2 cups sugar
1 cup butter, softened
4 egg yolks
1 teaspoon vanilla extract
1 cup buttermilk
4 egg whites
Coconut Pecan Frosting

Line three 8- or 9-inch cake pans with waxed paper.

Sift the cake flour, baking soda and salt into a bowl and mix well.

Combine the chocolate and boiling water in a bowl, stirring until the chocolate melts. Let stand until cool.

Beat the sugar and butter in a mixer bowl until light and fluffy, scraping the bowl occasionally. Add the egg yolks 1 at a time, beating well after each addition. Add the vanilla and chocolate mixture and mix well. Add the dry ingredients alternately with the buttermilk, beating well after each addition.

Beat the egg whites in a chilled mixer bowl until stiff peaks form. Fold into the chocolate batter. Spoon into the prepared cake pans.

Bake at 350 degrees for 35 to 40 minutes or until the layers test done. Invert onto wire racks to cool.

Spread the Coconut Pecan Frosting between each layer and over the top.
Yield: 12 servings.

Note: May double the frosting recipe and spread over the cake sides.

Coconut Pecan Frosting

1 cup evaporated milk
1 cup sugar
¹/₂ cup butter
3 egg yolks, lightly beaten
1 teaspoon vanilla extract
1¹/₃ cups shredded coconut
1 cup chopped pecans

Combine the evaporated milk, sugar, butter, egg yolks and vanilla in a 2-quart saucepan. Cook over medium heat for 12 minutes or until thickened, stirring constantly. Remove from heat. Stir in the coconut and pecans. Let stand until the frosting is of spreading consistency, stirring occasionally.

Every Sunday evening was dinner at Grandma's house. She always fixed plenty of food because friends and family would invariably "drop by." In the summer, we ate on the patio, and in the winter we were packed around the dining room table, sometimes with an extra card table set up. The highlight of these evening meals was German Chocolate Cake. No matter how much we had eaten, there was always room for that.

⌁ Janie Price ⌁

Heavenly Chocolate Roll

6 egg yolks, at room
   temperature
³/4 cup sugar
6 ounces semisweet
   chocolate
3 tablespoons strong
   coffee, cooled
6 egg whites, at room
   temperature
¹/8 teaspoon salt
Baking cocoa
1¹/4 cups whipping cream
2 tablespoons
   confectioners' sugar
¹/2 teaspoon vanilla
   extract

Line a 10x15-inch jelly roll pan with waxed paper. Butter the waxed paper.

Beat the egg yolks in a mixer bowl until creamy. Add the sugar gradually, beating until thick and pale yellow.

Combine the chocolate and coffee in a double boiler over boiling water. Cook until the chocolate melts, stirring constantly. Stir into the egg mixture.

Beat the egg whites and salt in a chilled mixer bowl until stiff but not dry peaks form. Fold into the chocolate mixture. Spread in the prepared pan.

Bake at 350 degrees for 15 minutes. Remove to a wire rack. Cover with a damp tea towel. Let stand for 1 hour or until room temperature.

Sift an even layer of baking cocoa on a sheet of waxed paper larger than the jelly roll pan. Invert the jelly roll pan onto the waxed paper. Remove the waxed paper from the top of the cake.

Beat the whipping cream, confectioners' sugar and vanilla in a mixer bowl until thickened. Spread over the baked layer; roll as for a jelly roll to enclose the filling. Arrange seam side down on a serving platter. Chill, covered, for several hours. Cut into slices. *Yield: 16 servings.*

Note: Rolling from the long side gives an elegant slender roll that can be cut into 14 to 16 small slices. Rolling from the short side produces a shorter, flatter roll and 12 to 16 larger slices.

Coconut Pecan Cake

2 cups sugar
1 cup butter, softened
5 egg yolks
1 cup buttermilk
1 teaspoon vanilla
  extract
2 cups flour
1 teaspoon baking soda
1/2 teaspoon salt
1 cup shredded coconut
1 cup chopped pecans
5 egg whites
Cream Cheese Frosting
1 cup chopped pecans

Beat the sugar and butter in a mixer bowl until creamy, scraping the bowl occasionally. Add the egg yolks 1 at a time, beating well after each addition. Add the buttermilk and vanilla, beating until blended. Stir in the flour, baking soda and salt. Add the coconut and 1 cup pecans, stirring until mixed.

Beat the egg whites in a chilled mixer bowl until stiff peaks form. Fold into the batter, stirring until blended.

Spoon the batter into 3 buttered and floured 9-inch cake pans. Bake at 350 degrees for 25 to 30 minutes or until the layers test done. Invert onto a wire rack to cool completely.

Spread the Cream Cheese Frosting between the layers and over the top and side of the cake. Press 1 cup pecans into the side and top. *Yield: 12 servings.*

Cream Cheese Frosting

12 ounces cream cheese,
  softened
3/4 cup butter, softened
1 (1-pound) package
  confectioners' sugar
1 teaspoon vanilla
  extract

Beat the cream cheese and butter in a mixer bowl until creamy. Add the confectioners' sugar and vanilla. Beat until of a spreading consistency, scraping the bowl occasionally.

Just before icing a cake, dust a little cornstarch or flour on top to prevent the icing from running off.

Almond Pound Cake

2/3 cup sugar
1/3 cup olive oil
5 tablespoons butter
12 ounces almond paste
3 tablespoons lemon zest
5 eggs
1 1/2 cups cake flour
1 1/8 teaspoons baking
   powder
Mascarpone Topping

Garnish:
Shaved chocolate
Toasted almonds

1/2 cup whipping cream
4 ounces mascarpone
   cheese

Line a 9-inch cake pan with parchment paper. Butter and flour the parchment paper.

Beat the sugar, olive oil and butter in a mixer bowl until smooth, scraping the bowl occasionally. Add the almond paste and lemon zest, beating until mixed. Add the eggs 1 at a time, beating well after each addition. Fold in the cake flour and baking powder. Spoon into the prepared cake pan.

Bake at 325 degrees for 45 minutes or until the cake tests done. Cool in the pan on a wire rack. Invert onto a cake plate.

Mound the Mascarpone Topping on the cake. Garnish with shaved chocolate and toasted almonds. *Yield: 6 servings.*

Mascarpone Topping

Chill a mixer bowl and beaters. Beat the whipping cream in the chilled bowl with the chilled beaters until soft peaks form. Stir the mascarpone cheese in a bowl. Fold into the whipped cream.

Cake flour is a specialty flour and is an excellent choice for biscuits, pastries, and fine-textured cakes. Store in an airtight container in a cool, dry place for up to fifteen months or in the refrigerator or freezer for longer periods.

Swedish Pound Cake

2 cups sugar
1 cup butter, softened
5 eggs
2 cups flour
1 1/2 teaspoons vanilla
    extract
1 1/2 cups chopped pecans
1 cup flaked coconut
1 cup chocolate chips
    (optional)
1/4 cup water
1/2 cup sugar
5 tablespoons butter
1 teaspoon almond
    extract

Beat 2 cups sugar and 1 cup butter in a mixer bowl until creamy. Add the eggs 1 at a time, beating well after each addition. Add the flour and vanilla and mix well. Fold in the pecans, coconut and chocolate chips.

Spoon into a buttered and floured bundt pan. Bake at 325 degrees for 1 hour.

Bring the water and 1/2 cup sugar to a boil in a saucepan. Add 5 tablespoons butter. Cook until the butter melts, stirring constantly. Stir in the almond flavoring. Pour over the hot cake.

Cool in the pan on a wire rack for 25 to 30 minutes. Invert onto a cake plate. *Yield: 20 servings.*

Note: May substitute 1/4 cup amaretto for the water as a variation, deleting the almond extract.

You get more volume from cakes if ingredients are at room temperature prior to mixing.

Tres Leches Cake

4 egg whites
4 egg yolks
1 cup sugar
1 cup flour
¹/4 cup ice water
1 teaspoon baking
   powder
1 (14-ounce) can
   sweetened condensed
   milk
1 cup whipping cream
¹/2 cup evaporated milk
1 cup confectioners'
   sugar
3 egg whites
1 teaspoon lemon juice
1 teaspoon vinegar
¹/2 teaspoon vanilla
   extract

Garnish:
Fresh berries

Beat 4 egg whites in a mixer bowl until foamy. Add the egg yolks, sugar, flour, ice water and baking powder. Beat for 1 to 2 minutes or until smooth, scraping the bowl occasionally. Spoon into a lightly buttered 9x13-inch cake pan.

Bake at 350 degrees for 25 minutes or until light brown; do not overbake.

Combine the condensed milk, whipping cream and evaporated milk in a bowl and mix well. Pierce the top of the warm cake with a wooden pick. Pour the milk mixture over the top. Chill, covered, until cool to the touch.

Beat the confectioners' sugar, 3 egg whites, lemon juice, vinegar and vanilla in a mixer bowl for 5 to 10 minutes or until peaks begin to form. Spread over the baked layer. Garnish each serving with fresh berries. *Yield: 15 servings.*

Note: When the cake is cut, a sauce covering the bottom of the cake pan will appear. Spoon the sauce over each serving or spoon the sauce into a dessert bowl and place the cake on top.

Process granulated sugar in a blender or food processor to make superfine sugar.

White Texas Sheet Cake

1 cup butter
1 cup water
2 cups flour
2 cups sugar
1/2 cup sour cream
2 eggs, beaten
1 teaspoon salt
1 teaspoon baking
   powder
1 teaspoon almond
   extract
Butter Pecan Frosting

Combine the butter and water in a saucepan. Bring to a boil, stirring occasionally. Remove from heat.

Add the flour, sugar, sour cream, eggs, salt, baking powder and almond flavoring, whisking until smooth. Spoon into a buttered and lightly floured 10x15-inch cake pan.

Bake at 350 degrees for 20 to 25 minutes or until light brown. Spread the warm cake with the Butter Pecan Frosting. *Yield: 24 servings.*

Butter Pecan Frosting

1/2 cup butter
1/4 cup milk
1/2 teaspoon almond
   extract
3 cups confectioners'
   sugar
1 cup chopped pecans

Combine the butter and milk in a saucepan. Bring to a rolling boil over medium heat, stirring occasionally. Remove from heat. Whisk in the almond flavoring. Add the confectioners' sugar gradually, whisking constantly until of spreading consistency. Stir in the pecans.

For a new twist on a chocolate sheet cake, try White Texas Sheet Cake.

Caramel Oatmeal Bars

1 cup flour
1 cup quick-cooking oats
3/4 cup packed brown
 sugar
3/4 cup melted butter
1/2 teaspoon baking soda
1/4 teaspoon salt
1 cup semisweet
 chocolate chips
1 cup shredded coconut
1/2 cup chopped nuts
3/4 cup caramel ice cream
 topping
3 tablespoons flour

Combine 1 cup flour, oats, brown sugar, butter, baking soda and salt in a bowl and mix well. Pat 1/2 of the oat mixture over the bottom of a greased 7x11- or 9x9-inch baking dish. Bake at 350 degrees for 10 minutes.

Sprinkle the chocolate chips, coconut and nuts over the warm baked layer.

Combine the ice cream topping and 3 tablespoons flour in a bowl and mix well. Spread over the prepared layers. Sprinkle with the remaining oat mixture.

Bake for 15 to 20 minutes longer. Chill for 30 to 45 minutes or until firm. Cut into bars. Chill for 2 hours longer before serving. Store leftovers, covered, in the refrigerator. *Yield: 24 bars.*

Country Fudge Brownies

1/2 cup flour
1/2 teaspoon baking
    powder
1/2 teaspoon salt
2 ounces unsweetened
    chocolate
2 cups confectioners'
    sugar, sifted
6 tablespoons unsalted
    butter
2 eggs
3/4 teaspoon vanilla
    extract
3/4 teaspoon dark rum or
    milk
3 ounces semisweet
    chocolate, grated or
    finely chopped
1/2 cup chopped pecans
Coconut Pecan Topping

Combine the flour, baking powder and salt in a bowl and mix well.

Heat the unsweetened chocolate in a double boiler until melted. Remove from heat and stir. Cool slightly.

Beat the confectioners' sugar and butter in a mixer bowl at medium speed until creamy. Add the eggs, vanilla and rum and mix well. Add the melted chocolate, stirring just until mixed. Add the dry ingredients. Beat at low speed just until moistened, scraping the bowl frequently. Stir in the semisweet chocolate and pecans. Spoon into a greased and lightly floured 8x8-inch baking pan.

Bake at 350 degrees for 35 minutes or until a wooden pick inserted in the center comes out clean. Cool in the pan on a wire rack.

Spread the baked layer with the Coconut Pecan Topping. Let stand until set. Cut into bars. *Yield: 16 bars.*

Coconut Pecan Topping

3/4 cup shredded coconut
1/2 cup chopped pecans
1/2 cup evaporated milk
2 egg yolks, lightly
    beaten
1/2 cup sugar
1/4 cup butter, cut into
    pieces

Spread the coconut and pecans in a single layer in a shallow baking pan. Bake at 350 degrees for 5 to 10 minutes or until golden brown, stirring once or twice. Heat the evaporated milk in a saucepan just to the boiling point. Stir a small amount of the hot milk into the egg yolks; stir the egg yolks into the hot milk. Add the sugar and mix well. Cook over medium heat until thickened, stirring constantly; reduce heat to low. Cook for 2 minutes, stirring constantly. Remove from heat. Add the butter, stirring until blended. Stir in the coconut and pecans. Let stand until cool.

A jar lid or a couple of marbles in the bottom half of a double boiler will rattle when the water gets low and warn you to add additional water before the pan scorches or burns.

Pumpkin Bars

2 cups flour
2 teaspoons baking
  powder
2 teaspoons cinnamon
1 teaspoon baking soda
$^1/_2$ teaspoon salt
2 cups sugar
1 cup minus 1 teaspoon
  vegetable oil
2 cups solid-pack
  pumpkin
4 eggs
1 teaspoon vanilla
  extract
Cream Cheese Frosting

Garnish:
Chopped nuts or pecan
  halves

Sift the flour, baking powder, cinnamon, baking soda and salt into a bowl and mix well.

Beat the sugar and oil in a mixer bowl until blended. Add the pumpkin and mix well. Add the eggs 1 at a time, beating well after each addition. Beat in the vanilla. Add the dry ingredients gradually and mix well. Spoon into a buttered 12x17-inch baking pan.

Bake at 350 degrees for 20 to 25 minutes or until the edges pull from the sides of the pan. Cool in the pan on a wire rack. Spread with the Cream Cheese Frosting. Let stand until set. Cut into bars. Garnish with chopped nuts or place a pecan half in the center of each bar. *Yield: 15 bars.*

Note: Add 1 teaspoon nutmeg and 1 teaspoon allspice for spicier bars. May freeze in single layers in an airtight container for future use.

Cream Cheese Frosting

4 cups (about) sifted
  confectioners' sugar
8 ounces cream cheese,
  softened
$^3/_4$ cup butter, softened
2 teaspoons vanilla
  extract

Combine the confectioners' sugar, cream cheese, butter and vanilla in a mixer bowl. Beat until of spreading consistency, scraping the bowl occasionally.

Chocolate Snowflakes

2 cups sifted flour, sifted
2 teaspoons baking
  powder
1/2 teaspoon salt
4 ounces unsweetened
  chocolate
2 cups sugar
1/2 cup vegetable oil
4 eggs
2 teaspoons vanilla
  extract
1/2 cup chopped nuts
1 cup confectioners'
  sugar

Sift the flour, baking powder and salt into a bowl and mix well. Heat the chocolate in a double boiler until melted, stirring frequently. Remove from heat. Stir in the sugar and oil. Add the eggs 1 at a time, beating well after each addition. Stir in the vanilla. Combine with the flour mixture in a bowl and mix well. Stir in the nuts. Chill for several hours to overnight. Shape into balls; roll in the confectioners' sugar. Arrange on a greased cookie sheet. Bake at 350 degrees for 10 to 12 minutes. Remove to a wire rack to cool. *Yield: 3 dozen.*

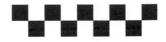

Keep cookies crisp by placing crushed tissue wrapping paper in the bottom of the cookie jar.

Sugar-n-Spice Chocolate Chip Cookies

1 cup butter, softened
1 cup sugar
1/2 cup packed brown
  sugar
2 eggs, beaten
2 1/4 cups flour, sifted
1 teaspoon salt
1 teaspoon baking soda
1 teaspoon cinnamon
1 teaspoon nutmeg
1/2 teaspoon mace
1 teaspoon vanilla
  extract
1/2 teaspoon hot water
2 cups semisweet
  chocolate chips
1 cup chopped nuts
  (optional)
2/3 cup raisins (optional)

Cream the butter, sugar and brown sugar in a mixer bowl until light and fluffy. Add the eggs, beating until smooth. Add the flour, salt, baking soda, cinnamon, nutmeg and mace and mix well. Make a well in the center of the mixture. Add the vanilla and hot water to the well and mix thoroughly. Fold in the chocolate chips, nuts and raisins. Chill, covered, until firm. Shape by teaspoonfuls into balls. Arrange on a buttered cookie sheet. Bake at 375 degrees for 10 minutes. Remove to a wire rack to cool. *Yield: 5 to 6 dozen.*

White Chocolate Blackberry Cookies

12 ounces good-quality
  white chocolate,
  coarsely chopped
1 cup sugar
1/2 cup butter, softened
1 teaspoon baking soda
1/2 teaspoon almond
  extract
2 eggs
3 cups flour
2/3 cup seedless
  blackberry jam
1/2 teaspoon shortening

Divide the white chocolate into 3 portions.

Heat 1 portion of the white chocolate in a saucepan over low heat until melted, stirring frequently. Remove from heat.

Beat the sugar and butter in a mixer bowl until creamy. Add the baking soda and almond flavoring and mix well. Add the eggs 1 at a time, beating well after each addition. Stir in the melted white chocolate. Add the flour gradually and mix well. The dough will be dry. Stir in 1 portion of the white chocolate.

Drop by teaspoonfuls onto a lightly buttered cookie sheet. Bake at 350 degrees for 8 to 10 minutes or until light brown. Remove to a wire rack to cool. Arrange on a sheet of waxed paper.

Heat the jam in a saucepan until melted, stirring occasionally. Cool slightly. Top each cookie with some of the jam.

Combine the remaining portion of white chocolate and shortening in a saucepan. Cook over low heat until blended, stirring constantly. Drizzle over the cookies. Let stand until set. Store the cookies in an airtight container.
Yield: 3 1/2 dozen.

Note: May substitute any seedless jam for the blackberry jam. There can be no substitutions for the butter in this cookie recipe.

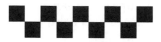

When making drop cookies, cool the cookie sheets between batches. This will prevent the dough from flattening during the baking process.

Chewy Chunky Chocolate Chip Cookies

1 cup plus 2 tablespoons packed brown sugar
1 cup sugar
1/2 cup butter, softened
4 1/2 cups quick-cooking oats
2 cups extra-crunchy peanut butter
3 eggs
2 teaspoons baking soda
1 teaspoon light corn syrup
1 teaspoon vanilla extract
1/4 teaspoon salt
2 2/3 cups chocolate chips

Beat the brown sugar, sugar and butter in a mixer bowl until creamy, scraping the bowl occasionally. Add the oats, peanut butter, eggs, baking soda, corn syrup, vanilla and salt and mix well. Stir in the chocolate chips. Drop by spoonfuls onto a buttered cookie sheet. Bake at 350 degrees for exactly 13 minutes; do not overbake. Cool on the cookie sheet on a wire rack. Remove to an airtight container.
Yield: 5 dozen.

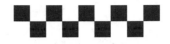

Heavy-gauge aluminum cookie sheets with low sides or no sides are the best for cookie baking. The lower sides provide for better air circulation and more evenly baked cookies.

Spanish Peanut Cookies

2 cups flour
1 teaspoon baking powder
1 teaspoon baking soda
1 cup shortening
1 cup packed brown sugar
1 cup sugar
1/2 cup peanut butter
2 eggs
2 teaspoons vanilla extract
2 cups quick-cooking oats
1 1/2 cups salted Spanish peanuts

Sift the flour, baking powder and baking soda into a bowl and mix well. Beat the shortening, brown sugar, sugar and peanut butter in a mixer bowl until smooth. Add the eggs and vanilla. Beat until fluffy, scraping the bowl occasionally. Add the dry ingredients gradually and mix well. Stir in the oats and peanuts. Drop by teaspoonfuls onto a cookie sheet. Bake at 350 degrees for 10 minutes or until light brown. Remove to a wire rack to cool.
Yield: 6 dozen.

German Apple Pie

1 recipe (2-crust) pie
  pastry
12 ounces apples, thinly
  sliced
1/4 cup raisins
2 tablespoons lemon
  juice
1/4 cup sugar
3/4 teaspoon cinnamon
1/4 teaspoon nutmeg
3/4 cup packed brown
  sugar
3 tablespoons flour
2 tablespoons butter
1/4 cup chopped pecans

Fit 1/2 of the pastry into a 9-inch pie plate. Spread the apples in the pastry-lined pie plate. Sprinkle with the raisins; drizzle with the lemon juice.

Combine the sugar, cinnamon and nutmeg in a bowl and mix well. Sprinkle over the prepared layers.

Combine the brown sugar and flour in a bowl and mix well. Cut in the butter until crumbly. Stir in the pecans. Sprinkle 2/3 of the crumb mixture over the prepared layers. Top with the remaining pastry, fluting the edge to seal. Sprinkle with the remaining crumb mixture and cut vents.

Bake at 450 degrees for 10 minutes. Reduce the oven temperature to 350 degrees. Bake for 40 minutes longer.
Yield: 8 servings.

A charming country-cooking cafe, Wunsche Bros. Cafe prepares everything, such as this German Apple Pie, from scratch. Customers delight in the unpretentious atmosphere that makes the place all the more endearing.

Banana Toffee Pie

4¹/2 ounces chocolate
  wafer cookies
²/3 cup pecans
7 tablespoons melted
  unsalted butter
1 (14-ounce) can
  sweetened condensed
  milk, caramelized
5 ripe bananas, thinly
  sliced
1¹/2 cups whipping cream

Garnish:
Dutch process baking
  cocoa
Confectioners' sugar
Bittersweet chocolate
  shavings

Combine the cookies and pecans in a blender or food processor container. Process until of a fine crumb consistency. Combine the cookie mixture and butter in a bowl and mix well.

Press over the bottom of a 9-inch fluted tart pan with removable bottom or a springform pan. Chill, covered, for 2 hours.

Spread the caramelized milk over the prepared layer. Top with the sliced bananas.

Beat the whipping cream in a chilled mixer bowl until stiff peaks form. Spread over the prepared layers.

Chill, covered, for several hours. Garnish with baking cocoa, confectioners' sugar and chocolate shavings just before serving. *Yield: 8 servings.*

Note: Do not caramelize sweetened condensed milk in a closed can. To caramelize, pour the condensed milk into a pie plate, cover with foil, and place in a hot water bath. Bake at 425 degrees for 1 hour or until thick and caramel colored.

Blueberry Tart

1 cup flour
2 teaspoons sugar
1/8 teaspoon salt
1/2 cup butter, softened
1 teaspoon white vinegar
3 cups fresh blueberries
1 cup sugar
2 teaspoons flour
1/8 teaspoon cinnamon
1 cup fresh blueberries
Confectioners' sugar to
    taste

Combine 1 cup flour, 2 teaspoons sugar and salt in a bowl and mix well. Cut in the butter and vinegar until blended. Press over the bottom and up the side of a tart pan with a removable bottom or a springform pan. Combine 3 cups blueberries, 1 cup sugar, 2 teaspoons flour and cinnamon in a bowl, tossing gently to mix. Spoon into the prepared pan. Bake at 400 degrees for 1 hour. Top with 1 cup blueberries. Let stand until cool. Remove the side of the pan. Sprinkle with confectioners' sugar just before serving.
Yield: 8 servings.

Buttermilk Pecan Pie

1/2 cup chopped pecans
1 unbaked (9-inch) pie
    shell
2 cups sugar
1/2 cup butter, softened
2 teaspoons vanilla
    extract
3 eggs
3 tablespoons flour
1/4 teaspoon salt
1 cup buttermilk

Sprinkle the pecans over the bottom of the pie shell. Add the sugar 1/2 cup at a time to the butter in a mixer bowl, beating until creamy. Beat in the vanilla. Add the eggs 1 at a time, beating well after each addition. Add a mixture of the flour and salt gradually and mix well. Mix in the buttermilk. Pour into the prepared pie shell. Bake at 300 degrees for 1 1/2 hours. Serve at room temperature.
Yield: 8 servings.

Buttermilk Pecan Pie is a Southern Comfort. With the tanginess of buttermilk and the nuttiness of pecans, it is unforgettable. This pie is a favorite at the Wunsche Bros. Cafe.

Cranberry Apple Pie

2 all ready pie pastries
³/4 cup packed brown
    sugar
¹/3 cup sugar
¹/3 cup flour
2 teaspoons cinnamon
¹/2 teaspoon nutmeg
¹/2 teaspoon allspice
4 cups thinly sliced
    Granny Smith apples
2 cups cranberries
2 tablespoons butter

Fit 1 of the pie pastries into a 9-inch pie plate. Combine the brown sugar, sugar, flour, cinnamon, nutmeg and allspice in a bowl and mix well. Add the apples and cranberries, tossing to coat. Spoon into the pastry-lined pie plate. Dot with the butter. Top with the remaining pie pastry, fluting the edge to seal and cutting vents. Bake at 400 degrees for 15 minutes. Cover the edge with foil to prevent excess browning. Bake for 30 to 35 minutes longer or just until golden brown. *Yield: 8 servings.*

Praline Pumpkin Pie

¹/3 cup chopped pecans
¹/3 cup packed brown
    sugar
2 tablespoons butter,
    softened
1 unbaked (9-inch) pie
    shell
1 cup solid-pack
    pumpkin
2 eggs, beaten
1 cup evaporated milk
²/3 cup packed brown
    sugar
1 tablespoon flour
¹/2 teaspoon cinnamon
¹/2 teaspoon ginger
¹/2 teaspoon ground
    cloves
¹/2 teaspoon mace
¹/2 teaspoon salt

Combine the pecans, ¹/3 cup brown sugar and butter in a bowl and mix well. Press over the bottom of the pie shell. Bake at 450 degrees for 10 minutes. Decrease the oven temperature to 325 degrees. Combine the pumpkin and eggs in a bowl and mix well. Add the evaporated milk, ²/3 cup brown sugar, flour, cinnamon, ginger, cloves, mace and salt, beating until blended. Spoon into the baked pie shell. Bake for 45 minutes. *Yield: 8 servings.*

Baking since the age of thirteen, Janice Lehmann decided to turn her passion into a business providing scrumptious baked goods to sweet-toothed patrons. The Praline Pumpkin Pie is one of her specialties.

Southern Fruit Pie

1/2 cup butter
1 cup sugar
1/2 cup dark or golden
  raisins
1/2 cup shredded coconut
1/2 cup nuts
2 eggs, beaten
1 tablespoon vinegar
1 teaspoon vanilla
  extract
1/8 teaspoon salt
  (optional)
1 unbaked (8-inch) pie
  shell

Heat the butter in a saucepan over medium heat until melted. Remove from heat. Stir in the sugar, raisins, coconut, nuts, eggs, vinegar, vanilla and salt. Spoon into the pie shell. Bake at 325 degrees for 40 minutes. *Yield: 8 servings.*

Sweet Pastry Shells

3 cups flour
2 tablespoons sugar
1/4 teaspoon salt
1 1/2 cups unsalted butter,
  chilled
3 tablespoons (about) ice
  water
1 egg, beaten
1 to 2 tablespoons water

Combine the flour, sugar and salt in a mixer bowl and mix well. Cut in the butter using the paddle attachment at low speed until crumbly. Add just enough ice water until the dough adheres and mix well. The addition of too much water will produce a tough dough. Chill for 30 minutes. Roll the dough to fit individual tart pans, allowing 1/4 inch overhang to allow for shrinkage. Blind bake the dough (see Note below) at 350 degrees for 15 to 20 minutes or until light brown. Remove the parchment paper and dried beans. Brush a mixture of the egg and water over the bottoms. Bake until light brown and the bottoms of the tart shells are beginning to get firm. *Yield: 12 tart shells.*

Note: To blind bake, score the bottom of the dough with a fork. Line with parchment paper and fill with dried beans to weigh down the dough and thus prevent puffing.

My mother shared her love of baking cakes, pies, and cookies with me at an early age. When I was a young girl, I enjoyed helping her create many wonderful things in the kitchen. I have shared this with my own son who has been cutting out and decorating cookies for the holidays since he could crawl onto a stool in the kitchen. Now that I have three children, we have many helping hands and always look forward to our day of baking for the holidays.

⌣ *Kim Klein* ⌣

Comfort
Foods

A Tribute to Grandma

by Gina Nelson Ebers

My grandma and I have spoken on the phone every week for as long as I can remember. Once we lived in the same town— now we are a thousand miles apart. It makes no difference... we continue to talk. We talk of daily activities, news, family members and inevitably food. You see, Grandma and I have always shared a great fondness for eating! She'll ask, "Are you making something good for dinner?" By now I know the proper response, "Of course I am." This makes her happy. To tell her I have just popped a frozen pizza into the microwave or that Mike is stopping for take-out is a whole other matter!

Grandma was born in 1908. She was the eldest daughter in a family of twelve. Her father was a cattle feeder. Her mother was a homemaker and a great cook.

Her Angel Food cakes, which stood ten inches high, were well known throughout the country. She worked her kitchen magic in an unregulated oven heated by corncobs.

Refrigeration was something of which she could only dream. Perishable items were stored in an underground cave near the house. Gathering eggs, milking cows, slaughtering animals, canning and gardening were part of the daily routine. Cooking and entertaining were also a way of life. As Grandma says, "We had nothing else to do in those days." She fondly recalls picnics under the trees and her mother's fried chicken. Life was slower and uncomplicated.

By the time Grandma was grown and married, the Great Depression was gripping the country. Times were hard. She had three children and a husband to feed. Like her mother, she planted a garden and counted on it to be fruitful. What she hadn't counted on was thousands of grasshoppers.

They moved through a field of grain and descended upon the garden stripping it bare. "They even ate my onions!" Grandma exclaims. "Still we managed. We never went hungry."

Towards the end of World War II, my grandparents moved to town. My grandpa worked for an ice cream factory for eighteen dollars a week. Rent was twelve dollars a month. A loaf of bread cost ten cents and milk was eight cents a quart. Ahhh, refrigerators and grocery stores at last!

Big family dinners continued to be a tradition. Imagine feeding the men, cleaning the table, doing the dishes, and resetting the table, feeding the women, cleaning the table, doing the dishes and resetting the table; and repeating the process once again for the children. Grandma remembers this took hours. One particular occasion, the menfolk were outside and did not come to eat when they were called. The women chose to go ahead and eat and were in the process when the men arrived. "You should have seen the looks on their faces!" said Grandma.

By the time my parents set up a household, my mother had a dishwasher. Grandma remembers how excited she was when she got it. The same went for the double oven. Mom had a choice of grocery stores and eating out was an occasional option. Family dinners were smaller and yes… we all sat down and ate at the same time! For some reason, however, my cousin and I still got stuck doing the dishes.

So…you may come to understand why my answer to my Grandma's question, "Are you making something good for dinner?" is so important. It's not that she wants to make me feel guilty (well, maybe a little), or that she wants to know exactly what type of food I'm having. She wants me to appreciate all of the options, even luxuries, available today—improved cookware, kitchen gadgets, microwaves, freezers, sealable plastic bags, coolers, pre-packaged food, signature stores with aisles and aisles of food, husbands who cook, restaurants and so much more.

To appreciate what you have, you must understand where you have been. Thanks to my grandma, I know making dinner has never been easier. What is hard to explain, though, is making time has never been harder!

Gina Nelson Ebers is an active member of the League. She considers herself a realist and says "what you see is what you get." Being the only woman in a household of men has challenged her in every way.

Hot Chocolate

3 cups half-and-half
³/₄ cup vanilla baking
  chips or milk
  chocolate chips
1 (3-inch) cinnamon
  stick
¹/₄ teaspoon nutmeg
1 teaspoon vanilla
  extract
¹/₂ teaspoon almond
  extract

Garnish:
Whipped cream
Cinnamon

Combine ¹/₄ cup of the half-and-half, vanilla baking chips, cinnamon stick and nutmeg in a saucepan. Cook over low heat until the baking chips melt, whisking constantly. Add the remaining 2³/₄ cups half-and-half. Cook until heated through. Remove from heat. Stir in the flavorings; discard the cinnamon stick. Ladle into mugs. Garnish with whipped cream and cinnamon. *Yield: 5 (6-ounce) servings.*

Hot Buttered Rum

1 pint vanilla ice cream,
  softened
2 cups confectioners'
  sugar
1 cup packed brown
  sugar
1 cup butter, softened
¹/₂ teaspoon each
  nutmeg, allspice and
  ground cloves
¹/₂ teaspoon cinnamon
Rum to taste
Cinnamon sticks

Process the ice cream, confectioners' sugar, brown sugar, butter, nutmeg, allspice, cloves and cinnamon in a blender until smooth. Freeze until firm. Scoop 2 to 3 tablespoons of the frozen mixture into a cup or mug. Add rum to taste and boiling water, stirring with a cinnamon stick until blended. *Yield: 24 servings.*

My brother once told Mom that he couldn't tell her what she was getting for Christmas, but it sounded like "perk, perk, perk."

⏖ Judy Schweitzer ⏕

Homemade Chicken Noodle Soup

1 (3- to 4-pound)
  chicken
4 cups chicken broth
4 cups water
2 ribs celery, cut into
  halves
1 large onion, cut into
  quarters
1 carrot, peeled, cut into
  halves
1/4 cup parsley sprigs
1 teaspoon salt
1 teaspoon freshly
  ground pepper
1 1/2 cups sliced celery
1 cup chopped onion
2 carrots, cut into 1-inch
  slices
1 teaspoon salt
1 teaspoon freshly
  ground pepper
8 ounces spaghetti,
  broken into 2-inch
  pieces
1/4 cup chopped fresh
  parsley

Rinse the chicken and discard the gizzard. Combine the chicken, broth, water, 2 ribs celery, 1 onion, 1 carrot, parsley sprigs, 1 teaspoon salt and 1 teaspoon pepper in a stockpot. Bring to a boil over high heat; reduce heat. Simmer for 45 minutes or until the chicken is tender.

Remove the chicken to a platter, reserving the broth. Cool slightly. Chop the chicken, discarding the skin and bones. Strain the reserved broth through a fine mesh colander or cheesecloth into a bowl, discarding the vegetables. Skim the broth. Rinse the stockpot to remove any fat.

Return the broth to the stockpot. Bring the broth to a simmer. Add 1 1/2 cups celery, 1 cup onion, 2 carrots, 1 teaspoon salt and 1 teaspoon pepper. Simmer for 15 minutes, stirring occasionally. Stir in the spaghetti. Increase the heat to medium. Cook for 8 to 10 minutes or until the pasta is tender, stirring occasionally. Stir in the chicken and parsley. May add additional water if needed for the desired consistency. Simmer just until heated through.

Ladle into soup bowls. Serve immediately. *Yield: 6 servings.*

Note: May substitute 6 ounces egg noodles for the spaghetti. Remove the egg noodles from the soup and store separately in the refrigerator or freezer as they will absorb all the broth.

To remove fat from the top of soup, place a lettuce leaf in the stockpot. This will absorb the fat and can be removed easily.

Creamy Tricolor Coleslaw

1 medium head green
  cabbage (about 5
  cups), shredded
1 medium head purple
  cabbage (about 5
  cups), shredded
2 cups grated carrots
$^1/_2$ cup mayonnaise
$^1/_2$ cup sour cream
$^1/_3$ cup cider vinegar
$^1/_4$ cup honey-mustard
2 tablespoons light
  brown sugar
2 teaspoons celery seeds
1$^1/_2$ teaspoons salt
1 teaspoon freshly
  ground pepper

Toss the cabbage and carrots in a bowl. Combine the mayonnaise, sour cream, vinegar, honey-mustard, brown sugar, celery seeds, salt and pepper in a bowl, whisking to mix. Pour over the cabbage mixture, tossing to coat. Chill, covered, for 4 to 10 hours. *Yield: 12 servings.*

Homemade Mayonnaise

1 egg
2 tablespoons fresh
  lemon juice
$^1/_2$ teaspoon salt
$^1/_4$ teaspoon dry mustard
1 cup vegetable oil

Combine the egg and lemon juice in a blender or food processor container. Add the salt, dry mustard and $^1/_3$ cup of the oil gradually, processing constantly at low speed until blended. Add the remaining $^2/_3$ cup oil gradually, processing constantly until the mayonnaise is of a firm consistency. Stop the processing periodically to scrape the side of the container. Spoon into a jar with a tightfitting lid. Store in the refrigerator for up to 3 days.
Yield: 1 cup.

    Note: Substitute fresh lime juice for the lemon juice and add 1 teaspoon finely chopped cilantro for Lime Cilantro Mayonnaise.

Hearty Beef Stew

2 pounds sirloin tips
1/4 cup flour
1/4 cup vegetable oil
1 pound onions, thickly
   sliced
3 cloves of garlic, minced
1/4 cup chopped fresh
   parsley
2 tablespoons red wine
   vinegar
1 tablespoon brown
   sugar
1 1/2 teaspoons salt
1 bay leaf
1 tablespoon chopped
   fresh thyme
Freshly ground pepper to
   taste
1 1/4 cups beef broth
1 (12-ounce) can dark
   beer
Steamed baby carrots
Steamed new potatoes

Combine the beef and flour in a sealable plastic bag, shaking until coated.

Heat the oil in a skillet until hot. Add the beef in small batches. Cook until brown on all sides. Remove the beef with a slotted spoon to a bowl, reserving the pan drippings.

Add the onions and garlic to the pan drippings. Cook until light brown, stirring frequently. Remove the onion mixture with a slotted spoon and mix with the beef. Stir in the parsley, wine vinegar, brown sugar, salt, bay leaf, thyme and pepper.

Deglaze the skillet with the broth. Pour over the beef mixture. Stir in the beer. Spoon into a greased baking dish.

Bake, covered, at 325 degrees for 2 hours. Discard the bay leaf. Serve over baby carrots and new potatoes.
Yield: 6 servings.

Note: May substitute good-quality stew beef for the sirloin tips.

Sauerbraten with Sour Cream Gravy

1 (4- to 5-pound) beef
    pot roast
1 tablespoon salt
2 cups water
1 cup sliced onion
1/2 cup dry red wine
1/2 lemon, sliced
10 whole black
    peppercorns
3 bay leaves
3 whole cloves
2 1/2 tablespoons
    vegetable oil
2 tablespoons flour
6 gingersnaps, crumbled
1 tablespoon sugar
Salt and freshly ground
    pepper to taste
1/2 cup dry red wine
1/2 cup sour cream

Rub the roast on all sides with 1 tablespoon salt. Place in a nonmetallic bowl.

Combine the water, onion, 1/2 cup red wine, lemon slices, peppercorns, bay leaves and cloves in a saucepan. Bring to a boil. Remove from heat. Let stand until cool. Pour over the beef, turning to coat.

Marinate, covered, in the refrigerator for 36 to 48 hours, turning the roast each morning and evening. Drain, reserving the marinade. Strain the marinade.

Heat the oil in a skillet until hot. Add the beef. Cook until brown on all sides. Place the roast on a rack in a roasting pan, reserving the pan drippings.

Brown the flour in the reserved pan drippings, stirring constantly. Stir in the gingersnaps, sugar, salt and pepper to taste and 2 cups of the strained marinade. Cook over medium heat until smooth and creamy, stirring constantly. Pour over the roast.

Roast, covered, at 325 degrees for 2 1/2 to 3 hours or until the beef is tender, adding 1/2 cup red wine 30 minutes before the end of the cooking process.

Arrange the roast on a serving platter and slice. Stir the sour cream into the pan drippings. Serve with the roast.
Yield: 8 servings.

Note: May substitute a beef top or bottom round roast for the pot roast.

Sauerbraten, or "sour roast," is authentic to the German families who settled much of what is today North Harris County. Many descendents of these early settlers still reside and operate businesses in this area today.

Texas Beef Brisket

1 (8- to 10-pound) beef
  brisket, trimmed
1 cup low-sodium soy
  sauce
1 cup Worcestershire
  sauce
2 teaspoons garlic
  powder
2 teaspoons seasoned salt
2 teaspoons freshly
  ground pepper
2 cups sliced onions

Place the brisket in a roasting pan. Pour a mixture of the soy sauce, Worcestershire sauce, garlic powder, seasoned salt and pepper over the brisket, turning to coat. Marinate, covered, in the refrigerator for 6 to 8 hours, turning occasionally. Arrange the onions on top of the brisket. Bake, covered, at 225 degrees for 8 to 10 hours. Remove the brisket to a serving platter. Slice against the grain. Serve with the pan drippings. *Yield: 10 servings.*

For as long as I can remember, my father has prepared and cooked brisket. It is the best in the world, so tender it literally melts in your mouth. I always look forward to coming home to visit my parents during the football season because I know Dad will have brisket waiting for me. A tradition in our family is to have large parties on Saturdays after the Texas A&M football games, and we always have brisket.

◆ Molly Whisenant ◆

Down-Home Meat Loaf

2/3 cup dry bread crumbs
1 cup milk
1 1/2 pounds lean ground
  beef
1/2 cup finely chopped
  onion
2 eggs, lightly beaten
1 teaspoon sage
1/8 teaspoon freshly
  ground pepper
1/2 cup tomato sauce
6 tablespoons dark
  brown sugar
2 teaspoons dry mustard
1/2 teaspoon nutmeg

Soak the bread crumbs in the milk in a bowl. Add the ground beef, onion, eggs, sage and pepper and mix well. Shape into a loaf in a greased loaf pan. Combine the tomato sauce, brown sugar, dry mustard and nutmeg in a bowl and mix well. Spread over the top of the loaf. Bake at 350 degrees for 1 hour and 20 minutes or until cooked through; drain. Remove the meat loaf to a serving platter. Let stand for 15 minutes before serving.
Yield: 10 servings.

Comfort Foods

Authentic Spaghetti and Meatballs

2 (28-ounce) cans peeled
  tomatoes
1 (15-ounce) can peeled
  tomatoes
1/4 cup olive oil
1 large pork chop
1/2 cup finely chopped
  onion
1 (6-ounce) can tomato
  paste
1 3/4 cups water
1 clove of garlic, cut into
  slivers
3 tablespoons olive oil
2 tablespoons sugar
1 tablespoon basil
1 teaspoon freshly
  ground pepper
Salt to taste
24 uncooked meatballs
Hot cooked spaghetti

Crush the undrained tomatoes in a skillet. Rinse each can with 1/4 cup water and add to the skillet. Simmer for 15 minutes, stirring occasionally.

Heat 1/4 cup olive oil in a heavy saucepan. Add the pork. Cook over medium heat until brown on both sides. Stir in the onion. Cook for several minutes, stirring frequently. Add the tomatoes and mix well. Simmer for 20 minutes, stirring occasionally. Stir in the tomato paste and 1 3/4 cups water.

Sauté the garlic in 3 tablespoons olive oil in a saucepan until brown. Add to the tomato mixture and mix well. Stir in the sugar, basil, pepper and salt.

Drop the meatballs 1 at a time into the tomato sauce and mix gently. Simmer, partially covered, for 1 1/4 hours, stirring occasionally to prevent the sauce from scorching.

Remove the pork chop bone from the sauce and break up any large pieces of pork. Serve with the meatballs and sauce over hot cooked spaghetti or pasta of your choice. *Yield: 6 to 8 servings.*

Deliver half this recipe to a family "in need" and serve the other half to your family. Even the kids like this one, and it freezes well.

Meatballs

2 pounds ground round
2/3 cup freshly grated
  Parmesan cheese
1/3 cup bread crumbs
1/4 cup coarsely chopped
  fresh parsley
1 clove of garlic, coarsely
  chopped
Salt and freshly ground
  pepper to taste
4 eggs, beaten
3/4 cup water

Combine the ground round, cheese, bread crumbs, parsley, garlic, salt and pepper in a bowl and mix well. Add the eggs, mixing until blended. Add the water gradually, mixing constantly until blended. Shape into 24 meatballs.

Pork Chops with Apple Walnut Stuffing

12 thick boneless pork
    chops
Salt and freshly ground
    pepper to taste
1 cup seasoned bread
    crumbs
2 Rome apples, peeled,
    chopped
1/2 cup chopped celery
1/2 cup chopped walnuts
1/4 cup golden raisins
1 egg, beaten
2 tablespoons minced
    fresh thyme
2 cups whipping cream

Cut a slit in the side of each pork chop to form a pocket or request your butcher to perform this task. Season both sides with salt and pepper. Combine the bread crumbs, apples, celery, walnuts, raisins, egg and thyme in a bowl and mix gently. Spoon some of the mixture into the pocket of each pork chop. Arrange in a lightly greased baking dish. Pour the whipping cream over the pork chops. Bake at 350 degrees for 1 1/2 hours or until cooked through. *Yield: 12 servings.*

    Note: Serve with Make-Ahead Mashed Potatoes on page 222 and Baked Apples and Cranberries on page 144. They can be baked at the same time.

When preparing stuffed pork chops, make a pocket in each chop. Cut from the fat side of the chop nearly to the bone. After adding the stuffing, hold the pocket closed with a wooden pick if needed.

Baked Ham with Brown Sugar Glaze

1 (5- to 6-pound) fully
    cooked smoked ham
    half
3/4 cup fresh orange juice
1/2 cup dry sherry
Whole cloves
1 cup packed brown
    sugar
2 tablespoons prepared
    mustard

Garnish:
Kale
Orange slices

Place the ham, orange juice and sherry in a sealable plastic bag and seal tightly. Shake to coat the ham. Place in a large bowl. Marinate in the refrigerator for 8 hours, turning occasionally. Drain, reserving 1 tablespoon of the marinade. Trim the ham, leaving an even layer of fat. Place the ham fat side up on a hard surface. Carve a diamond design into the fat; stud with cloves. Place the ham fat side up on a rack in a shallow roasting pan. Insert a meat thermometer in the thickest part of the ham; do not allow the thermometer to touch fat or bone. Bake at 325 degrees for 1 1/2 to 2 hours or until the meat thermometer registers 150 degrees. Mix the brown sugar, mustard and reserved marinade in a bowl. Spoon over the ham. Bake, covered with foil, for 15 minutes longer. Remove to a serving platter. Garnish with kale and orange slices. *Yield: 10 servings.*

Comfort Foods

Chicken with Rosemary and Thyme

1 (3½-pound) roasting
   chicken
1½ tablespoons unsalted
   butter, softened
Salt and freshly ground
   pepper to taste
Paprika to taste
4 whole heads unpeeled
   fresh garlic, cut
   horizontally into
   halves
12 (2-inch) sprigs fresh
   rosemary
12 (2-inch) sprigs fresh
   thyme
¼ cup water
½ cup Rainwater
   Madeira

Rinse the chicken and pat dry. Rub with the butter and season with salt, pepper and paprika. Place the chicken on its side in a baking dish. Arrange the garlic cut side up around the chicken. Lay 6 sprigs of the rosemary and 6 sprigs of the thyme on top of the chicken. Place the baking dish on the center oven rack.

Roast at 425 degrees for 20 minutes. Discard the rosemary and thyme and replace with the remaining 6 sprigs of rosemary and 6 sprigs of thyme. Add the water and turn the chicken on its other side.

Roast for 20 minutes. Turn the chicken breast side up. Add the wine. Roast for 20 minutes or until golden brown.

Reduce the oven temperature to 400 degrees. Roast for 15 minutes. Let stand vertically for 10 minutes or longer. This makes the bird perfectly moist, as the juices flow down through the breast meat. When you roast a chicken breast side up, the delicate white meat drys out.

Cut the chicken into 4 portions and arrange on a heated serving platter. Drizzle with the pan drippings. Arrange the garlic around the chicken. *Yield: 4 servings.*

Note: Use a free-range chicken if available. If a larger chicken is used, the cooking time should be increased.

This will make your kitchen smell wonderful! Serve with green beans and new potatoes. The initial investment in the Rainwater Madeira is a good one as you will make this recipe again and again.

Chicken Potpie with Cheese Dumplings

1 (3-pound) chicken
3 cups clear chicken
  broth
3 carrots, sliced
3 ribs celery, sliced
1 large potato, coarsely
  chopped
1 large onion, chopped
1 chicken bouillon cube
3 tablespoons cornstarch
1/4 cup water
Cheese Dumpling Dough

Rinse the chicken. Combine the chicken and broth in a stockpot. Add water if needed to cover the chicken. Cook until the chicken is tender. Remove the chicken to a platter, reserving the broth.

Chop the chicken, discarding the skin and bones. Arrange the chicken in a 9x12-inch baking dish.

Skim the broth and strain. Return the broth to the stockpot. Add the carrots, celery, potato, onion and bouillon cube. Simmer for 5 minutes, stirring occasionally. Stir in a mixture of the cornstarch and water. Cook until thickened, stirring constantly.

Pour the vegetable mixture over the chicken. Drop the Cheese Dumpling Dough by tablespoonfuls over the top.

Bake at 400 degrees for 20 to 25 minutes or until brown and puffy.
Yield: 6 servings.

Cheese Dumpling Dough

1 cup water
1 chicken bouillon cube
1/2 cup butter
1 tablespoon chives
1/2 teaspoon salt
1 cup flour
4 eggs
1/2 cup freshly grated
  Parmesan cheese
1/4 cup sesame seeds,
  toasted

Combine the water, bouillon cube, butter, chives and salt in a saucepan. Bring to a boil, stirring frequently. Add the flour all at once, stirring constantly until blended. Cook over medium heat until the mixture forms a stiff ball, stirring constantly. Add the eggs 1 at a time, mixing well after each addition. Stir in the cheese and sesame seeds.

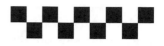

Clean wooden chopping boards meticulously to prevent cross-contamination or use nonporous cutting boards.

Classic Chicken Tetrazzini

1 pound mushrooms,
    sliced
3 ribs celery, sliced
1 medium onion,
    chopped
1/4 cup butter
2 1/2 tablespoons sherry
Salt and freshly ground
    pepper to taste
8 ounces spaghetti,
    broken into halves,
    cooked al dente
1 pound roasted chicken,
    cut into bite-size
    pieces
Freshly grated Parmesan
    cheese to taste
2 cups Velouté Sauce

Sauté the mushrooms, celery and onion in the butter in a skillet until tender. Add the sherry and mix well.

Cook for 1 minute, stirring constantly. Stir in salt and pepper.

Combine the pasta, chicken and sautéed vegetables in a bowl and mix gently. Sprinkle in Parmesan cheese. Add the Velouté Sauce and toss gently. Spoon into a 9x12-inch baking pan. Top generously with Parmesan cheese.

Bake at 400 degrees for 25 minutes or until brown and bubbly. *Yield: 6 servings.*

Note: May substitute 1 pound poached chicken breast or 1 pound chopped turkey for the roasted chicken.

This dish may be divided between two 8x8-inch baking dishes, one for your family and one to share. Or, freeze one for use after a hectic day at work.

Velouté Sauce

1/4 cup butter
5 tablespoons flour
2 cups rich canned or
    homemade chicken
    broth
1/4 teaspoon salt
Freshly ground pepper to
    taste
2/3 cup whipping cream

Heat the butter in a saucepan until melted. Stir in the flour. Cook for 2 minutes, stirring constantly. Add the broth, whisking constantly. Bring to a simmer. Simmer until smooth but not too thick. Season with the salt and pepper. Remove from heat. Whisk in the whipping cream until blended.

Four-Cheese Lasagna

16 ounces lasagna
  noodles
15 ounces ricotta cheese
3 cups shredded
  mozzarella cheese
1 cup freshly grated
  Parmesan cheese
1/2 cup freshly grated
  Romano cheese
1 egg, beaten
Homemade Tomato
  Sauce (at right)
Freshly grated Parmesan
  cheese to taste

Cook the noodles using package directions; drain. Let stand until cool.

Mix the ricotta cheese, mozzarella cheese, 1 cup Parmesan cheese, Romano cheese and egg in a bowl.

Reserve a small amount of the Homemade Tomato Sauce for the top. Spread a thin layer of the Homemade Tomato Sauce in a greased lasagna baking dish. Layer the noodles, cheese mixture and remaining Homemade Tomato Sauce 1/2 or 1/3 at a time in the prepared dish, ending with the noodles. Spread with the reserved Homemade Tomato Sauce. Sprinkle with Parmesan cheese to taste.

Bake, covered with foil, at 350 degrees for 55 minutes. Remove the foil. Bake for 5 minutes longer or until light brown. Let stand for 10 minutes before serving.
Yield: 12 servings.

Note: This recipe works well with oven-ready lasagna noodles. The lasagna may be frozen unbaked for future use. Bake frozen lasagna at 350 degrees for 1 1/2 hours or until bubbly.

For Homemade Tomato Sauce, sauté 1 cup finely chopped onion and 1 teaspoon minced garlic in 1 tablespoon olive oil in a saucepan until tender. Stir in three 8-ounce cans tomato sauce, 3 tablespoons chopped fresh parsley, 2 tablespoons minced fresh basil, 2 tablespoons minced fresh oregano, 1 tablespoon sugar and 1/2 teaspoon freshly ground pepper. Cook over low heat for 30 minutes, stirring occasionally. Stir in 5 coarsely chopped seeded Roma tomatoes gently. Simmer for 10 minutes longer, stirring occasionally.

Triple-Cheese Macaroni

2¹/₂ cups elbow macaroni
Salt to taste
6 ounces sharp Cheddar
    cheese, shredded
6 ounces Monterey Jack
    cheese, shredded
5 tablespoons plus 1
    teaspoon butter,
    softened
3 ounces cream cheese,
    softened
1¹/₂ cups evaporated
    milk
2 tablespoons plus
    2 teaspoons butter
1 cup fresh bread crumbs
1 tablespoon melted
    butter
¹/₂ teaspoon paprika

Cook the macaroni in boiling salted water in a saucepan using package directions; drain.

Combine the macaroni, ¹/₂ of the Cheddar cheese, ¹/₂ of the Monterey Jack cheese and 5 tablespoons plus 1 teaspoon butter and mix well. Spoon into a buttered shallow 3-quart baking dish.

Beat the cream cheese in a mixer bowl while gradually adding the evaporated milk. Beat until blended. Spoon over the macaroni mixture. Sprinkle with the remaining Cheddar cheese and Monterey Jack Cheese. Dot with 2 tablespoons plus 2 teaspoons butter.

Bake at 425 degrees for 20 to 25 minutes or until bubbly.

Combine the bread crumbs, 1 tablespoon butter and paprika in a bowl and mix well. Sprinkle over the baked layer.

Bake for 10 minutes longer.
Yield: 8 servings.

Note: If prepared in advance, do not add the cream cheese mixture until just before baking.

Make-Ahead Mashed Potatoes

8 white boiling potatoes,
　peeled, coarsely
　chopped
8 ounces cream cheese,
　softened
1 cup sour cream
1 cup chopped green
　onions
1 teaspoon garlic salt
1 teaspoon onion salt
Butter to taste
Paprika to taste
1½ cups freshly grated
　Parmesan cheese
　(optional)

Combine the potatoes with enough water to cover in a saucepan. Bring to a boil. Boil until tender; drain. Beat the cream cheese and sour cream in a mixer bowl until blended. Add the hot potatoes and green onions gradually, beating constantly until light and fluffy. Beat in the garlic salt and onion salt. Spoon into a 2-quart baking dish. Dot with butter; sprinkle with paprika. Sprinkle with the Parmesan cheese. Bake at 350 degrees for 45 minutes or until brown. May prepare 1 day in advance, store in the refrigerator and bake just before serving time. Add 5 to 10 minutes to the baking time.
Yield: 8 servings.

This recipe takes the last-minute fuss out of preparing mashed potatoes.

Maple Sweet Potatoes and Apples

2 pounds sweet potatoes
2 cups chopped peeled
　Granny Smith apples
¾ cup maple syrup
¼ cup melted butter
1 teaspoon salt

Combine the sweet potatoes with enough water to cover in a saucepan. Bring to a boil. Boil until tender; drain. Peel the sweet potatoes and cut into slices lengthwise. Place the potatoes in an 8x12-inch baking dish. Arrange the apples over the potatoes. Combine the syrup, butter and salt in a bowl. Pour over the prepared layers. Bake, covered, at 350 degrees for 45 minutes. Remove the cover. Bake for 15 minutes longer or until the apples are tender. *Yield: 8 servings.*

Heavenly Jam

2 pints fresh
    strawberries, sliced
5 cups sugar
Grated zest of 1 orange
Grated zest and juice of
    1 lemon
1 cup crushed pineapple,
    drained
1 envelope fruit pectin

Combine the strawberries, sugar, orange zest, lemon zest, lemon juice, and pineapple in a 6- to 8-quart saucepan and mix well. Bring to a boil. Stir in the fruit pectin. Bring to a rolling boil, stirring constantly. Boil for 5 minutes, stirring constantly; do not overcook. Remove from heat. Cool slightly. Skim off foam. Spoon into 12 hot sterilized 4-ounce jars, leaving $1/4$ inch headspace; seal with 2-piece lids. Cool to room temperature before storing. *Yield: 12 (4-ounce) jars.*

Gourmet Peanut Butter

2 cups unsalted dry-
    roasted peanuts
3 tablespoons peanut oil
2 teaspoons honey
1 teaspoon salt

Process the peanuts in a blender or food processor until ground. Add the peanut oil gradually, processing constantly until smooth. Add the honey and salt. Process until blended. Spoon into a crock with a good seal or a jar with a tightfitting lid. For a more sophisticated version of this childhood staple, substitute cashews for the peanuts and substitute a mild-flavor oil for the peanut oil, increasing the amount to $3^{1}/2$ to 4 tablespoons. *Yield: $1^{1}/2$ cups.*

   Note: Homemade peanut butter is not homogenized, and therefore does not have the shelf life of commercial peanut butter. Store in the refrigerator for up to 2 weeks.

Perfect Apple Crisp

1/2 cup sugar
2 teaspoons cinnamon
1/4 teaspoon nutmeg
2 1/2 pounds Granny
   Smith apples, peeled,
   sliced
2 cups flour
1 cup sugar
1 cup packed brown
   sugar
1/2 cup butter, chilled

Combine 1/2 cup sugar, cinnamon and nutmeg in a bowl and mix well. Add the apples, tossing to coat. Spoon into a 9x13-inch baking pan. Combine the flour, 1 cup sugar and brown sugar in a bowl and mix well. Cut in the butter until crumbly. Press 1/2 of the crumb mixture over the apples. Sprinkle with the remaining crumb mixture. Bake at 350 degrees for 25 minutes or until light brown and bubbly. Serve warm with ice cream or whipped cream. *Yield: 6 servings.*

Vanilla Bean Ice Cream

4 eggs
2 1/4 cups sugar
1 quart half-and-half
1 quart whipping cream
1 1/2 tablespoons vanilla
   extract
1/2 teaspoon salt
2 vanilla beans, split
   lengthwise into halves
Milk (optional)

Beat the eggs in a mixer bowl until frothy. Add the sugar, beating constantly until blended. Add the half-and-half, whipping cream, vanilla and salt. Beat until blended. Scrape the vanilla seeds into the mixture, discarding the pods. Beat until mixed. Pour into an ice cream freezer container. Add milk to the fill line if a thinner "icier" consistency is desired. Freeze using manufacturer's directions. *Yield: variable.*

   Note: To make Oreo Cookie Ice Cream, leave air space in the freezer container and freeze just until partially set. Add crumbled Oreo cookies and freeze until hard. Any type of fresh fruit may be added to the basic recipe.

Extra whipped cream may be frozen for future use. Spoon the whipped cream into mounds on a baking sheet lined with waxed paper. Freeze until firm. Transfer the whipped cream mounds to an airtight freezer container. The whipped cream mounds may be stored for up to three days. Let stand for five minutes before serving.

Amaretto Sauce

1 1/2 cups sugar
1/2 cup butter, softened
1 (5-ounce) can
   evaporated milk
1 egg, beaten
3 1/2 tablespoons amaretto

Beat the sugar and butter in a mixer bowl until light and fluffy. Add the evaporated milk and egg and mix well. Pour into a double boiler. Simmer until thickened, stirring constantly. Cool slightly. Stir in the amaretto. Serve over Vanilla Bean Ice Cream on page 224 or over Traditional Pound Cake on page 231. *Yield: 8 servings.*

Serve these quick and easy sauces with assorted ice cream at your next summer ice cream social.

Spiced Apple Pie Sauce

1/2 cup butter
3 pounds chopped peeled
   Granny Smith apples
1 1/2 teaspoons apple pie
   spice
1 teaspoon cinnamon
1 cup raisins
1/2 cup packed brown
   sugar
2 tablespoons light corn
   syrup
1 1/4 cups apple cider
2 teaspoons cornstarch
2 1/2 teaspoons fresh
   lemon juice

Heat the butter in a skillet until melted. Stir in the apples, apple pie spice and cinnamon. Cook over medium heat for 12 to 15 minutes or just until the apples are tender, stirring occasionally. Add the raisins, brown sugar and corn syrup and mix well. Cook until the brown sugar dissolves, stirring constantly. Stir in a mixture of the apple cider and cornstarch. Cook until bubbly, stirring frequently. Cook for 2 minutes longer, stirring constantly. Add the lemon juice and mix well. Spoon into a sauce boat. Cool slightly. The sauce will thicken as it cools. Serve warm over ice cream. May store, covered, in the refrigerator until serving time. Reheat just before serving.
Yield: 12 servings.

Sweet Cherry Sauce

1³/4 pounds Bing
  cherries, stemmed,
  pitted
3¹/2 cups sugar
³/4 cup water
¹/2 teaspoon almond
  extract
1 tablespoon fresh lemon
  juice

Layer the cherries and sugar ¹/4 at a time in a nonmetallic saucepan, beginning with the cherries and ending with the sugar. Macerate for 1 hour. Add the water and almond flavoring. Bring to a boil, stirring frequently; reduce the heat. Simmer for 10 to 15 minutes or until the mixture begins to thicken, stirring frequently. Skim off the foam. Remove from heat. Stir in the lemon juice. Cool to room temperature. Chill, covered, until serving time. Serve over your favorite ice cream.
Yield: 12 servings.

Note: May store, covered, in the refrigerator for up to 1 month.

Fresh Pineapple Topping

4 cups (¹/4-inch) cubes
  fresh pineapple with
  juice
1 cup sugar
1 tablespoon plus ³/4
  teaspoon (about)
  minced crystallized
  ginger

Combine the pineapple and juice in a nonmetallic saucepan. Add the sugar and ginger gradually and mix well. Bring to a boil, stirring constantly; reduce heat. Simmer for 10 to 15 minutes or just until the sauce begins to thicken, stirring frequently. Remove from heat. Cool to room temperature. Chill, covered, until serving time. *Yield: 12 servings.*

Note: This sauce should be used within 24 hours since it may begin to ferment. May add additional crystallized ginger if desired.

To make Favorite Hot Fudge Sauce, combine 2 cups sugar and ¹/2 cup hot water in a saucepan. Cook over medium heat until the sugar dissolves, stirring frequently. Add 7 ounces coarsely chopped bittersweet chocolate 1 ounce at a time, stirring after each addition until melted. Bring to a boil, stirring constantly. Add 1¹/3 cups sweetened condensed milk and mix well. Serve immediately over your favorite ice cream. The sauce may be stored, tightly covered, in the refrigerator for months. Reheat in a double boiler just before serving.

Pecan Sticky Buns

3 to 3 1/2 cups flour
1 envelope dry yeast
1 cup warm water
3 tablespoons sugar
2 tablespoons shortening
3/4 teaspoon salt
1 egg, at room
    temperature
4 tablespoons melted
    butter
1 cup sugar
1 tablespoon cinnamon
1 cup packed brown
    sugar
1/4 cup butter
1/4 cup light corn syrup
1 1/2 cups coarsely
    chopped pecans

Combine 1 1/2 cups of the flour and the yeast in a mixer bowl and mix well.

Combine the warm water, 3 tablespoons sugar, shortening and salt in a saucepan. Heat just until the shortening melts, stirring frequently. Add to the flour mixture. Add the egg.

Beat at low speed for 30 seconds. Beat at high speed for 3 minutes, scraping the bowl occasionally. Stir in just enough of the remaining flour to make a soft dough. The last amounts may have to be kneaded in.

Place the dough in a buttered bowl, turning to coat the surface. Let rise, covered, in a warm place for 1 hour. Punch the dough down.

Let rest for 15 minutes. Divide the dough into 2 equal portions. Roll each portion into a 10x18-inch rectangle on a lightly floured surface. Brush each rectangle with 2 tablespoons of the melted butter. Sprinkle with a mixture of 1 cup sugar and cinnamon. Roll as for a jelly roll, starting with the long side. Cut each roll into 15 slices.

Heat the brown sugar, 1/4 cup butter and corn syrup in a saucepan over low heat until blended, stirring constantly; do not boil. Spread the mixture evenly in the bottom of two 5x9-inch loaf pans. Sprinkle with the pecans. Arrange 15 slices in a single layer in each prepared loaf pan, 3 across and 5 down.

Let rise for 45 minutes or until doubled in bulk. Bake at 375 degrees for 25 minutes or until light brown.

Let stand for 6 to 7 minutes. Invert onto a serving platter. *Yield: 30 sticky buns.*

My mother has always been a great baker. One of the family's favorites was caramel rolls (aka Sticky Buns). She made them for very special occasions. My first year out of college, I had my family over for Easter brunch. I stayed up until 1:00 a.m. making the caramel rolls. The rolls looked great, but they were hard as rocks and could have been used as hockey pucks. My dear dad was the only one who attempted to eat them, after soaking them in his coffee. As it turns out, my father-in-law is the baker in his family, and he, too, makes caramel rolls for special occasions. I have now mastered the art, and we have caramel rolls every Christmas morning.

᭟ Cynthia Jarosh ᭠

Best Banana Pudding

1 cup sugar
3 tablespoons flour
1 1/2 cups milk
3 egg yolks, lightly
  beaten
3 egg whites
1/4 cup sugar
Vanilla wafers
4 to 5 bananas, sliced

Combine 1 cup sugar and flour in a sauce-pan and mix well. Add the milk gradually and mix well. Cook over medium heat until thickened, stirring constantly. Stir a small amount of the hot mixture into the egg yolks; stir the egg yolks into the hot mixture. Beat the egg whites in a mixer bowl until foamy. Add 1/4 cup sugar, beating constantly until stiff peaks form. Fold into the custard. Layer the vanilla wafers, bananas and custard alternately in a trifle bowl or deep dish with straight sides until all the ingredients are used, ending with the custard. Decorate with vanilla wafers around the edge of the bowl or dish. Chill until serving time. *Yield: 6 servings.*

Most banana pudding recipes call for the meringue on top, however this has the egg whites incorporated into the pudding. Your family and friends will think this is the best!

Maple Bread Pudding

1/2 (1-pound) loaf firm-
  texture bread, cut into
  3/4-inch slices
1/4 cup butter, softened
2 cups milk
1/2 cup raisins
1/2 cup maple syrup
2 eggs
1 tablespoon
  confectioners' sugar

Trim the crust from the bread and toast the slices until light brown. Butter 1 side of each slice; cut diagonally into halves. Arrange butter side down and overlapping in a single layer in a buttered loaf pan or 6-cup baking dish. If there are too many slices for a single layer, use half and reserve the remaining slices. Scald the milk with the raisins in a saucepan. Beat the maple syrup and eggs in a bowl until blended. Stir in the milk mixture. Pour in just enough of the milk mixture to cover the bread. If only half the milk mixture is used, make a second layer of bread and pour the remaining milk mixture over the top, making sure the raisins are scattered evenly through the layers. Sprinkle with confectioners' sugar. Bake at 300 degrees for 25 minutes or just until set. Serve warm. *Yield: 4 servings.*

Comfort Foods

Mixed Berry Shortcake Hearts

3½ cups mixed seasonal
  berries
¼ cup sugar
3 tablespoons fresh
  lemon juice
2 cups flour
¼ cup sugar
1 tablespoon baking
  powder
½ teaspoon salt
6 tablespoons butter, cut
  into pieces, chilled
½ cup plus 2
  tablespoons whipping
  cream
1 egg
1 egg yolk
1 tablespoon whipping
  cream
Vanilla Bean Whipped
  Cream (at right)

Garnish:
½ cup mixed seasonal
  berries

Combine the berries, ¼ cup sugar and lemon juice in a bowl and toss gently. Let stand at room temperature for 1 hour to allow juices to form.

Combine the flour, ¼ cup sugar, baking powder and salt in a bowl and mix well. Cut in the butter with a pastry cutter until crumbly.

Combine ½ cup plus 2 tablespoons whipping cream and the egg in a bowl, whisking until blended. Add to the crumb mixture, stirring with a fork until the dough begins to form a ball; do not overmix.

Pat the dough into a 6- or 7-inch square on a lightly floured surface; cut into 6 hearts with a heart-shape cutter. Arrange on a lightly buttered baking sheet.

Whisk the egg yolk and 1 tablespoon whipping cream in a bowl until blended. Brush the tops of the hearts with the mixture.

Bake at 375 degrees for 25 to 30 minutes or until light brown. Transfer to a wire rack. Cool slightly.

Cut the warm shortcakes into halves horizontally. Arrange the bottom halves on a serving platter or on individual dessert plates. Spoon the undrained berries over the halves. Spread with some of the Vanilla Bean Whipped Cream. Top with the remaining shortcake halves. Spoon the remaining Vanilla Bean Whipped Cream over the top. Garnish with the berries. Serve immediately. *Yield: 6 servings.*

Note: May substitute a round biscuit cutter for the heart-shape cutter.

For Vanilla Bean Whipped Cream, place a metal bowl in the freezer. Scrape the seeds of 1 split vanilla bean into 1 cup whipping cream in a bowl 1 day prior to serving or early the day of serving, discarding the pod. Chill for several hours to overnight. Strain the whipping cream mixture into the chilled bowl, discarding the vanilla seeds. Add 2 tablespoons confectioners' sugar. Beat for 6 minutes or until soft peaks form, scraping the bowl occasionally. May substitute 1 teaspoon vanilla extract for the vanilla bean.

Red Velvet Cake

1 tablespoon vinegar
1 teaspoon baking soda
2¹/₂ cups flour
1 teaspoon salt
1¹/₂ cups sugar
¹/₂ cup shortening
2 eggs
3 tablespoons baking
  cocoa
¹/₄ cup red food coloring
1 cup buttermilk
1 teaspoon vanilla
  extract
Red Velvet Frosting

Combine the vinegar and baking soda in a cup and mix well. Combine the flour and salt in a bowl and mix well.

Beat the sugar and shortening in a mixer bowl until creamy, scraping the bowl occasionally. Beat in the eggs.

Combine the baking cocoa and food coloring in a bowl, stirring until of a paste consistency. Add to the creamed mixture and mix well. Add the buttermilk and flour mixture alternately, mixing well after each addition. Beat in the vanilla. Stir in the vinegar mixture. Spoon into 2 buttered and floured 8-inch cake pans.

Bake at 350 degrees for 30 minutes. Split the warm layers into halves horizontally. Cool the layers on a wire rack.

Spread the Red Velvet Frosting between the layers and over the top and side of the cake, making lavish swirls with the knife. Store, covered, in the refrigerator. *Yield: 12 servings.*

Note: Dental floss or thread, pulled slowly through the middle of each layer with a back-and-forth motion, makes a clean cut.

Many baby boomers will remember this classic cake from their childhood. With its deep red layers framed in creamy white frosting, it is ideal for Christmas or Valentine's Day.

Red Velvet Frosting

¹/₂ cup flour
2 cups milk
2 cups sugar
1 cup shortening
1 cup butter, softened
2 teaspoons vanilla
  extract

Whisk the flour into the milk in a saucepan. Cook over medium heat until thickened, stirring constantly. Remove from heat. Let stand until room temperature, stirring frequently. Cover the mixture with waxed paper. Chill for 1 to 2 hours. Beat the sugar, shortening and butter in a mixer bowl until creamy. Stir in the milk mixture. Add the vanilla. Beat at high speed until light and fluffy or of the consistency of whipped cream.

Traditional Pound Cake

3 cups flour
1/2 teaspoon salt
1/4 teaspoon baking soda
3 cups sugar
2 cups butter, softened
6 eggs, at room
   temperature
1 teaspoon vanilla
   extract
1 teaspoon almond
   extract
1 teaspoon lemon extract
1 cup sour cream

Combine the flour, salt and baking soda in a bowl and mix well. Beat the sugar and butter in a mixer bowl until creamy, scraping the bowl occasionally. Add 2 of the eggs, beating until blended. Add the flour mixture alternately with the remaining 4 eggs, beating well after each addition. Stir in the flavorings and sour cream. Spoon into a buttered and floured 10-inch tube pan. Place the pan on the middle oven rack of a cold oven. Bake at 325 degrees for 1 1/2 hours. Do not open the oven door during the first hour of baking. Cool in the pan on a wire rack for 10 to 15 minutes. Remove to a cake plate. Slice and serve with Mango Curd on page 146 or Amaretto Sauce on page 225. *Yield: 16 servings.*

Note: May bake in 2 buttered and floured 5x9-inch loaf pans.

To test baking soda's usability, combine 1/4 teaspoon with 2 teaspoons vinegar. If the mixture bubbles, the baking soda is active. To test baking powder, combine 1 teaspoon with 1/3 cup hot water. If the mixture bubbles, the baking powder is suitable for use.

Cookie Pops

12 wooden craft sticks
12 fun-size chocolate-
   peanut candy bars
1/2 cup sugar
1/2 cup packed brown
   sugar
1/2 cup butter, softened
1/2 cup peanut butter
3/4 teaspoon vanilla
   extract
1 egg
1 1/4 cups flour
1/2 teaspoon baking soda
1/2 teaspoon baking
   powder

Push a craft stick into the small end of each candy bar to resemble a lollipop. Beat the sugar, brown sugar, butter, peanut butter, vanilla and egg in a mixer bowl until blended. Add the flour, baking soda and baking powder and mix well. Shape 1/4 cup of the dough around each candy bar, making sure the candy bar is completely concealed. Do not allow any of the dough to touch the wooden handles to avoid it baking on the sticks. Arrange 4 inches apart on an ungreased cookie sheet. Bake at 375 degrees for 14 to 16 minutes or until golden brown. Cool on the cookie sheet for 10 minutes. Remove to a wire rack to cool completely. *Yield: 1 dozen.*

Try substituting your favorite chocolate chip cookie dough recipe and fun-size dark caramel nougat candy bars for variety.

231

Jumbo Oatmeal Walnut Raisin Cookies

1 cup flour
1 1/2 teaspoons cinnamon
1 teaspoon baking soda
1/2 teaspoon salt
1 cup packed brown
    sugar
3/4 cup sugar
3/4 cup butter, softened
1 egg
2 tablespoons water
1 teaspoon vanilla
    extract
3 cups rolled oats
1 cup raisins
1/2 cup coarsely chopped
    walnuts

Sift the flour, cinnamon, baking soda and salt into a bowl and mix well. Beat the brown sugar, sugar and butter in a mixer bowl until creamy, scraping the bowl occasionally. Beat in the egg. Add the water and vanilla and mix well. Stir in the flour mixture. Add the oats, raisins and walnuts, stirring until mixed. The dough will be stiff. Shape into large balls using the bowl of a wooden spoon. Arrange on a greased cookie sheet; press lightly. Bake at 350 degrees for 15 to 17 minutes or just until the centers are done. Remove to a wire rack to cool. *Yield: 20 servings.*

Note: Substitute dried cranberries for the raisins during the holiday season.

These are those big chewy cookies that you buy for one dollar apiece at cookie stands. You'll love them!

Triple-Chip Cookies

2 1/2 cups quick-cooking
    oats
1 cup butter, softened
1 cup packed brown sugar
1 cup sugar
2 eggs
1 1/2 teaspoons vanilla
    extract
2 cups flour
1 teaspoon baking
    powder
1 teaspoon baking soda
1/2 cup each semisweet
    chocolate, milk
    chocolate and white
    chocolate chips
1 (6-ounce) chocolate
    candy bar, grated
1 1/2 cups chopped nuts

Process the oats in a blender until powdery. Beat the butter, brown sugar and sugar in a mixer bowl until creamy. Add the eggs and vanilla, beating until blended. Add the oats, flour, baking powder and baking soda and mix well. Stir in the semisweet chocolate chips, milk chocolate chips, white chocolate chips, candy bar and nuts. Roll into 1-inch balls. Arrange 2 inches apart on a cookie sheet. Bake at 375 degrees for 10 minutes. Remove to a wire rack to cool. *Yield: 4 dozen.*

Fresh Lemon Meringue Pie

1¹/₂ cups sugar
¹/₄ cup plus
    2 tablespoons
    cornstarch
¹/₂ cup cold water
¹/₂ cup fresh lemon juice
3 egg yolks, beaten
2 tablespoons butter,
    softened
1¹/₂ cups boiling water
1¹/₄ teaspoons lemon zest
2 drops of yellow food
    coloring
1 baked (9-inch) pie
    shell
3 egg whites
¹/₄ teaspoon cream of
    tartar
6 tablespoons sugar

Combine 1¹/₂ cups sugar and cornstarch in a 2-quart saucepan. Add the cold water and lemon juice gradually, whisking until smooth. Stir in the egg yolks. Add the butter. Add the boiling water gradually, stirring constantly.

Bring to a boil gradually, stirring constantly. Boil just until thickened; reduce the heat to medium. Cook for 1 minute. Remove from heat. Stir in the lemon zest and food coloring. Spoon into the pie shell. Let stand until a thin film forms over the filling.

Beat the egg whites in a mixer bowl until foamy. Add the cream of tartar. Beat at high speed until soft peaks form. Add 6 tablespoons sugar 1 tablespoon at a time, beating constantly at medium speed until blended. Beat at high speed until stiff and glossy.

Drop scoops of the meringue around the edge of the hot filling, spreading with a rubber spatula to the edge of the pie shell to seal. Spread the meringue toward the center of the pie, making decorative swirls with the spatula until the entire filling is covered.

Bake at 350 degrees for 12 to 15 minutes or until golden brown. Let stand at room temperature away from drafts for 2 hours before serving. Store, covered, in the refrigerator. *Yield: 8 servings.*

Note: For easier, neater slicing, use a sharp knife dipped in hot water after each cut.

Pecan Pie

6 eggs
2 cups dark corn syrup
1 cup sugar
1/2 cup melted butter
2 teaspoons vanilla
  extract
2 cups pecan halves
1 unbaked (9-inch) pie
  shell

Beat the eggs in a mixer bowl. Bring the corn syrup and sugar to a boil in a saucepan over medium heat. Boil for 3 minutes, stirring constantly. Remove from heat. Add the hot syrup mixture to the eggs gradually, beating constantly until blended. Stir in the butter and vanilla. Add the pecans and mix well. Spoon into the pie shell. Bake at 425 degrees for 5 minutes. Reduce the oven temperature to 300 degrees. Bake for 55 to 60 minutes longer. Let stand until cool.
Yield: 8 servings.

Old-Fashioned Pumpkin Pie

2 cups solid-pack
  pumpkin
1 cup sweetened
  condensed milk
3/4 cup sugar
2 eggs, beaten
1 teaspoon cinnamon
1/2 teaspoon salt
1/2 cup chopped pecans
1 cup whipping cream
1 unbaked (9-inch) pie
  shell

Combine the pumpkin, condensed milk, sugar, eggs, cinnamon and salt in a bowl and mix well. Stir in the pecans. Beat the whipping cream in a chilled mixer bowl until soft peaks form. Fold into the pumpkin mixture. Spoon into the pie shell. Bake at 425 degrees for 15 minutes. Reduce the oven temperature to 350 degrees. Bake for 40 to 45 minutes longer.
Yield: 8 servings.

Index

Additional copies of *Texas Ties* may be obtained by writing or calling:

The Junior League of North Harris County, Inc.
5555 Fellowship Lane
Spring, Texas 77379
(281) 376-5754
WATS (888) TEX-TIES (888-839-8437)
FAX (281) 251-8200